THE PROFIT PARADOX

The Profit Paradox

HOW THRIVING FIRMS THREATEN
THE FUTURE OF WORK

JAN EECKHOUT

PRINCETON UNIVERSITY PRESS

PRINCETON & OXFORD

Published by Princeton University Press
41 William Street, Princeton, New Jersey 08540
6 Oxford Street, Woodstock, Oxfordshire OX20 1TR

press.princeton.edu

Library of Congress Cataloging-in-Publication Data

Names: Eeckhout, Jan, author.
Title: The profit paradox : how thriving firms threaten the future of work /
    Jan Eeckhout.
Description: 1st Edition. | Princeton : Princeton University Press, 2021. |
    Includes bibliographical references and index.
Identifiers: LCCN 2020052907 (print) | LCCN 2020052908 (ebook) |
    ISBN 9780691214474 (hardback) | ISBN 9780691222769 (ebook)
Subjects: LCSH: Labor market. | Manpower policy. | Business enterprises—
    Technological innovations. | Work. | Wages. | Working class.
Classification: LCC HD5706 .E35 2021 (print) | LCC HD5706 (ebook) |
    DDC 331.1—dc23
LC record available at https://lccn.loc.gov/2020052907
LC ebook record available at https://lccn.loc.gov/2020052908

British Library Cataloging-in-Publication Data is available

Editorial: Joe Jackson, Josh Drake
Jacket/Cover Design: Karl Spurzem
Production: Erin Suydam
Publicity: James Schneider, Kate Farquhar-Thomson

Cover lettering: Shutterstock

This book has been composed in Arno

Printed on acid-free paper. ∞

Printed in the United States of America

10 9 8 7 6 5 4 3 2 1

The trouble with competitions is that somebody wins them.

—GEORGE ORWELL

Labor was the first price, the original purchase—
money that was paid for all things.
It was not by gold or by silver, but by labor,
that all wealth of the world was originally purchased.

—ADAM SMITH

CONTENTS

1

Introduction

IT WAS LIKE a science fiction movie. While I was on another phone I saw Erin, who was a few thousand miles away, enter my daughter Elena's smartphone and move around among apps to troubleshoot. The high-speed data transmission was not working, and I had called technical support. After talking to several lower-level technicians who each did the same checks, switching the phone on and off or toggling the carrier settings, I was transferred to Erin, a senior technical advisor. It was pretty clear that she had a deeper knowledge of the technical characteristics of the device, and she asked me to change settings I was not even aware existed.

She spoke with an emphatic and confident voice, further accentuating her technical know-how. She gave the impression from the first instant that she would be able to resolve the issue. And she did. As a senior technical advisor, Erin's job is to analyze issues lower-level technicians cannot resolve. She gets the hard technical problems. In all we had four phone conversations for a total of more than three hours spread over several days. During that time she got several other people on the phone, including the telecom provider, to find out if it was an issue with the SIM card. At stages where she could not resolve a particular technical issue, she would do research and call me back the following day. In the end, she found out what the problem was: one batch of an older-model phone was incompatible with the newest SIM technology.

After everything was done, I wondered why it made business sense for a senior technical advisor to spend over three hours on the case.

Surely her hourly cost—her wage, the employer contribution, and the overhead associated with her work space—must be considerably higher than the replacement cost of the older-model smartphone, which at that point was sold for around $300, but the production cost to the company must be substantially lower, estimated to be around $150. Why not spend $150 on a replacement phone instead of spending the high labor cost of a skilled technical advisor? Additionally, to compensate for the technical failure and the time it took to resolve the problem, the company even let me choose a $150 accessory from their store. After the issue was resolved I asked Erin to talk outside the troubleshooting environment in order to find out.

Erin has two bachelor's degrees, one in journalism and one in social psychology from different universities. She also has a master's degree in sociology from another university, where she was a teaching assistant. When I first talked to her, I was surprised to learn that she had no schooling in engineering or the sciences. She told me that personal skills are the most important asset necessary to earn a promotion.

These social skills—which include things such as being able to show empathy or to understand the situation a customer is in—can't really be learned at school, in part because they are rarely taught. Erin described people getting angry on the phone, which required all her composure to remain even-tempered in order to deescalate the situation without taking things personally. The technical skills came later and required no formal education. Once you got the customer in the right place, you could comfortably get to the technical issues.

When she first took the job, she started at the bottom of the ladder, and within less than a year she had made her way to the highest technical advisor level. Despite being at the highest technical level, she didn't supervise others. Lower-level technicians passed problems on to her but they did not report to her.

After finishing her graduate degree and enjoying life in New Mexico, Erin decided to stay on as a technical advisor. The local establishment of her company had only one client, a large smartphone company. While the smartphone manufacturer outsourced the technical support work, the parent company closely monitored the operations and set the quality standards of the service provided. Externally it looked like the parent company interacted with the customer: the technical advisors identified themselves with the name of the parent company, and their email addresses ended in @the-parent-company-name.com. The technical support they provided was by telephone, email, and by remotely accessing a customer's device.

Work was closely monitored and measured by all kinds of metrics, such as the average duration of the handle time, the after-call time, whether the technical advisor kept the commitment to a scheduled out-call, and of course by customer surveys.

Calls were recorded, and the representatives of the smartphone manufacturer listened in. The physical environment, as it was before the COVID-19 outbreak at least, was unappealing, with a lot of people crammed into a large open space. To get a space to work, you had to arrive early. Still, Erin said, the interaction with coworkers was very pleasant. You could ask colleagues questions on how to handle difficult problems, management was friendly, and the trainers were extremely helpful. "It is definitely a lot more pleasant than working for small companies, which I did through a temp agency. In a way, it is much less impersonal here in such a giant service firm dotted with half-cubicles than in those small firms. But the company management in those firms is much more aggravating."

With two bachelor's degrees and a master's degree, Erin is highly educated, in the top 15 percent of US citizens in terms of education.[1] But years of schooling is of course not the best measure of productivity. Many without college degrees earn outrageous amounts of money on Wall Street, and others with advanced degrees in the arts wait tables. Erin is doing a technical job and has excellent social and interpersonal skills, but despite her job title as a senior technical advisor, the substance of her job does not require higher education. She does this job because she cannot find a more gratifying job for which she has trained.

When Erin told me how much she earns, I was astonished: twelve dollars an hour before taxes, and no paid holidays. She works around forty hours a week, thus making $480 a week, or $23,000 a year when working forty-eight weeks. That is substantially below the country-wide median wage of $917 per week ($47,684 per year over 52 weeks).[2] Typical jobs in the area for recent high school graduates without experience pay even less—$9 per hour. But hers is the job of a senior technical advisor with experience, and she has a postgraduate degree, yet her pay is only just over half the median wage.

Now it makes sense why the smartphone company chooses to spend three hours of a senior technical advisor's time resolving a technical problem instead of sending a new phone. At an hourly wage of $12, her total labor cost including employment contributions is somewhere between $15 and $20. The troubleshooting labor cost was probably $50–$60, substantially below the replacement cost. In fact, the company spent more on the $150 gift.

Erin Is Not Alone

Erin's earnings are representative of work for most in the current economy. Since the 1980s, for workers who do not supervise others, for those who perform routine tasks, and for those with fewer years of schooling, wages have stagnated. These three categories make up the majority of all jobs. Fewer than one in five people have a supervisory role, and even today many jobs involve a routine activity such as secretarial work or driving a car,[3] and more than 55 percent of all workers do not have college degrees.[4] In real terms after adjusting for inflation, those wages have been virtually constant.

What's more striking is that during that same period, from the 1980s to the present, workers have become increasingly productive. Worker productivity, the total value produced in the economy divided by all workers, including higher-paid workers, has grown at a steady rate of 1.7 percent on average per year, as shown in figure 1.[5] The value of the output workers produce has grown, yet what most workers get in exchange for producing that output has not kept up. Since 1980 there has been a clear break between the evolution of worker productivity and that of wages for most workers.

This growing wedge between flat wages for most workers and rising productivity clearly indicates that the majority of workers are getting a

Real wages and productivity, 1948 = 1

FIGURE 1. Average wages of nonsupervisory production workers and productivity of all workers. *Source*: U.S. Bureau of Labor Statistics, Current Employment Statistics. For further details, see www.TheProfitParadox.com.

smaller share of the pie. The striking development is therefore not so much that wages in dollar terms are stagnating, it is that workers are now doing worse relative to the wealth they generate. The share of output in the economy that goes to wages—what economists call the labor share—is declining.

Ordinary working people notice that they are doing worse than their parents. Despite working hard, they're moving down the social ladder. And it's not like workers walking but staying in place—they're walking fast and moving backward.

Not All Workers Are Worse Off

Wage stagnation is not equally distributed. Figure 2 illustrates that the evolution of average wages is very different depending on education. Workers with only a high school diploma or those who have dropped out of high school have seen their wages decline by 15 percent. Even those with some college education—for example, a two-year professional

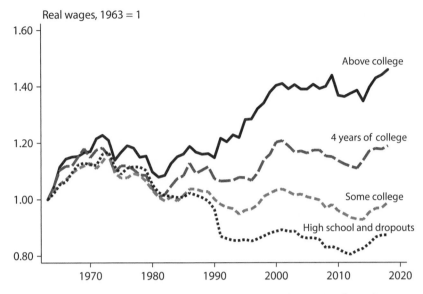

FIGURE 2. Wages by education. *Source*: U.S. Census Bureau, Current Population Survey.
For further details, see www.TheProfitParadox.com.

degree—have not experienced any increase. The workers in these two education categories are the vast majority of the working population (80 percent in 1980).

While the wages of the less educated have languished, the wages of the more educated have increased. Those with a four-year college degree have seen a 20 percent increase since 1980, and especially those with higher-level education such as master's degrees and PhDs have experienced the highest wage increase. The sharp rise since the 1980s in the wage gap between those with a full college education and those without is often called the college premium. In the United States, a worker with a college degree or higher now on average earns 96 percent more than a worker with at most a high school diploma, up from 46 percent more in 1980.[6]

The evolution of the college premium is hard to rationalize with standard explanations. Nearly twice as many workers have a college degree today compared to workers in 1980. With more skilled workers vying for the high-skilled jobs, it should be easier for firms to hire high-skilled employees. Therefore we expect that the wages firms need to pay to hire those college graduates would be lower.

The idea that tougher competition among college graduates leads to lower wages is clearly at odds with what the data tells us—that there is a rise in the college premium. This is all the more striking if we acknowledge that there are many workers like Erin who do have a college degree but who perform a noncollege job—and as a result earn low wages. How many of our brightest college-educated musicians wait tables in Nashville?

Something else is going on. The most prominent explanation is that technology has changed in a way that makes skilled workers disproportionately more productive. Information technology (IT) allows a logistics manager to change the efficiency in thousands of stores of a wholesale distributor like Walmart or Amazon. Cheaper capital goods, such as computers and software, affect productivity of the central office software developer at Uber much more than it affects the drivers. For example, the technology makes the drivers more productive because downtime is minimized, but those gains originate from the input of the developers, not from the input of the drivers.

The workers who generate those gains also get compensated proportionately to what they generate. And then there is the extent of the market. With better communication technology and cheaper transportation and shipping, the reach of technology is extremely far. With a minor innovation businesses now can capture the world market, whereas before 1980 they were much more constrained by the local market. In the case of Uber, this creates a winner-take-all payoff that is extremely lucrative for those whose input in production changes the product, the efficiency, or the sales, but very little changes for the driver. Likewise, a new attractive feature of a cell phone developed at headquarters may substantially raise sales, but it does little for a senior technical advisor like Erin.

Such technological change is most visible in the economics of superstars.[7] Before high-quality recording technology became available, the only way to listen to music or see a play was to go to a concert hall, the opera house, or the theatre. There are only so many seats in each hall, and there are only so many performances an artist can give. The best opera singer might demand a slightly higher ticket price and the largest opera house, but there is not much else that scales his or her better skill.

Once radio, television, and general recording technology became widely available, the people who could claim to have heard Maria Callas sing jumped from a few thousand to millions or even billions. Superstar pay then simply reflects the fact that her voice and persona generate enormous economic value. In the same way, Mick Jagger and Adam Levine command astronomical incomes because millions of people pay to stream their music; Leo Messi and Neymar Jr. earn millions in salary and royalties because of the television rights to their games, and the shirts with their names on them that are sold from Beijing to Buenos Aires.

This does not necessarily mean that the best opera singer today is better than the best opera singer a hundred years ago, or that superstar earnings reflect an equally abysmal difference in their abilities and performances. The role of the superstar phenomenon is to amplify even minor differences in ability into huge differences in stardom and in earnings.

These are the winner-take-all markets. The winner who not only takes the trophy but sells more jerseys will have more viewers for the next game, and so on. The superstar who can do this commands a share of the output that corresponds to the amount of profits that his or her contribution generates. Superstar pay reflects how much a star's ability contributes to the output it generates. Technological change in a globalized economy screens the superstar's game to more eyes and leads to the sale of more jerseys with their name around the globe. The same skill now commands a higher income for the winner.

Whether it is the famous superstar or the not-so-famous data scientist, medical doctor, or Wall Street banker, technological change has made some workers disproportionately more productive. As a result, they earn multiple times what Erin makes as a senior technical advisor. However, technological change is not the only driver behind the rise in income inequality. The same determinants that lead to a decline in the wages of the common worker also create a wedge between the high- and low-earnings workers: the rise of market power by dominant firms.

The force behind the atrophying labor market is the decline of competition in the marketplace for goods and services. From tech to textiles, our age is marked by rapid technological progress—progress that means just a few companies now dominate the railway lines of wireless technology. These technological advances bestow enormous power to those few firms. In turn, the accompanying lack of competition creates brutally unequal outcomes among workers.

It is evident that firms play a crucial role when we look at the origins of the increase in wage inequality. The lion's share of the rise in wage inequality is driven by the fact that firms now increasingly look different from one another. Most firms used to have a solid share of both low- and high-skilled workers on the books. Now, some firms almost exclusively house the highly valued and highly paid workers, where they rely on outside companies for more menial services such as cleaning and food preparation.

This is true even in the high-tech industry, where there are a number of firms full of extremely high-skilled workers with high salaries and benefits, especially in Silicon Valley. Who doesn't want to be a well-paid programmer at Google headquarters, where subsidized amenities such as high-end food, laundry service, and day care are available in the building?

But in that high-tech industry there are also firms such as the one where Erin works as a senior technical advisor, where she and most other employees are on the low end of the pay scale, especially compared to the salaries at the Google headquarters in Silicon Valley. You can think of Erin's firm as the help-desk function within any company. Only now, the help-desk function is outsourced at a different firm.

The result is two firms, one with low salaries performing the help-desk tasks, and the headquarters with the design and development tasks. Some time ago the two tasks were most likely in the same firm. In the same way that the cleaners and security personnel were hired within the firm, now most firms outsource all those functions.

As a result, the increase in wage inequality that we observe is nearly entirely due to the fact that businesses now look more different from one another. Those who design the phones, as well as the coders and developers, have high wages, and those working for the firm sourcing the help-desk function have low wages. The rise in wage inequality that we observe is mainly driven by the increase in inequality between firms, with some firms paying high wages to all their highly productive workers whose work is scalable and other firms paying low wages to their workers who perform menial services.

While inequality between firms has increased, there is little increase in inequality in wages within firms. The top 1 percent worker now earns on average twenty times more than the bottom 99 percent worker in the same firm, which is only slightly higher than what it was in 1980. Nonetheless, there has been a much sharper increase in wage inequality economy-wide, and more than two-thirds of that rise in wage inequality is due to the increase in inequality between firms.[8]

The implication of course is that firms look very different from each other: working at Google headquarters with one day per week to work on your own project is very different from Erin's environment with cubicles, low ceilings, and stained and curled-up wall-to-wall carpet. Until 1980 they might all have been located at the same site, neither as fancy as Google nor as basic as the tech support site. And if the sites where people work are different, so are the wages. The gap between companies and the wages that they are paying has grown since 1980. The rise in economy-wide wage inequality is driven by this gap between companies.

The higher earnings of a minority of workers are not enough to offset lower earnings for the majority, the common workers. Even if we consider the salaries of all workers, including those in high-paying jobs and the superstars, the amount the economy spends on labor has decreased steadily since 1980. The labor share, the total expenditure on wages as a share of production in the economy, has historically been around two-thirds, or 65 percent. The remaining one-third is expenditure on capital and profits. Today the labor share is below 58 percent.[9] A decline of seven percentage points—or 10 percent—may seem tiny, but that includes the salaries of all those top earners, not just the low-paid workers. It means that work in total takes a 10 percent smaller share of the pie.

This is a huge decline, and it is unprecedented. It is even more surprising if we add that the capital share has declined. Firms also spend a smaller share investing in capital. What has happened since 1980 is that the profits have risen sharply economy-wide.

This is evidence that large firms dominate the market of the goods they sell. This is a fundamental change in the economy that reduces the compensation workers receive for their labor, while those owning the firms—including all of us who own pension funds that invest in those firms—are doing better.

However, the decline in the labor share is not simply the re-distribution from those who work to those who own capital, with some winners and some losers. In this book I will argue that what is happening in the economy is to the detriment of all, except for a few capital owners. The big loser is work, but the economy as a whole, including most of the owners of capital, is worse off, too.

The Gold Watch Myth

Wage stagnation and the rise in wage inequality are not the only developments in the market for work. Since 1980, other long-term trends are profoundly transforming work. In this book I offer a bird's-eye view of the state of work in modern times. Some of the facts about work are well known and others are less so, or even counterintuitive.

There are several myths about the economics of work. Relying on data and research, I will attempt to debunk these myths. One is the Gold Watch myth. Most people believe that the generations of our parents and grandparents had jobs that were safer and lasted longer. A job used to be something you could count on for your entire professional life. As a youngster you would start work at a corporation or the local factory and you would gradually get promoted until the day you retired, when you received your gold watch in appreciation and a handshake from the boss.

This Gold Watch moment is a myth because jobs today on average last substantially longer than they used to. It may not fit our view of what is happening in the economy, but the data tells us that the duration of jobs has become longer. On average, jobs today last one year longer than in the 1980s.[10] This is a huge change.

If job duration is longer, it necessarily means that people switch jobs less frequently. It is like children going to the local fair. If the horse carrousel rides are longer, then they switch less frequently to a different attraction. Job duration and the frequency of job switching are therefore inversely related. When we look at the data, we find that the decrease in job switching is striking. The likelihood of switching a job in a given month is 31 percent lower than what it was in 1994, the first year the data was collected.[11] This decline in the dynamism of the labor market is massive. And if workers switch jobs less often, then we naturally see a decline in the adjustment of the workforce. In other words, there is a decline in business dynamism.

Another way of examining this labor market dynamism is to look into migration rates between cities. Since most people who relocate from one city to another do so because of a job change, the data naturally also shows a substantial decrease in the migration rates within the country. Migration rates have decreased by about half. Whereas thirty years ago the fraction of the population that migrated between states in a given month was 3 percent, now it is 1.5 percent.[12]

This large decline in the dynamism of the labor market is a cause for concern. I will argue that despite the desirability of job security, the slowdown in job switches is harmful. It hampers social mobility, as workers get promoted at a lower rate and they climb up the job ladder at a slower pace, which affects some workers much more than others, in particular the young and new graduates. It now takes the young longer before they can find a job, which hurts them and the economy because they lose out on the largest growth in their productivity.

The absence of job prospects when young is also the reason why many people in European countries live with their parents until their mid-thirties, and why they marry and have children late or not at all.

With low labor market dynamism, older workers who happen to lose their jobs at or after the age of fifty are doomed because it is much harder to find a new job. A telling example is that of the Danish labor market. Until the 1990s, workers in Denmark experienced low labor market dynamism and hence long unemployment durations comparable to workers in Mediterranean countries today. The Danish government introduced policies that would do away with the rigidity of job security precisely to make job finding more fluid. Now both old and young Danish workers can find jobs more quickly, and that compensates for their lack of job security because there are no doomsday scenarios for those above age fifty (this is discussed in greater detail in chapter 11).

Every new job originates at a firm that expands, and whether a firm expands is driven by innovation. Young firms create disproportionately more jobs than older and more established firms do.[13] One of the most striking facts is that currently there are fewer new startup firms than there were four decades ago.

If at a cocktail party you insist that startups are down, you risk not being taken seriously. Surely, with fast technological change and the new, fast-growing firms out of Silicon Valley, there are more startups than ever, people argue. And yes, some are startups like pets.com that never live up to their promise, but at least they try and they innovate. But this is not what the data tells us.

Across the economy in all sectors, such as retail, manufacturing, transportation, energy, banking, and so on, about half as many new businesses are started every year compared to forty years ago.[14] The decline in startups is true even in the tech sector![15] After all, who will enter to compete with Google or Facebook? It may have come as a surprise, but the startup boom is a myth.

Modern Times Then

All these ailments that affect the current state of work—lower wages for the common worker, rising wage inequality, a declining labor share, declining labor dynamism and mobility, declining startups—are new since 1980. The main aim of this book is to go on a quest to discover why work has lost its luster.

Undoubtedly, the past forty years has been a period of remarkable technological change, globalization, and changing demographics. These profound changes are the first candidates to explain this evolution and development. And technology deserves particular attention. But technology is not the villain in this murder mystery. Rather, it resembles Javier Pereira in the series *Good Behavior* (2016–2017), where all are bad and he is the least bad. More importantly, when you watch the series, you tend to sympathize with him. It is the same with technological change: many of the ailments that we observe in the data about work originate in technology. And while technological change is very often the cause, it is also the solution.

To find the real villain we need to take a detour, because even if what is going on with work in the past forty years is remarkable, it is not unique in history. The current state of work is not all that different from a hundred years ago, so our detour takes us to the original "modern times."

In the full onslaught of the Great Depression, Charlie Chaplin's silent film *Modern Times* tells the story of a factory worker whose labor is dehumanized—where the meaning of his work is equated to that of a cog, a screw, or a coil. In conjunction with the repetitiveness of his actions, he fights in frustration against the effect of the machine and the assembly line from the Industrial Age. For the last time Chaplin plays his favorite character, the Little Tramp, who first appeared on screen in 1914 and made him a familiar and popular persona around the world.

Poor and destitute, well-mannered and educated, and with a heart of gold, the Tramp is from a lost generation that is doing worse than their parents. Whenever he can, he dresses up elegantly with a white collar, a hat, and a three-piece suit. Even if he only has one pea to eat, he serves the meal on white linen.

He is poor because as a middle-class worker, he has been dealt a bad hand. He has received some education and is well prepared for doing any job, but the only jobs he can get are those on the assembly line where it is hard work for little pay, and where his middle-class background and education is not valued. Work conditions are harsh, the pay is low, and the work is dehumanizing. By the time Chaplin makes *Modern Times*, his focus is on the origins of why work is so miserable.

Modern Times premiered in February 1936 at the Rivoli Theatre in New York City. The movie was not an immediate box-office success in the United States, but it had a big impact in Europe, both popularly and with intellectuals. Jean-Paul Sartre and Simone de Beauvoir used the title of the movie to name their French existentialist literary magazine (*Les Temps modernes*), which was published from 1945 to 2019. The images the movie portrayed had a lasting legacy. The idea of Big Brother screens controlling the workers made it into George Orwell's novel *1984*, which was not published until 1949, and the assembly line scene has been an inspiration for many other comedy features.

When the movie was made, the economy was at the height of the Great Depression.[16] It was the first global economic recession after the first truly global conflict, World War I. The global conflict and economic downturn came on the heels of of the first global economic epoch, which had seen unprecedented expansion of industrial production, technological innovation, and an enormously dense network of international trade routes.

The Second Industrial Revolution, between 1870 and World War I, saw an explosion of inventions in manufacturing in the use of machine tools and steel production, as well as in the spread of electrification, the use of petroleum, and the development of new materials and chemicals. Those technological developments in manufacturing gradually led to a large increase in mobility and communication—a massive expansion of the railroad network around the world, the introduction and dissemination of the internal combustion engine, the development of the electric engine, the introduction of the manufacturing production line, and the use of new communication technology such as the telegraph, the telephone, and the radio.

While the groundwork for these developments was often laid decades earlier, in the first half of the nineteenth century, it was not until the availability of other technologies that large-scale production led to rapid economic development toward the turn of the twentieth century.

Trade and mobility of goods, people, and ideas contributed to the spread of technology and growth. Both nationally and internationally, the interdependence of economic flows and interests was greater than ever. International trade before World War I, with 30 percent of output, was at its highest level ever following rapid growth during the preceding decades.[17] Then, following World War I and the Great Depression in the 1930s, trade dropped back to 10 percent and would not reach 30 percent of gross domestic product until more than half a century later, in the mid-1970s.

In conjunction with rapid economic growth and progress, the rise of technological change also allowed firms to organize in ways that enabled them to exert more market power. Firms that opened up new markets not only were the first to enter new markets, but the technology also allowed them to build on the first-mover advantage to maintain market dominance.

Lack of entry of firms competing away those profits was due either to the technological aspects (huge entry costs for railroads), to the implicit protection by government policies, to the lack of enforcement of antitrust, or to explicit collusion. The individuals behind the business empires that they managed to build were often accused of unscrupulous and amoral tactics, lending the name "robber barons" to those entrepreneurial heavyweights such as Andrew W. Mellon, J. P. Morgan, Andrew Carnegie, Charles M. Schwab, Leland Stanford, Russell Sage, Cornelius Vanderbilt, and John D. Rockefeller.

While some have argued that the robber barons were captains of industry who created economic progress, many historians view them in a negative light, as obstructionists who plundered and cheated investors, customers, and the government. John D. Rockefeller's Standard Oil, for example, had been buying up many smaller firms to exert market power in an industry where competition would bring down profits; and J. P. Morgan reorganized and consolidated competing railroad companies along the US East Coast and in the Midwest, where he created the controversial Northern Securities Company, which had a virtual monopoly around Chicago.

A by-product of that period of enormous wealth accumulation in the hands of a few companies and individuals has left us with a long-lasting legacy of philanthropy, much of it to the benefit of universities and research institutions that got their names from those wealthy families, such as Stanford, Carnegie-Mellon, Duke, and Vanderbilt Universities and the Russell Sage Foundation. Andrew Carnegie gave away 90 percent of his wealth, much like the Giving Pledge campaign launched by Bill Gates and Warren Buffett, inspiring contemporary billionaires to give away at least half their wealth.

Interestingly, a nonnegligible share of last century's wealth accumulated in the hands of a few gigantic corporations has ended up in the richest foundations that fund social intervention as well as research into social issues. Cynically, those causes are often related, directly or indirectly, to putting right the wrongs of the moneymaking activities of the founders of the foundations.

Massive wealth also made for amazing architecture. Impressive buildings like Grand Central Station or the offices of General Motors in New York would probably not have been built if Vanderbilt or Ford had very thin margins.[18] This was not exclusive to the United States. Major architectural achievements at the turn of the century would not have been built without philanthropy of the rich: the Eiffel Tower in Paris, the art nouveau buildings by Horta in Brussels, and the modernist buildings by Gaudí in Barcelona.

The wealth accumulation and the economic growth that technological progress brought looked extremely good on paper. The extreme global interconnectedness of the economic activity even led people to believe that finally the world had reached a point where there was no way back: the economic prosperity was there to stay. Recall, this is the period in which international travel across most advanced countries was unrestricted and no passports were needed.[19]

In 1910 Norman Angell published *The Great Illusion*, arguing that the economies of different countries were so interdependent through trade flows and credit that the economic losses of this economic independence would be too great to ever curtail it, and no nation would have any incentive to wage war. Even if a country conquered another and seized its property, the need to maintain the conquered population would require the occupying country to grant property rights, as well as to incur the cost of occupation.[20] It is the ultimate view of capitalism: capital, human or physical, in a modern open economy does not see borders or respond to nationalities or countries.

Of course, Angell's thesis was itself a great illusion and proven wrong only four years after publication with the onset of World War I. In the ensuing years he reformulated his thesis, saying that given economic development and interconnectedness, war was not impossible but pointless and economically irrational. Underneath this unbridled optimism reflecting unprecedented average economic growth and average wealth accumulation, however, was the entirely skewed distribution of those gains.

Chaplin's *Modern Times* illustrates that those gains were not equally spread and that the vast majority of the working population was worse off despite the progress. Even Angell's refurbished view did not take into consideration the fact that for the economic system the gains must be distributed sufficiently evenly, or else the majority of the population has nothing to lose if the whole progress machine is destroyed.

Modern Times Now

The central tenet of the profit paradox is that rapid technological change creates enormous potential for economic and social progress. Innovating firms improve efficiency and the lives of citizens. At the same time, the new technology lets firms build up market power and dominance that is detrimental for work.

The profit paradox, and its development since 1980, has a lot in common with how it developed over a century ago. Modern times now are not unlike Chaplin's *Modern Times*. A well-trained, educated worker like Erin who works as a senior technical advisor in IT earns strikingly low wages, while her parent company reports enormous profits and reaches an unprecedented stock market valuation.

Just like the development of electricity, the telegraph, and the combustion engine in the eighteenth century, technological development after World War II gave rise to computers, the internet, and mobile communication. Half a century after those individual discoveries, the democratization and the resulting scale of the operations at the turn of the twenty-first century led to the widespread adoption of mobile phones and the transformation of many sectors, retail not the least. This huge technological disruption has not only brought progress, but it has also created the possibility for first movers to develop market power and to stifle competition.

The highway of digital communication today is the equivalent of the railways of the early twentieth century. Just like J. P. Morgan created market power by consolidating competing operators and raising prices, in current times Mark Zuckerberg has consolidated the large social media platforms Facebook, Instagram, and WhatsApp.

That market power has brought enormous profits and has created huge wealth. In fifty years our grandchildren and great-grandchildren are likely to apply for grants from a Zuckerberg Fund, if it exists, or the Bezos Family Foundation, and buildings and museums with those family or company names will be on the list of landmarks, just like the Guggenheim Museum today.

Most of today's bankers, hedge fund owners, entrepreneurs, and Silicon Valley billionaires still do not have bad reputations, at least for now. Let us hope that the economic impact of today's market power is less acute than it was a century ago.

Even the robber baron's market power in the Gilded Age was a decaffeinated version of full monopoly power that the Crown granted to the Dutch East India Company in the seventeenth century.[21] However, there is no doubt a parallel that market power by firms in the output market has far-reaching implications for work today, as it did over a century ago.

The point of this book is to document that the evolution of work we have seen in the past forty years is the result of a rise in market power, and that the causes and implications bear a remarkable resemblance to what happened in Chaplin's *Modern Times*.

I am taking the liberty to describe current times as "modern" because in economic terms, our times resemble that period usually identified as modern—the turn of the twentieth century. It is a similar socioeconomic epoch with fast technological progress, with globalization and economic interdependence, and with substantial disparities in how the economic gains from this progress are distributed.

Interestingly enough, there is a double meaning to the word "modern." More colloquially, with *modo* (meaning "just now") as its root, "modern" stands for something current, or an event in the not-too-distant past. For example, modern batteries now give electric cars a range of up to 350 miles. The terms "modern" and "contemporary" are synonyms in vernacular English. At the same time, it indicates a particular epoch.

The focus of the book is on documenting all aspects of work and how they have evolved in the past four decades. I will report the facts and what we know, as well as how things have changed and are in the process of changing. In addition to the facts, we have a wealth of economic research that analyzes and interprets the facts from current times. This allows us to search for the causes.

What follows is a quest for what is the cause of the current state of work, based on the facts and economic research. But this book is also inspired by Studs Terkel's book *Working* (1974), which recounts what ordinary (and not-so-ordinary) people do all day. Throughout the book I will accompany my quest for the facts and statistics with the stories of individuals like Erin that are related to work. While there is a sharp scientific contrast between the large number of observations with statistical significance and the singular experience of an individual worker, I cannot state it more lucidly than Stefan Zweig that both are valuable: "It is not the cold fact which has meaning, but rather the human and emotional element contained within it."[22]

PART I

The Origins
of Market Power

2

The Art of Managing
the Moat

WARREN BUFFETT DESCRIBES the ideal business he wants to invest in as follows: "I don't want a business that's easy for competitors. I want a business with a moat around it. I want a very valuable castle in the middle, and then I want the Duke in charge of the castle to be honest and hard-working and able, and then I want a big moat around the castle." He goes on to say that if you've got a beautiful castle, people are going to try to attack it, so he has one message for his managers, which is to widen the moat and to throw crocodiles and sharks into the moat to discourage competitors.[1]

If you think about it, it is an entrepreneur's dream to be a monopolist, the only firm active in the market. Without competitors, the monopolist sets a price that maximizes profits. There is probably no pure monopoly anywhere in the world, but in the early 2000s cable television providers like Comcast were pretty close to monopolistic in many local markets. When they were the only provider in rural states, they could set prices without consideration of competitors.

Higher prices directly increase revenue because each unit is sold at a higher price than what it costs to manufacture. Higher prices also indirectly decrease revenue because fewer buyers can afford to buy, and hence Comcast sells fewer contracts. The profit-maximizing price trades off higher revenue from the direct effect of higher prices with lower revenue from the indirect effect of selling fewer contracts.

Comcast was never a pure monopoly because there were alternative providers that offered substitute services such as satellite, and internet providers increasingly started to compete. When only a small number of firms compete, then the market is an oligopoly. Firms face limited competition, and they can still set prices above costs and make excess profit without being undercut completely. High profits are difficult to sustain, however, because they attract competitors who want a share. Easy entry by competitors and the resulting competition is the entire paradigm on which the capitalist system within a competitive economy is built.

In a competitive market without market power, firms make no more profit than the return on capital, appropriately compensating the investor for risk and other costs.[2] We can thus define market power as the ability of a firm to raise prices above costs and generate excess profits to compensate for investment, risk, and innovation. And as Warren Buffett eloquently explained, successful entrepreneurs always look for markets where they face limited competition. The reason why an entrepreneur sets up a firm and enters into a market in the first place is to generate a return that is higher than what they can make by just leaving the money in a bank account.

Of course, excess profits are not equal to all. When Walmart started to dominate the retail market, its profits went through the roof while those of their competitors slumped. The whole point of entrepreneurship is to take risky gambles with the objective of coming out on top, which involves a substantial amount of luck in addition to savvy decisions and skillful development of new technologies.

The whole objective is to come out as a winner in this race to innovate and become more productive, but the monopoly power obtained is supposed to be temporary. That is Joseph Schumpeter's theory of growth and creative destruction: firms innovate in order to gain temporary market power, while in the process destroying the existing, inferior technologies.[3]

The innovations also open up opportunities for competitors to adopt the new technologies or even surpass them, thus eating away at the positions of the leaders in the process. This continuous game of leapfrog is the driver of technological change. Tesla dominates the electric car market, but competitors are already threatening their lead with better or cheaper technology.

The monopoly power provides incentives for innovation and growth, yet that power is temporary and will eventually vanish once competitors adopt the same or a superior technology. Moreover, it should not lead to excess profits because in order to make the leap and eventually benefit from the temporary market power, the firm needs to invest. With rivals competing to make the leap, firms will invest up front as much as the profits they expect the investment to generate.

As a weathered investor like Warren Buffett prescribes, the objective of a profit-making firm is not necessarily to innovate in order to come up with new products and technologies or to make producing cheaper. Just as often, the objective is to make sure that other firms cannot enter the market and grab a share of those profits.

Rather than a dynamic of leapfrogging firms whose temporary monopoly power gives them incentives to innovate, Buffett's entrepreneur cements the castle into a permanent monopoly by building a moat around it to limit entry of competitors. If the investor accumulates those castles and uses the profits from them to acquire other castles with large moats around them, then the Schumpeterian growth story turns into a Monopoly board game.

Incidentally, the Parker Brothers, who own the Monopoly board game as it is played today, liked to market it as an American dream story of an unemployed worker who invented Monopoly during the Great Depression and became a millionaire after he made it into arguably the most popular board game.

The truth is somewhat more complicated, however. Today's Monopoly is based on the Landlord's Game, designed in 1903 by Elizabeth Magie, which she made as a pedagogical device to illustrate the perils of monopoly. She had two sets of rules. First, the game as it is played under today's rules leads to one dominant owner and the winner of the game. But she also included a second set of antimonopolist rules where growing wealth was distributed to all. The antimonopolist rules were based on the ideas of the nineteenth-century economist and politician

Henry George, who had proposed a land value tax as the least distortionary way of generating government revenue instead of taxing labor income.[4]

Magie's board game was a rebuke of the wealthy industrialists such as J. P. Morgan and John D. Rockefeller, who had become rich winning the monopoly game of the real economy. During that epoch there was a perception that technological innovation would lead to the creation of dominant and uncontested firms, instead of a Schumpeterian dynamic with leapfrogging of firms enjoying temporary monopoly power.

Several decades later, George Orwell, in his review of *The Road to Serfdom*, argued that Friedrich Hayek was painting too rosy a picture of competition in a free market economy. Orwell alleged that "the trouble with competitions is that somebody wins them."[5] Hayek was a brilliant economist and philosopher; Orwell was not an economist but he was an equally gifted thinker. Economists have long known that certain conditions (full information as well as the absence of externalities, economies of scale, and frictions) need to be satisfied for competition to yield the beneficial outcomes of Adam Smith's "invisible hand" and generate the greatest good for the greatest number of people.

The difference in opinion between Hayek and Orwell rests on whether the premise of those conditions for competition to be beneficial were satisfied. Hayek considered those conditions for perfect competition were largely satisfied, whereas Orwell argued they were not and that "free capitalism necessarily leads to monopoly."[6]

At the turn of the twentieth century, a handful of firms had managed to become the dominant players in their markets, without the beneficial competition that Hayek advocated for. Through consolidation, often with shady practices, a few firms in oil and railways, for example, managed to control entire networks of production that made it prohibitively expensive for competitors to enter the market. Firms were engaging in competitions "for" a market rather than facing competition "in" a market. They fiercely competed to become the dominant firm in the market, but once they won their competitions, the winners subsequently faced no further competition. It took Orwell's literary genius to add an "s" to Hayek's "competition" to underscore their disagreement.

I will argue that just as over a century ago, between 1890 and 2014, in the last decades of rapid technological progress, Schumpeter's theory has failed and firms have managed to extend market power more permanently. Using the disruption of fast technological change, those successful firms have managed to become highly productive, and at the same time they have managed to exploit that same technological advantage to fend off competitors. Technological innovation gives both the advantage to become the leader and it builds a permanent moat.

Let us turn to the evidence on market power and we can see whether, and how much, the current economy bestows market power on firms.

Evidence of the Rise of Market Power

Casual evidence about market power is everywhere. This is most often illustrated by how a few firms dominate any given market. Eighty-nine percent of pacemakers are produced by three firms, with the market leader, Medtronic, having more than half the market share. Sixty-nine percent of baby formula sold in the United States is produced by two firms. Fifty-seven percent of dry cat food sold in the United States is produced by one firm, Nestlé. Unilever and Kraft account for 87 percent of US mayonnaise sales. Seventy percent of all social networking is in the hands of Facebook; Twitter and LinkedIn jointly only account for 15 percent. The four major airlines have a 76 percent share of the domestic US airline market. The Home Depot and Lowe's have an 81 percent share of the US market for home improvement. And if you ever decide to plan your funeral before you die, you are likely to choose one of two manufacturers for coffins and caskets who have an 82 percent market share.[7]

The concentration of firms—the fact that there are few options to buy from—is an indication of market power, but it does not tell the whole story. In some sectors, such as utilities and heavy industry, the cost of setting up a firm is so high that there is space only for a few firms. Therefore we need more precise tools and measures to analyze market power in order to map the current state of affairs and how market power has changed over time.

In early 2017, Jan De Loecker, then at Princeton and now at the University of Leuven, and I were investigating the effect of market power on the salaries of executives. Our hypothesis was that an increase in market power would lead to an increase in executive salaries. To test this hypothesis, we needed to derive a measure of market power for all the largest firms.

Interestingly enough, while there were detailed studies on market power in narrowly defined markets, little was known about market power economy-wide. The view of most experts was that it is impossible to calculate market power indicators for the whole economy because the data needed to do so is not available using existing methods.

Going back to a method in a 1988 research paper by Bob Hall from Stanford to calculate the market power sector by sector,[8] we used accounting data for publicly traded firms in order to back out a market power measure for each individual firm rather than the entire sector. Because accounting data goes back to the 1950s and publicly traded firms account for over one-third of the economy, for the first time we managed to calculate measures of market power for each firm, across all sectors and over seven decades. What we measured is usually called a markup—the price a firm charges over the unit cost of production. For a car manufacturer, that would be the cost of steel, tires, and other materials, as well as the wages for the workers who work on the assembly floor. If a firm sells one car for $12,500 and the unit cost is $10,000, then the markup is 1.25. The markup is relevant because it informs about how costly a good is relative to its price.

This new series of data that documents the evolution of market power turned out to be full of surprises even for two nerdy economists. To our astonishment, the data showed a remarkable pattern over time. As we can see in figure 3, the average markup in the United States began to rise sharply, from 1.21 in 1980 to 1.54 in 2019. That means that initially firms were selling 21 percent above cost and now they are selling 54 percent above cost. There was a particularly sharp rise in the 1980s and 1990s, followed by a decade of markup stagnation in 2000, followed in turn by a new sharp rise in 2010 after the Great Recession.

The pattern of this increase is not just an artifact of the US economy—it is spread across the globe with similar evolutions in Europe,

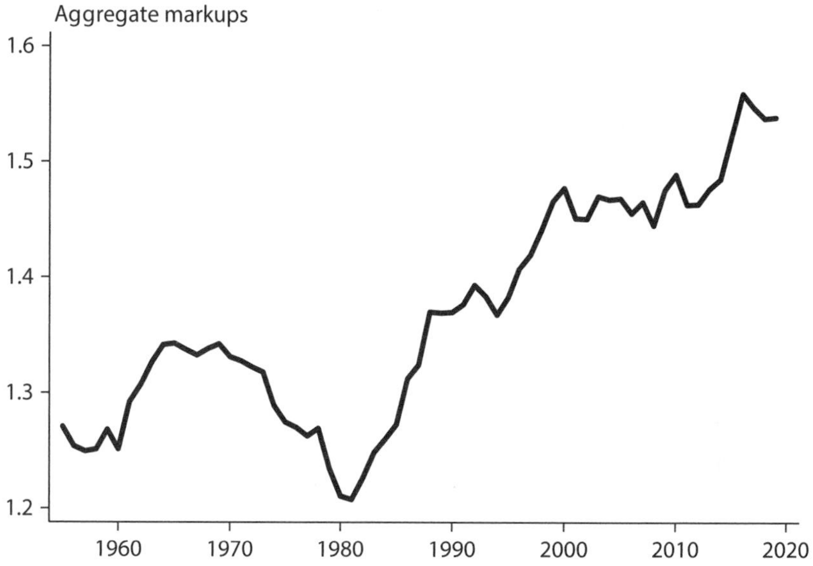

Aggregate markups

FIGURE 3. Aggregate markups in the United States. *Source*: De Loecker, Eeckhout, & Unger (2020), 575. For further details, see www.TheProfitParadox.com.

North America, and Asia. Worldwide, markups increased from 1980 through 2000 (see figure 4). Then, in the first decade of the twenty-first century, markups stagnated, only to rise sharply again in 2010 after the Great Recession. It is quite striking how similar this pattern is across most continents around the world. In particular, the pattern of markups in Europe is virtually identical to that in the United States, even if Europe started off somewhat lower.[9] Some of the emerging economies in South America and Africa have seen less of an increase, but they had higher markup levels to start with. In sum, we find that the rise of market power is a global phenomenon.

When we started to dig deeper, to our even greater surprise we found that the rise in markups is a phenomenon that we see from tech to textiles. It is not just the usual suspects, namely the Googles and Apples in the tech industry, that are driving the rise. Some of these tech firms do have high markups, but there are also some firms in more traditional sectors, such as textiles or retail, that have seen a similar or even larger increase in markups. New technologies in any sector, including the traditional sectors, appear to be driving the rise in markups.

Aggregate markups

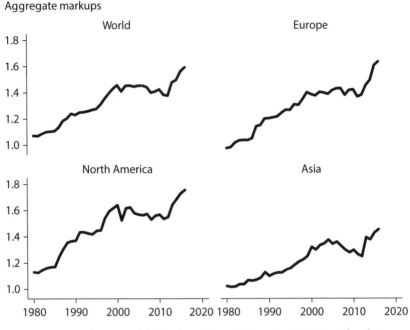

FIGURE 4. Aggregate global markups. *Source*: De Loecker & Eeckhout (2018), 6.
For further details, see www.TheProfitParadox.com.

The firms in these traditional sectors that adopted new technologies have higher markups. The Spanish clothing producer and retailer Zara, for example, uses advanced data science technologies for design, production, and logistics. These new technologies allow the firm to save on costs and increase sales by responding more rapidly to customer demand for fashionable clothing items. In addition, lower costs allow Zara to price the goods competitively, which increases their market share.

There are always differences across sectors. For example, retail is a notoriously low-markup business. Walmart has become the largest firm in the world precisely because it has kept undercutting the prices of its competitors. Walmart gets its profits from volume on relatively low markups, though it still has higher markups than its competitors.

In contrast, many businesses in much more specialized markets, such as for medical devices, have enormous margins. The US company

Mylan, for example, has had high markups in recent years. They are the producers of EpiPen, the anti-allergy device that sells for $609, up from $94 in 2007. The estimated production cost is $35 and has not changed over the same period. EpiPen's unscrupulous pricing strategy has been controversial, but unfortunately it is not an isolated case.

When the results of my collaboration with De Loecker first came out, Jim Bullard, an economist and the chairman of the Federal Reserve Bank of St. Louis, told me that the business leaders in his district, covering Arkansas and parts of Illinois, Indiana, Kentucky, Mississippi, Missouri, and Tennessee, tell him a very different story.[10] The executives of those manufacturing and retail firms all experience a squeeze by overseas competitors or by local firms with superior technologies.

Because the firms in the St. Louis area face competitors from all over the world that massively deploy robots, data-driven logistics, and artificial intelligence, the competition leaves these more traditional companies zero or no margins and many are forced to close down. I agree with the assessment that most firms are having harder times than ever because we see exactly that in the data—just looking at the average markups and their rise is misleading.

The most shocking observation is that the median markup, the markup of the firm exactly in the middle of the distribution, has remained unchanged. This tells us that for at least half of the firms, there has been no rise in markups at all! Yet, at the same time, markups for a few firms have grown outlandishly. The ninetieth percentile of the markup distribution—those firms with the highest markups—has grown from 1.5 in 1980 to a whopping 2.5 in 2016. Ten percent of the firms now sell their goods 250 percent above cost!

There is not only a rise in markups from which thriving firms benefit. Those firms that run high markups also obtain a high share of the sales. This reallocation of business from low-markup firms to high-markup firms is what leads to the large, dominant firms.

The Amazons of this economy are not only able to produce at higher margins, but they also dominate their competitors. What has happened over the past forty years confirms George Orwell's assessment: the trouble with competitions is that somebody wins them. Not only does the economy pick winners, the prize pot for those winners has grown enormously. All other firms are struggling.

To make a caricature of the point, the St. Louis Federal Reserve has jurisdiction over giant companies like Anheuser-Busch. Sadly, it is unlikely that the CEO would meet with the Federal Reserve Bank of St. Louis. This is because Anheuser-Busch is now owned by AB InBev, and its headquarters are located in Leuven, Belgium, rather than in St. Louis.

Rising Profits

The sharp rise in market power has been confirmed using different measurements and methods by other researchers.[11] But markups alone do not paint the full picture of market power. To complete the picture we need to consider all costs, not only the direct costs needed for production but also the cost of capital and overhead costs, which are large upfront investments, the benefits of which are only obtained gradually.

Capital includes expenditure on machines and buildings, and overhead consists of expenditure on R&D, marketing, and advertising, as well as salaries of management. These expenditures do not vary directly with the amount of output produced. Once installed, the cost of a robot to assemble a car is the same whether the robot is used at full capacity or whether it sits idle. This renders capital and overhead costs fixed.

Of course, over a long time horizon, the firm adjusts those fixed-cost investments to the capacity and productivity needed. If a firm was in the business of transporting people across the river using a ferry, then building a bridge is an extremely costly investment that makes the transportation cost virtually zero. The fixed cost of buying the ferry and building the pier is considerably lower, but there is a much higher variable cost of operating the ferry.

Now, the data shows that these overhead costs and capital are fairly small as a share of a firm's total costs, but they are growing, especially overhead costs. In 1980, overhead costs were on average around 15 percent of total costs, and now they are 22 percent. The cost of capital is even smaller (around 9 percent of total cost). But again, capital and overhead costs vary substantially across firms. For some biotechnology firms, for

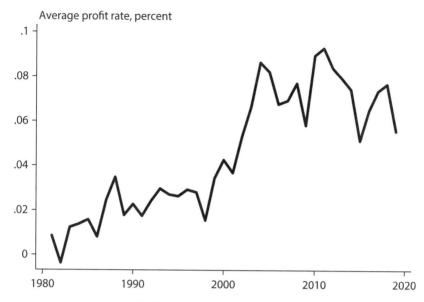

FIGURE 5. Average profits of publicly traded firms in the United States. *Source*: De Loecker, Eeckhout, & Unger (2020), 595. For further details, see www.TheProfitParadox.com.

example, overhead costs are the vast majority of their expenses, and they have little variable costs. I will turn to this below, because who incurs those large fixed-cost investments is key to understanding the evolution market power.

To calculate the profitability of a firm, we need to account not only for the variable cost but also for the cost of capital and overhead. That is a fundamental difference between a markup, based exclusively on variable costs, and profits, based on all costs, both variable and fixed.

When we calculate the profit rate, the percentage of profits a firm makes as a share of its sales, we find that those have seen a sharp increase as well, from 1–2 percent of sales in 1980 to 7–8 percent in 2016, as shown in figure 5.[12] That is a gigantic increase!

To see how large an 8 percent profit rate is, consider that firms on average spend around 20 percent of their sales on payroll. That includes wages for production workers, salaries for managers, and incentive compensation, payroll taxes, and pension costs. The remainder of the firm's expenses goes to buying materials, overhead costs, and the cost of capital. Whatever is left over of sales is profits.

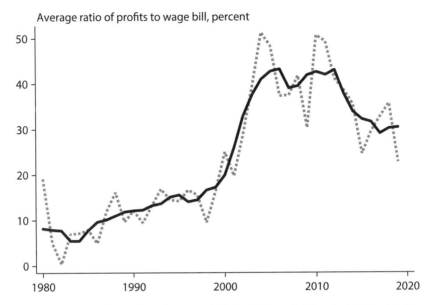

Average ratio of profits to wage bill, percent

FIGURE 6. Average of ratio of profits to wage bill of publicly traded firms in the United States. *Source*: De Loecker, Eeckhout, & Unger (2020) and author's own calculations. For further details, see www.TheProfitParadox.com.

So there is an enormous increase in the ratio of profits as a share of payroll, from as low as 5 percent in 1984 to as high as 43 percent in 2012. As figure 6 illustrates, in the 1980s firms on average made profits that were less than one-tenth of payroll—profits were on average around 1–2 percent of sales and payroll was 20 percent. By the mid-2000s that ratio had jumped above 30 percent. Part of the driving force behind the rise in the ratio of profits to payroll is a moderate decline in payroll as a share of sales. But the majority of the increase is the rise in profits as a share of sales to around 7–8 percent.

The fact that firms obtain profits that are nearly half of what they spend on all compensation for employees, from production workers to executives, is clear evidence of an increase in market power, and that increase is enormous.

As is the case with profits, there are huge differences across firms in the ratio of profits to payroll. Most firms have very low ratios, and a few dominant firms have very high ratios. Moreover, the extremely high ratios for some firms is a recent phenomenon that did not exist in the 1980s. Since then, most firms still have profits that are a small share of payroll, but a few firms have outlandish ratios. For example, Apple and Facebook have ratios that are well over 300 percent. But this phenomenon is not confined to the tech sector. In the pharmaceutical sector, Pfizer had a profit-to-payroll ratio of 210 percent in 2019, up from 41 percent in 1980.[13] The dominance of a few firms in terms of profitability reflects precisely what the profit paradox is about: the success of thriving firms is not beneficial for workers.

The rise of market power shows that inside the firm there is a shift of money flowing from compensation for work to compensation for profits, and hence to ownership of the firm. Ownership goes from getting a tiny fraction of sales to getting nearly half of what employees get. This is a clear sign that something fundamental has changed. Market power is not merely about paying high prices for goods, it is as much about the enormous impact it has on work. This book is about exploring the massive ramifications market power has for work.

We also embark on a journey to explore what causes market power. With this new evidence of the rise in market power and the growing size of dominant corporate castles, the most pressing question is: What is the origin of the widening moat that protects those castles? Only if we understand the causes can we formulate effective policy responses to remedy the calamitous impact of market power on work. Each dominant firm has its own story, but I will classify the moat origins in two categories.

First, moats that result directly from the market structure and the systematic creation of dominant firms through mergers and acquisitions and the concentration of ownership in the hands of the few. An example of such a moat is the one that protects the castles in the beer market. Second, moats that result from organic growth and technological change, an example of which is Amazon. Let's start with beer.

More Choice Is Less: Mergers and Acquisitions

When I was finishing high school in Belgium, I started going out with friends to school parties, the soccer club championship celebration, or simply to the local village bar. Every bar had its own flagship beer, as well as a selection of a few other beers on offer. There were as many beers as there were towns. And at the time there were as many brewers as there were brands. In our neighborhood it was Safir, a fairly standard pilsner, and De Ryck, a beer produced with high fermentation and with secondary fermentation in the bottle, called a *Spéciale Belge*. Safir gave you the typical headache and De Ryck did not, but you did notice the tertiary fermentation in the stomach the day after.

The colorful diversity in beer choice, however, was reaching its end, and by the early 1990s thousands of brands were consolidating. De Ryck managed to remain an independent niche beer, currently brewed by An de Ryck, the great-granddaughter of its founder. But that is a rare and unique story in the brewing industry.

Meanwhile, one brewer named Stella Artois, which in 1988 changed its name to Interbrew, acquired many of the most popular Belgian beer brands. At the same time many brands went bankrupt and disappeared. By the end of the millennium beer brands started to internationalize. The Safirs of the world now no longer exist, but today anywhere around the globe where you can find Coca-Cola, you can find Stella Artois and Hoegaarden.

The internationalization of the brands required distribution channels and a toehold to get entry into the pubs, which was best achieved by mergers with dominant firms in local markets. Interbrew first merged with the Canadian Labatt, followed by the merger in 2004 with the Brazilian brewer AmBev to form the new InBev. Finally, in 2008 InBev acquired Anheuser-Busch, the St. Louis brewer of Budweiser.

Back then, the Anheuser-Busch takeover was painted in the popular press to be the culmination of a dysfunctional Busch family saga with underperforming management that led to the loss of a national icon, Budweiser. Unknown to most, though, even before the Interbrew takeover, the Busch family had already sold most of its stake in the company that was owned by shareholders around the globe. It was in fact the worst of both worlds: the family no longer owned the company, so the national icon was already foreign owned. More importantly, management under the new ownership continued the parochial thinking of the Busch family. Anheuser-Busch and its Budweiser brand were destined to become the world leader in the global beer market, but their management was hardly thinking beyond St. Louis.

When the InBev management team landed in St. Louis in 2006 to complete the due diligence process of Anheuser-Busch, they knew immediately that there was a huge potential to be realized with the company's brands. Budweiser was marketed and sold nearly exclusively to the North American market. The success of InBev had been that its brands could be sold not only in Belgium but also from Buenos Aires to Shanghai, and from Toronto to Cape Town. After a week in St. Louis, the InBev management knew that Anheuser-Busch was not thinking of Budweiser as a global brand anytime soon when they realized that hardly anyone on the Anheuser-Busch management team held passports. Traveling outside North America, perhaps, was not on their agenda.

InBev, the relatively small player with management from Brazil and headquarters in Belgium, formed the current brewing giant AB InBev. InBev offered a 30 percent premium on Anheuser-Busch shares over the stock price before the offer. They would surely generate efficiency gains cleaning up the mess of Augustus IV Busch's reign and turning Budweiser into a global brand.

The customer benefited from these global brands because there was more choice, since anywhere in the world there were more and better beers on offer. But the reason why the merger was so valuable was not just the efficiency gains that resulted from establishing global brands. Most importantly, with this deal, the newly formed company AB InBev became the largest player in the beer market, where competition was limited. After yet another merger in 2016, with SABMiller, AB InBev is estimated to hold 28 percent of the global beer market—46 percent in the United States, 56 percent in Belgium, and 68 percent in Brazil.[14]

A company that controls half of the sales in any given market surely is a dominant player. The moat around the company is an intricate combination of advertising, exclusivity deals with bars and distributors, cross-subsidization of brands, and a powerful distribution network that keeps competitors out. The abundance of brands on tab at the bar may make it appear to the customer that they have choice, but a choice of many products does not mean competition among many providers and therefore lower prices. In economic terms, it is only an illusion of choice.

The customer is choosing from the same beer producer who has an exclusivity contract with the bar that sells beers by one owner only. With only a few of those giant beer producers, the customer can choose the brand but they cannot choose the competitor.

Moreover, research shows that these giant firms are not more efficient than the smaller firms.[15] AB InBev has created an unbridgeable moat for its beer castles, and with it comes the ability to set high prices and therefore make excess profits. With operations on all continents in a global marketplace, AB InBev is one of the most profitable multinational companies. It is a remarkably successful company, headquartered in Belgium, with Brazilian management, and selling American beer. Imagine the ideal scenario where they are based in Brazil, have American management, and sell Belgian beer.

Quips aside, the reality is that the fiscal headquarters are located in Belgium because of the low corporate tax rate, with operational headquarters in New York, and that the gutsy takeover philosophy originates with the Brazilian investment fund that is a major shareholder.

The apparent wealth of choice from a dominant provider with market power is not exclusive to the beer industry. Other so-called competitive industries give a perception of choice while the ownership is highly concentrated. The car dealer market in the United States, for example, has become highly concentrated. Often one or two businesses own all car dealerships. The customer gets the impression that they can buy a Toyota and compare the price with a Ford, or a BMW with a Volvo. They can even be lulled into the illusion they can haggle with the competitor to obtain a better deal. But when they walk over to the dealership next door, the showroom with the different brand is under the same ownership. Not surprisingly, it is hard to come away with a good deal from the competitor, and prices are far from competitive. It is like bargaining at the butcher's over the price of lamb and threatening to buy veal. There is evidence that concentration of ownership in car dealers in US cities has risen remarkably, especially since the Great Recession.[16] Again, a portfolio of choice does not guarantee competitive prices. Only diverse ownership leads to competition.

Even the ownership of supposedly free services such as Facebook, Instagram, and WhatsApp by one company (Facebook) gives the customer choice but not competitive prices—and often not even real choice. Advertisers who compete for eyeballs are paying more than what they would pay if these companies were independently owned.

Then there is the market power that arises from killer acquisitions.[17] Companies like X (formerly Google X) or pharmaceutical companies buy up promising startup companies before they make it big. The pharmaceutical company is not really interested in the value of the product or service of the acquired company—though they may be interested in keeping some of the brightest minds—rather, it wants to take down a direct competitor who obstructs the pharmaceutical's potential to charge high prices.

The killer acquisition in antitrust is the equivalent of the catch-and-kill practice in media; for example, the *National Enquirer* buys Stormy Daniels's exclusive rights to the story of her affair, with the objective to never publish it. In the same manner, dominant firms like X take over a small competitor to close the competitor down. This is just another way of widening the moat.

In recent years, researchers have discovered yet another hidden way in which firms stifle competition, called common ownership. Under the motto "If you can't beat 'em, join 'em," financial firms own significant stakes in direct competitors. It is a bit like the competing auto dealerships that are owned by the same company, only the businesses are so vast that these financial firms own only a share of those companies. For example, investment firms like BlackRock, Berkshire Hathaway (the conglomerate of which Warren Buffett is chairman and CEO), and Vanguard are the largest shareholders in the largest companies in many sectors, including the major airlines. Interestingly enough, the shares in those large investment funds are owned by people like you and me through index funds for our pensions. Even the late John Bogle, inventor of the index fund and founder of Vanguard, became concerned that index funds are becoming so dominant that their concentration is not in the national interest.[18]

Research shows that on routes where competitors have a significant share of common ownership, ticket prices are higher.[19] Tacit collusion—the practice where competitors follow the price setting of the dominant firm—is prevalent, even though it is illegal in the European Union and Canada. But more than price-fixing practices, common ownership is particularly influential at the level of strategic decision making.[20] When an airline company decides which routes to enter or exit, they will have in mind who the competitors are. Delta will think twice about entering an American Airlines route when both companies are owned by the same majority shareholder.

In addition to common ownership, the airline industry in the United States has become increasingly concentrated over the past twenty years due to an extensive sequence of mergers and acquisitions, going from ten to four major airlines.[21] Remember US Airways, Continental, or TWA? The customer pays for this lack of competition with higher prices and fewer options. Prices in the United States are roughly double what they are on comparable routes in competitive markets around the world.[22] Not surprisingly, profit margins for US airlines are higher as well.

Over a beer, some economists argue that the rise in market power is due to economics teaching and the spreading of MBA graduates. When we teach the prisoner's dilemma to undergraduates, we tell them the story of the tragedy of the commons, where shepherds let their flock of sheep overgraze to the point where there is no more green left. Each shepherd is better off free riding and letting their flock graze a lot, but as a community they are worse off if all shepherds do so. We then think about ways in which we can overcome this free-rider problem. Those solutions include monitoring, fencing off the green, contracts, and social norms that can be enforced because the common-goods problem is among citizens who have repeated interactions.

When we turn from twenty-year-old undergraduate students to the twenty-six-year-olds who are enrolled in MBA programs, we explain exactly the same game but we frame it differently. It is between competitors in a duopoly who flood the market with their goods and thus drive down the price and the firm profits. If only the firms could cooperate, both firms would be better off and realize higher profits. Overt collusion to fix high prices is illegal because it is to the detriment of the customer, so we tell students about all the strategies to solve the free-rider problem that are similar to the strategies that solve the tragedy of the commons. Rather than cooperation for the common good, now it is about cooperation to collude and raise prices and profits.

Not all market power stems from grabbing market share via mergers, hostile takeovers, or from wealthy funds owning multiple competitors. Another reason for market power is technology: enter Amazon.

3

Technological Change and Superiority

WE ALL LOVE AMAZON because it brings a book, a pack of lightbulbs, or sportswear at rock-bottom prices right to our doorsteps, barely a day after we add the items to our shopping carts. Better and faster service at lower prices is great for the customer. Amazon can do this because they are a technologically superior firm that has lower costs than any of its competitors. The company has grown organically as a result of innovation and huge investments in logistics instead of through mergers and acquisitions taking over competitors.

Technological progress leads to lower costs and hence lower prices. Still, that technological superiority is not all good news. Technology that is lopsided also creates scope for market power. Smaller bookstores, for example, can no longer compete against those low prices and better service, and as a result they are forced to remain within a marginal market share or to close. These closures can be desirable as long as the dominant firm cannot exploit its technology to exert market power.

The reduction in the number of competitors due to closures or the reduction in the size of existing competitors then leads to excess profits. Prices are lower, but they could have been even lower had there been more surviving competitors and had those that did survive been more dominant. Amazon does great things for customers, but in the process they also destroy rivals. This lets them charge higher prices and keep a significant part of the value they create for themselves, which is to the detriment of the customer. Such organic growth leads to market power when there is a winner-take-all race toward dominance in the market. This is particularly acute in times of fast technological change. New technologies and inventions allow for rapidly changing ways of producing goods and services.

The objective of the race is to be technologically superior, producing either cheaper and/or of better quality, so that competitors are either driven out of the market or their market share is sharply reduced. But if that technological superiority is simply based on a blueprint that any competitor can copy, then the market power will not last very long. As soon as it is invented, competitors will copy the blueprint and the competitive field will level again.

However, new technologies that are difficult to copy or reproduce give rise to permanent technological superiority. Typically they require vast upfront investments that often lead to economies of scale. Information technologies have contributed to the increase in market power because increasing those economies of scale results in what is usually called a natural monopoly. The cost of setting up a business is so high that there is room for only one competitor.

The early tech startups committed enormous amounts of money to win the race; many of them lost their investments. A few companies, such as Amazon, that stated early on that they were not in the race to dominate the books market but to dominate retail full stop, came out as winners. Via a massive upfront investment and new technology, Amazon dominates either because the investment lowers the cost of production or because it increases the quality.

There is fierce competition for the market, with many losers and few winners. Because there is limited competition in the market, the winners who have gained an initial advantage can use the disruptive technology to build and maintain an advantage, often based on economies of scale, to which we turn next.

Of Railway Tracks: Supply

Broadly speaking, there are three sources of economies of scale due to technological superiority, and each of them is a breeding ground for market power: economies of scale from supply, from demand, and from learning.

First, the classical source of market power stems from supply returns to scale, such as railways, utility provisions, and cable television. They originate in the scale of production, so we call them supply returns. The transcontinental railroad in the United States that opened in 1869 completely transformed the country. Travel from New York to San Francisco was instantaneously cut to ten days, down from four to six months by horse-drawn carriage.

There was not only the time gain; the same trajectory could be delivered at 10 percent of the cost and at superior comfort. This shows how unequal the technology of competing suppliers of transportation were at the time. It was a good thing that horse-drawn carriages were forced out of the market. The question is why no firm simply copied the superior technology and competed for the customers—in this case, passenger and freight transportation. The answer: with a high setup cost and a relatively low cost of operation, there was little room to duplicate the investment in railway tracks.

If a private firm first builds a rail track, it faces little threat of entry. A competitor would have to incur the same enormous investment building a parallel track, to then find itself in a price war with the incumbent firm once the investment is complete and make little profit. Moreover, it is highly wasteful to build parallel rail tracks if there is enough capacity. The high upfront investment leads to economies of scale and thus market power. As a result, the incumbent can set prices high without any competitor contesting the market.

When a firm like the Northern Securities Company—a railroad holding company formed, among others, by J. P. Morgan in the early twentieth century—holds the monopoly for transportation over land, it will not set prices at cost. Even if it costs only 10 percent of alternative means of transportation, the ticket price is closer to 90 percent of the cost of a horse-drawn carriage ride. Low enough to beat the competition and grab the lion's share of the market but as high as possible to make maximal profits.

The huge profits don't mean there wasn't fierce competition before the railway system was consolidated. Initially there was overinvestment in railway lines around Chicago, until J. P. Morgan managed to consolidate ownership and build a moat with exclusive deals for operation. Once those deals were chiseled out, there was no competition left in the market.

Those classical supply returns to scale are still at work today in retail. Amazon is the third of three big waves in retail, each marked by technological change that led to a new form of distribution, guarded by an expensive moat of dense logistics.

Over one hundred years ago, Sears revolutionized retail via the distribution of goods through its mail-order service. They sent a catalog to households who could order anything that could be delivered to their homes via the US Postal Service. Initially their target customers were located in rural areas and were forced to buy from overpriced local stores that had a limited selection of goods on offer. Sears saved money by not relying on the distribution network of those local shops, and they could ship everything straight to the customer from their warehouses: lower cost, higher quality, and more variety. This allowed Sears to be highly competitive, undercutting the traditional retail outlets. Technological change (catalogs and shipping by post) led to lower prices and an infinitely more diverse offering. At the same time, it brought the company market power and generous profits.

The cost savings are clear, but what is less obvious is why Sears could build up market power and maintain it. Why did other firms fail to enter this market and grab some of these profits? The answer is in Sears' letterhead from 1907: "We sell everything by mail order only. Your money will be promptly returned for any goods not perfectly satisfactory and we will pay freight or express charges both ways."[1] This sounds very similar to what Amazon Prime offers today. Sears too had exploited a new and faster transportation technology and built a network of warehouses and logistics around the country. With an enormous upfront investment of the distribution network in rural areas, there was space for only one firm with such a costly network given demand.

The second wave in retail is the emergence of Walmart. Out of Bentonville, Arkansas, Sam Walton gradually built a network of retail stores that had everything to offer at the lowest prices. Within four decades of opening the first store, Walmart dominated retail in the United States and increasingly around the world. Low prices guaranteed scale; new technologies and scale guaranteed low costs. With the use of data-driven logistics, Walmart is able to respond quickly to changes in consumer demand before any competitor could. For example, Walmart logistics can increase the supply of energy bars and bottled water at short notice to stores in an area where a hurricane is predicted to make landfall.

Recent research shows that the process of organic growth of the distribution network of Amazon is very similar to that of Walmart. This brings us to the third wave in retail with online shopping. Amazon fulfillment centers were opened as a function of the density of the market and the proximity of the supply chain. The next distribution node is opened where the demand is most dense, which in turn alters the future density of demand. All this requires huge investments in physical capital.[2]

Like railways in the nineteenth century, Amazon experiences enormous economies of scale, limiting the space to only a few competitors. Economies of scale generate low costs, but not all of the cost savings are passed on to the customer. Hence both lower prices and more market power—that is, prices set competitively would be even lower.

From a historical perspective, how unusual is the concentration and market power in retail that we experience in current times? Just before the Great Depression of 1929, the two largest retailers, Sears and A&P (the Great Atlantic & Pacific Tea Company, then the country's largest grocery chain) jointly held 3 percent of all retail sales. At the time, such a market share was considered extraordinarily large. The concern about their market power gave rise to the 1936 amendment of the Clayton Antitrust Act, in particular preventing unfair price discrimination. Today Walmart and Amazon jointly account for 15 percent of retail sales,[3] yet there is no movement toward reining in the market power of these large retailers.

The rise of these behemoth firms through organic growth based on economies of scale is not exclusive to pure retail. In the textile industry, the Spanish company Inditex, with brands like Zara, Pull and Bear, and Bershka, has become the largest producer and retailer of clothing in Europe, Asia, and Latin America. Inditex has grown organically through innovation in logistics and its novel concept of retail. Zara renews the products in its stores weekly, and rather than committing to a collection for the whole season, it tests prototype pieces of clothing. Based on sales figures and customer feedback, it then launches larger volumes of that model. The production cycle is very short: it takes less than fifteen days from design to distribution in stores.

In order to be able to deliver on such short notice, Zara makes heavy use of information technology in the logistics process, in a manner that is similar to the tracking of goods that Walmart distributes in response to changes in meteorological conditions. Walmart's logistics apparatus can respond in a short time frame to sudden demand changes.

For Zara as well as for Walmart, such an information-driven logistics operation requires sufficient density of the distribution network: enough stores per population density to support the distribution network of warehouses. As a result, with this technological change these firms can realize substantial reductions in costs. Some of those cost savings are passed on to customers in lower prices, but not all. That is precisely where the rise in profits comes from. Hence again the impact of technological superiority: with a drop in prices, there is also an increase in markup. The only reason there is a rise in markup is because the scale required to achieve the cost savings limits the space to only one or a few firms. That implies large firms, low costs, low prices, and yet, high markups.

Of Platforms: Demand

Of the three sources of market power, we started with the classical economies of scale in supply, as in the case of the railways and retail. The second source of market power originates in demand returns to scale, where economies of scale are created by usage instead of the cost of building. This is often referred to as network externalities.

When looking for a vintage watch, a buyer goes to the site where there are the most sellers, such as eBay. Buyers are most likely to find an interesting piece, and the competition among sellers is fiercest. Sellers will choose the platform with the most buyers because they are more likely to sell, and with higher demand they can get a higher price. Both buyers and sellers coincide in that they would rather choose the platform with the most users, the platform with the highest market thickness. As a result, the platform with most users attracts even more participants, and these economies of scale lead to a dominant position of one main platform. The owner of the dominant platform can offer the best value to the users and extract some of that surplus by charging high fees. The seller of vintage watches would rather pay a 10 percent fee and sell quickly at a high price than pay a 1 percent fee and sell slowly at a low price.

A competitor can try to come in, but they can never offer the same market thickness that eBay can because eBay has over 90 percent of the online auction market. Competitors have tried by offering lower fees, for example. In the United States, eBay started in 1995 and Yahoo! Auctions launched in 1998. Despite Yahoo!'s Herculean efforts to compete and get a toehold in the market—Yahoo! did not charge a fee and financed its site with advertising—eBay has always been the market leader and is virtually the only player in the online auction market business.

Even if platforms are set up in parallel, it typically does not pay to have multiple platforms running at the same time (just as it doesn't pay to set up two parallel railways). It is not because eBay has a superior technology that it dominates the market; it is simply because it built the user base first. In fact, Yahoo! Auctions dominates the market in Japan, where eBay cannot get a toehold in. When there are economies of scale from the user base, the winner takes the entire market. Orwell is right again: the trouble with competitions is that somebody wins them. The company that wins the competition for the market dominates, and can then live off the profits without competitors in the market.

These platforms, which are marketplaces that facilitate bringing together buyers and sellers, existed long before the internet. Such economies of scale or network effects are inherent in technology adoption—for example, the adoption of QWERTY keyboards in the United States and AZERTY keyboards in other countries. These scale effects can even lead to the adoption of an inferior technology, simply because the scale effect is so large. The VHS magnetic tape technology was considered technologically inferior to Betamax. However, because more people used VHS, it was easier to find movies on VHS and therefore consumers chose to buy VHS players. You can easily see that it is possible that there could have been a better eBay. Even more worrisome is that without competitive pressure, eBay has little incentive to continue to improve its services and technology.

Most of the pre-internet platforms facilitate trade by bringing buyers and sellers together in a centralized marketplace. One example is newspapers or television channels, where the owner brings together advertisers and eyeballs. As the user, you think about reading an interesting op-ed piece or watching an Academy Award–winning movie; as the owner you think about monetizing this interest in the best writers and the award-winning movies by maximizing the number of viewers and the number of advertising dollars.

Another example is the stock exchange, where the owner brings together buyers and sellers to trade publicly held stocks. Some other examples, such as credit card platforms or networks, do not bring buyers and sellers together per se, but they facilitate the transaction.

Even though in all these markets the network externalities give rise to a dominant platform, multiple platforms may coexist if there is specialization in a selective group of clients. Some dating platforms, for example, cater exclusively to those select groups with preference for religion (for example, Jdate for Jewish daters), sexual orientation (Grindr for gay daters), and wealth (the League for elite daters). Larger platforms are always better from the point of view of the user because there is more choice, but there is no point wasting time sifting through profiles of heterosexual partners if you are not heterosexual. There is a trade-off between the scale of the network and the selective composition of the platform participants.

There are many newspapers competing for readers, many television stations, and several stock exchanges. Despite the returns to scale inherent in these platforms, they often differentiate and specialize in order to cater to a more limited audience: local newspapers focus on regional news, American Express offers credit cards to wealthier customers who spend more, and the Weather Channel caters to those who are worried about storms and floods.

These are mostly examples of markets that operate under old technologies. Still, there are plenty of platform markets with new technologies. The online auction market dominated by eBay is one example, as well as all the social media networks such as Facebook, Twitter, Instagram, and LinkedIn; the app stores such as Apple and Google Play; media platforms such as Pandora and Spotify; the car- and house-sharing platforms such as Uber and AirBnB; and the dating apps and websites such as Tinder and OkCupid. They all have enormous scale advantages and create benefits for their users from network externalities.

There are enormous gains from specialization and differentiation in these networks, but they also generate economies of scale that allow the platforms to create market power. Again, technological progress generates enormous gains, but because of the network features the owners exploit that same technology to raise prices (and hence the firm's profits), which undoubtedly hurts the customer, and as I will argue below, it hurts work.

On the demand side, beyond platforms, there are also consumer preferences that are a source of market power. Producers of consumer goods invest enormous amounts in marketing to differentiate their goods, which in turn creates market power. Anyone who says, "For all practical purposes, any differences between Coke and Pepsi are negligible" makes Coca-Cola and Pepsi users cringe. Yet, blind taste tests confirm few people can discern the difference between the two.[4]

Marketeers have known for the longest time that marketing can create the perception that goods are differentiated, even if the goods are identical. When buyers perceive a greater attachment to one good, they are willing to pay more. With advertising campaigns, firms create brand-name products in order to build a customer base of loyal customers who pay a premium. Because building that customer capital is expensive, only the larger, dominant firms can afford those upfront expenditures. Marketing strategies are thus a source of market power. All these upfront investments make up intangible assets, a subject to which we will turn later in this chapter.

Of Self-Driving Cars: Learning

We now get to the third source of market power. We already discussed the economies of scale in supply (railways and retail) and in demand (platforms with network externalities). The third source of market power through economies of scale is learning. Self-driving cars are trained on huge data collected from millions of hours of driving time. This requires enormous investments to collect those data. The more quantity and quality of data there is, the better it works.

For some applications, the vast amount of data needed to operationalize these machine-learning algorithms is already available in the public domain. For example, to build a reliable language translation service, companies such as Google can use translations of existing texts from novels, reports, and other texts that are in the public domain. Most often, though, the data requires costly collection efforts of vast amounts of new observations.

Firms have become very ingenious in obtaining those huge amounts of information in relatively cheap manners. For example, when making a purchase online, how often have you been asked to identify pictures with a storefront or a traffic light in them? You have been a provider of data for one of the image-recognition applications based on machine-learning algorithms. Even if you have not been paid to do so, the firm collecting the data must pay the websites that include these annoying image-recognition exercises to ensure that you are "not a robot." Cynically enough, as more people provide data, the robots will become able to recognize the images. The bottom line is that huge amounts of data are needed, and the collection of that data is costly.

Costly learning and data collection create a first-mover advantage for the firm that has collected the data first. Just like building costly railway lines, there is little benefit in collecting those databases twice. This costly investment process is again a source of economies of scale, a moat that firms can transform into market power.

Unlike building a second, expensive railway line, though, these costly databases collected once can be copied at virtually no cost; it is simply a matter of transferring the data from the server of one company to another. The ability to copy the data at little cost has important implications for policies that are aimed at leveling those moats and the resulting market power. Later in the book, when discussing the role of artificial intelligence and machine learning, I will return to the role of learning in creating (and fighting) market power.

These three sources of economies of scale create moats and render the resulting market power long lasting. New technologies are an essential force in creating the first-mover advantage and, consequently, in generating those economies of scale to fend off competitors. The different sources are often present simultaneously. In addition, the presence of costs of switching for customers among products is an important determinant for economies of scale to translate in market power.

Amplifiers of Market Power

Many different circumstances other than returns to scale can give rise to market power, and many factors amplify it. For example, firms use the buying power in given markets to affect the firms in their value chain, both their suppliers and their customers. They may take over those firms to stifle competition or simply to force them to trade at better terms. Large retailers like Walmart and Amazon have been known to exert a lot of clout over their suppliers. Vertical integration is a highly controversial issue associated with market power.

The largest amplifier of economies of scale is probably globalization and the growth in international trade. Globalization affects each of the three sources of returns to scale (supply, demand, networks) by magnifying the tiny impact in a local market into an enormous effect worldwide. Research estimates that the component parts of a car produced in the United States have crossed the borders with Canada and Mexico on average eighteen times.[5] Current economic activity is a remarkable web of international connections and trade relations.

Like technological change, globalization and trade is disruptive. In a way, trade is another form of technological change. First off, trade is relative to the size of a country. In Luxembourg, the share of imports and exports is a much larger portion of the economy than in the United States. Going to the bakery across the border in France counts as international trade because you consume in Luxembourg and import from France. Yet, the sale of a car produced in Alabama to a household in Vermont is not.

Falling transportation costs help international trade between Poland and Spain as much as they help national trade between Alabama and Vermont. And the fact that information technology allows a smartphone engineer to design a product in Silicon Valley today and have it produced in China tomorrow equally facilitates Erin, the New Mexico–based senior technical advisor discussed in chapter 1, who can troubleshoot your smartphone anywhere in the United States.

Globalization is thus closely related, if not identical, to technological change. Lower transportation cost bring goods manufactured in China closer to the United States in the same way that highways and information technology bring Alabama closer to Vermont. And information technologies fully integrate production processes of workers who are located far away from each other. Sending a blueprint over to your colleague across the hallway is as fast and as cheap as it is to send it from California to Shenzhen.

These advances in technology that facilitate international trade could easily be mistaken for a decrease in the economies of scale. The global market is larger, so the initial investment may appear to make up a smaller share of sales. Quite to the contrary, to be successful in international trade and global production, using goods and services from different internationally sourced markets requires enormous investments and, above all, a large enough scale of operations.

Operating globally means more and more international specialization, with many small inputs from many different countries of origin. That in turn demands economies of scale, which facilitates market power. Research indeed finds evidence that firms that export and import tend to have higher markups and thus exert more market power.[6]

Economies of scale arise from technological change and globalization. Unlike the advent of investment in machines, physical technologies, and transportation infrastructure, such as railroads during the Second Industrial Revolution at the turn of the twentieth century, the current wave of new technologies that create economies of scale is particularly driven by investment in intangible assets, such as ideas and research. The dominant firms that have market power have often gained that position from investment in the railway lines of wireless information technology. We turn to the role of intangibles next.

Intangibles Make Winners

When analyzing the evolution of market power, we find that since 1980 the markups of a select number of firms have gone through the roof. Still, the markup of the median firm remains unchanged, so at least half of the firms are no better off, and most of them are worse off. Under pressure from the high-performing firms, many smaller firms see their profits decline, and some are forced to close. This has created a handful of large and dominant firms with exorbitant profits. Not all of that is bad news, however. Like the railway companies a century ago that made transportation better and cheaper, many of the high-markup firms sell at cheaper prices. The problem is that there is not enough competition, and therefore they are not selling cheaply enough.

The data on markups give away one more crucial revealing fact. Those firms with the highest markups also spend most on overhead costs. By investing in new technologies, marketing, and R&D, firms manage to become so superior technologically that no other firm can compete on price, nor can any other firm enter the market. These facts are consistent with the view on how market power works that the economist John Sutton from the London School of Economics put forward thirty years ago. An Irishman in London, since the 1990s Sutton has quietly been arguing for a new view of how firms operate in order to gain market power. In addition, he has collected detailed evidence documenting that his view indeed closely matches the facts.

Sutton posits that firms invest heavily to gain an edge over competitors, especially in markets where they can exploit strong economies of scale.[7] Investment in R&D enables a firm to design new products or to enhance the technical characteristics of existing products and services. Cost-reducing product innovation makes production cheaper.

Intangible investments are made not only to gain a technological edge. Investment in advertising improves the brand image of a product, with the objective of differentiating the good and thus charging higher prices. This is not technological, but rather through the preferences of consumers. Investments in advertising to build brand reputation create barriers to competitors, not in production or technology but in a loyal base of customers that competitors cannot easily access. There are barriers to entry that generate economies of scale because they discourage entry by competitors. Such investments are a substantial share of expenditure on intangibles and an equally important source of market power.

Even expenditure on management salaries can help firms come up with better strategies to produce and compete. All of these investments often involve expenditure on human capital, such as hiring better designers and programmers, assets that are intangible in nature.

With the investment in overhead, firms compete not only in setting prices—they also compete in becoming the most efficient producer. Again, in the presence of economies of scale, firms that invest most heavily and are first to see results become dominant. It is the lopsidedness of the productivity of firms, with one firm becoming much more productive than all the others, that creates the lack of competition. What technological innovation and disruption does is create a winner-take-all contest. The first to develop the logistics network of warehouses and distribution will be able to get the goods most cheaply to the customer, and, as with railway networks, there is limited space for multiple Amazon-like distribution networks. The first to set up an auction platform like eBay becomes the market leader with virtually no competition; an unregulated capitalist economy naturally leads to market power in the presence of fast technological change with winners.

Currently, with the rise of information and communication technology, we are riding a wave of rapid technological change, another technological revolution. Like prior technological revolutions, the current one is full of rapidly arising occasions to crown the winners in a market with economies of scale. The First Industrial Revolution introduced steam to power machines that transformed manufacturing processes between 1760 and 1820; the Second Industrial Revolution built on the invention of electricity to further transform manufacturing and to mobilize mass transportation, which led to the first wave of globalization between 1870 and 1914. The Third "Industrial" Revolution is a bit of a misnomer because the current revolution has made industrial manufacturing so efficient and hence so cheap that it barely has a share of 8 percent of GDP. But digitization and information technologies have transformed production not only of goods but also of services.

The rise in investment in R&D, advertising, and human capital of high-skilled workers is, to a large extent, a rise of investment in intangible capital. What is different about the current digital economy is that intangible capital plays a much more important role than it used to. Indeed, those overhead costs as a share of total expenditure of firms have gone up from 15 percent in 1980 to over 20 percent in 2020.[8] Of course, not all overhead expenditures are intangibles, but the vast majority are. Intangible capital is now larger than tangible brick-and-mortar capital. If firms invest in intangibles, it is because they realize a return on those investments, just like firms make a return on tangible investments.

Intangible expenditures are extremely unequally distributed across different firms. Some firms have nearly none, and a few firms spend a lot on intangibles. This is most striking for R&D investment: most firms do not report any expenditure on R&D, whereas some firms have huge expenditures.

Many startup biotechnology companies that are built around one product, often with one patent only, are high intangible-cost firms. These small companies do clinical research, but often they don't even have a laboratory. They outsource the labs because they have highly risky life cycles. If the results are positive, they continue doing another round of experiments, advancing in the FDA approval process, hopefully until going to market.

But if the lab results are repeatedly negative, then the investors will soon shut down the financing and the operation will be closed. With an entire laboratory installation and researchers on the payroll, winding down the unsuccessful biotechnology company becomes very expensive. With a high-risk and short–time horizon venture, it is much more cost beneficial to outsource these activities. The result is that this company hardly has any variable costs; nearly 100 percent of its expenditures is in intangibles.

Intangibles are on the rise,[9] they are very unequal across firms, and they are a key determinant of market power. But unlike traditional capital, intangibles pose a really difficult problem of how to value them. People often make the step to conclude that because assets are intangibles, the dollar amounts of those investments are intangible, too.

Now, that is a misconception. In part this misconception has a good reason for its existence because accounting for the value of intangibles in the total value of an economy is difficult. When measuring GDP, the value of an economy, it is important how intangibles are accounted for. The traffic app Waze allows users to get from one part of town to another more quickly. This benefit is probably not accurately measured in GDP, as is anything we derive benefit from but that is not priced in the market, such as cooking at home or Wikipedia.

The role of such intangible benefits has led to revisions of how GDP is calculated. For example, in recent years software that used to be a service is accounted for as an investment.[10] Rather than attempting to value the utility to the user, which is virtually impossible, we value the cost of investment to the firm, which is a lot easier. We do that for bread (and for all other products) where we use the price at which bread is sold rather than the benefit it gives to the consumer, which could be substantially above the price, especially when the consumer is hungry.

Any expenditure on intangibles, such as R&D, advertising, or executive salaries, enters the firm's income statement one way or another. The cost might be an understatement of the value of the intangible, just as the price of bread is an understatement of the value of bread to the consumer. Because the value of intangibles (and bread) is intangible, we use what it costs rather than what it's worth to measure it. To add a further complication, most intangible assets are not even obtained with investment in R&D by scientists in white lab coats or with advertising on billboards and on TV, but they are as often simply the result of ideas. IKEA, for example, became hugely successful because its founder, Ingvar Kamprad, started to think about transporting furniture in flat packaging so that people could take their furniture home in their cars. Still, the investment to obtain the idea is accounted for with the salary of the employee or owner who comes up with it.

So, whether intangible capital is due to the idea of an employee, or is built by expenditure on advertising, as in the case of Coca-Cola, any expenditure is accounted for. If anything, in order to reduce the firm's tax base, accountants will book too many costs (for example, the CEO's private jet), not too few. I still need to meet the CFO who refuses to book legitimate costs, whether they are incurred to acquire tangible or intangible assets.

Like tangible assets, the cost of intangible assets is properly ac-counted for in the firm's income statement. In dollar terms, the cost of intangibles is fully tangible! But by their very nature, intangibles are not easily identified. First, there is the difficult task of determing which ex-penditure corresponds to which intangible. Second, unlike tangible as-sets, intangibles are not easily transformed from a flow of annual expen-ditures on intangibles into a "stock," the cumulative value of those expenditures. That is easy for a physical asset like a building, where the stock value is equal to the sum of the discounted monthly rental income minus all the costs. With intangible capital there is often no monthly rental income, which makes it hard to put a dollar value on how much intangible capital a firm has. The investment in the brand Coca-Cola a hundred years ago is still paying off today.

Our research on markups reveals that investment in intangibles is higher in firms that have the most market power, so intangibles are no doubt a tool to build and widen the moat. In order to create a vaccine, a pharmaceutical company has to spend a large amount on R&D; Coca-Cola spends more than half of its total costs on overhead, mostly advertising and marketing; and Google has market power nearly exclusively from investing in ideas, software, and people. For most of these firms that have created market power through investment in intangibles, there seems to be no substantial difference compared to firms that invest in tangible assets. In fact, most firms have both. Key to maintaining market power is whether there are economies of scale, irrespective of whether market power is obtained with tangible investment (such as railroads) or intangible investment (such as R&D).

In some markets the creation of a moat is a transitory process because the economies of scale get eroded quickly by competitors. Initially the winner takes the entire market, but depending on how strong the economies of scale are, eventually competitors enter the market and start eating away some of the profits. This is in the spirit of Schumpeter's view that creative destruction with temporary monopoly power leads to growth.[11]

The developments of the past four decades paint a picture that is different from Schumpeter's; it is the picture of the profit paradox. Like the earlier industrial revolutions, the technological change of the information revolution has been very profound, leading a handful of firms to make vast investments in overhead to become the winner in these winner-take-all contests. The winners of these contests use the same technological disruption that has brought lower costs and better services to build and maintain a moat. They now enjoy much higher markups and profits than any firm could have dreamed of forty years ago.

The source of the excess profits generated by the dominant firms is a truly high fixed cost, just like the cost that granted monopoly power to the railway companies. These successful firms have built a moat that will not be bridged anytime soon. There is literally nothing the customer can do in order to get some of those efficiency gains in lower prices, except to wait for new technologies—it took at least half a century before air travel became a viable substitute to rail travel—or for the government to bust the trusts, as Teddy Roosevelt did.

Of course, not all market power stems from size and economies of scale. The work of James Schmitz of the Federal Reserve Bank of Minneapolis draws the attention to another source of market power, sabotage monopoly. Firms of premium goods sabotage cheap substitutes, either illegally or through lobbying and regulation. Examples include cheap dental care or cheap housing construction services. Rather than a large firm dominating the market selling at high prices, these sabotage practices simply shut down markets, and as a result there are no prices at all. The consequences, to which we turn extensively in part 2, are borne predominantly by the low-income households. The harm comes from not being able to consume at all.[12]

Sabotage monopoly aside, the technological change in the Third Industrial Revolution that we are currently going through has a protagonist in intangible assets, simultaneously driving growth and progress as well as market power. But there is also another key player, the sharp reduction in costs.

The Cost-Cutting Cult

Market power is often synonymous with high prices. But prices are only relative to costs, and higher markups arise either because firms raise prices or they cut costs. When a firm like AB InBev builds market power through mergers and acquisitions, at constant costs the merged firms tend to increase prices. To further boost their market power, those firms may further reduce costs, but they gain profits from charging a higher price for a bottle of beer.

Instead, when a firm such as Amazon deploys a disruptive innovation that results in organic growth, it does so because it lowers costs and offers better services. Those lower costs result in lower prices. To a large extent, this is beneficial to society in general and the customer in particular. Unfortunately, the disruptive technology also serves to keep out competitors, which does not force the firm to sell at cost and lower prices even more. Herein lies another dimension of the profit paradox: firms that cut costs and gain dominance in the market do so by selling at lower prices while at the same time charging higher markups (price over cost). Sweet and sour. Moreover, if there is only one firm that has a significant cost advantage, market power is larger. The customer would be a lot better off if there were two identical low-cost Amazons. But no one seems to be able to bridge Amazon's moat, not even Alibaba, the Chinese equivalent of Amazon founded by Albert Ma, who is keen to compete in the United States.

More than pure investment in technologies that lower the cost of production, large firms have paid careful attention to cutting costs. The tailor in a local community who produced clothes half a century ago would have bought materials from a wholesaler, designed and produced the clothes, and sold them exclusively in the one store in town.

Now, instead, chains optimize the supply chain, which often amounts to cutting costs. This is often the greatest innovation that chain stores achieve. Better deals with suppliers, lower costs of production due to scale, and most of the time at lower wages. These firms are organized differently, of course. Instead of a tailor who is a professional cutting fabric, clothing stores like the Gap have management cutting costs. That is possibly the success of a business school education. MBAs have learned finance, how to act strategically, and how to minimize expenses. This cost-cutting cult achieves lower costs for the firm, higher profits for the shareholders, and lower prices for the customer.

But the extent to which the cost cutting requires sufficient economies of scale to keep competitors out, and cost cutting creates large advantages for one firm over all other firms, leads to market power where one firm dominates the market and generates higher profits. Cost cutting that results in such market power is not entirely beneficial to the customer because the dominant firm does not pass the entire cost reduction on to the customer, and it keeps part of those savings in their own accounts as profits.

Some of the cost cutting is in payroll—pay workers less or hire fewer of them in order to reduce the cost of labor. Note, though, that the reduction in the number of workers hired is due in part to market power itself, as we will discuss at length below. In addition, if market power is widespread across the economy, it also leads to lower wages. That is a windfall gain that leads to higher markups, which is the output price over the payroll cost.

The Human League: We're Only Human

Making money is, of course, not evil: it is the primary objective of a corporation. Sometimes, however, the way in which this objective is achieved is harmful. For example, some firms make money from the fact that customers are not always rational. Selling snake oil with unproven remedial properties is as old as the market and barter. But unlike the obvious false snake-oil claims, with the power of current information technologies, firms can keep the perception of cheating under the radar. Firms carefully analyze people's behavioral biases and exploit them to build market power. With bait-and-switch tactics, for example, firms announce extremely attractive terms to enter into a long-term arrangement. After a while the price increases and, once locked in, the inattentive consumer does not cancel the contract when the terms are no longer beneficial. With gym memberships, when we sign the contract we are certain that we will take that spinning class three times a week, only to find out later on that a Netflix series and the couch are more enticing. With the gym membership and the locked-in Netflix, Spotify, and cable contracts that all raise their prices, we may be making a choice among a portfolio of contracts, each of which we should have canceled anyway.

The tactics are as numerous as the number of anomalies that psychologists detect in individuals. Firms obscure information; they give the illusion of choice. They artificially build costly product differences to extract a higher price from some customers. It is fairly clear that doubling the memory on a smartphone does not increase the production cost by $200. In fact, given the low cost of memory, it might be cheaper to only offer the high-memory phone because running different production lines is costly. Artificially differentiating products is as old as the street, and they are not necessarily a *bias*; sometimes it is as simple as using different colors—people are willing to pay more for red cars, for example. But with new technologies it has become a lot easier to use personalized information to fine-tune the pricing to the individual customer, and with it to exploit behavioral biases and create market power.

One behavioral bias is the illusion that goods are sold "for free." When I use Google Maps or I install Yelp, my life changes for the better. Who would have thought twenty-five years ago that I would be walking in a city I have never visited before with a tiny device in my hand that not only shows me a changing map and directions on how to get where I wish to go, but also my real-time location? This is from a science fiction movie. And it is even more incredible if you acknowledge that this amazing technology, which infinitely improves the practicalities of our lives, is offered for free.

The illusion of free goods, however beneficial they are, is exactly that—an illusion. Any exchange, whether it is a labor contract, buying bread, or bartering antiques, involves an exchange that is mutually improving. I am willing to part with $2 in exchange for a loaf of bread, and the baker prefers dollars over keeping the bread. That is no different for Google Maps or the restaurant rating app: the app offers the service I love to use, but in exchange I offer my data and my eyeballs to look at advertising. And my data can be used for making the experience of other users (including myself) better. For example, Google Maps uses my location in traffic to update real-time delays and reroute drivers in order to get them to their destinations in the fastest estimated time of arrival. Most often the data is used by the app provider to make money from advertising or from selling my data to direct marketing firms who will target me to buy their goods.

Now, as with an antique exchange, if I trade my coffee table for your dining table, which is more valuable, we might agree that I should pay you some money on top of just offering my coffee table to make the deal agreeable to you. To me the price is positive; to you, who receives the money, the price is negative. A negative price means that you are the net seller. In these barter situations it is nearly impossible to find a perfect match where the value of goods exchanged is exactly equal. Therefore a zero price is an anomaly and suspicious. Yet, in antiques barter and in Google Maps, zero prices are prevalent, even if on net you are selling because your data is more valuable than the service provided. When the price is zero, in most situations one party is missing out. As they say, if the price of an app is zero, then most likely you are the seller, and you should have received money.

In the case of Google Maps, the value of the user's data to Google from advertising revenue exceeds the cost of providing the service of Google Maps, so we should compensate the users for the excess value that they bring to the exchange, just like the owner of the dining table. Usually the value of my data is peanuts—estimated to be a few dollars per year to all apps I use. The gains to the app producer come from the large numbers. With millions or even billions of users, even at a few cents per app, we are talking big money.

Ultimately, the problem with zero-price goods is that the customer does not *perceive* this as a price, and they do not recognize that as a net seller the price should be negative. This behavioral bias allows the app producer to build market power and charge prices that are higher than they would be under fully competitive pricing. I will return to how to deal with market power and zero prices in chapter 12.

The most obvious bias, if we can call it that, is addiction as a tool to create market power. Just like many other soft drinks, Coca-Cola contains caffeine—and even the residual of cocaine leaves in the original recipe—and sugar, which creates addiction. Even the attractiveness of Starbucks is due to more than just the tasty hot drinks and the cozy armchairs. Starbucks tends to have the highest caffeine concentration in their drips.[13] Caffeine is not only a less-than-innocent drug that has negative side effects on our health—it is a source of market power.

And the ultimate substance that gets us hooked is information. Social media like Instagram, Facebook, TikTok, and YouTube feed us information to maximize our time on their apps, which in turn maximizes advertising revenue. Social media companies are unscrupulously playing on our addictions to induce us to consume more, pay higher prices, and stay longer on their platforms.

The main reason why such addiction-inducing practices need regulation is the health and social damage they create. The severe psychological damage that is starting to appear is only the tip of the iceberg of the calamitous consequences that individuals, families, and society will have to deal with in the near future. Social media companies are behaving just like the tobacco companies of the 1950s that targeted advertisements to pregnant women, knowing full well the health consequences for unborn babies. And as if that is not harmful enough, these addictive practices create dependence that locks in consumers, whose psychological barriers to switch to competitors leads them to pay higher prices. There is no doubt that addiction-inducing practices need much closer scrutiny and regulation, also merely from an economic view.

Dealing with behavioral biases is complicated, and it may involve regulation of the behavior of the provider of the app as well as regulating the behavior of the user. People are averse to any kind of regulation of our behavior, but we have learned to accept some regulation where we are clearly biased and acting against our own interests. Take the obligation to wear seat belts, for example. In the past I often chose not to wear my seat belt in an airplane. It was inconvenient and, I reasoned, if a crash does happen, a seat belt won't do much to prevent certain death. However, during one flight at cruising altitude, our plane was hit by unexpected thermal turbulence, resulting in a sudden drop in altitude of the aircraft. That time I was lucky to be wearing a seat belt because a flight attendant had asked me to do so. Four other passengers were not, including some standing in line for the restrooms. Due to the sudden drop in altitude and inertia, they hit their heads against the ceiling of the plane. We had to return to the nearest airport and make an emergency landing to take the injured passengers to the hospital. Since then I have worn my seat belt religiously. In my case it took a bad experience to overcome my ignorance and behavioral bias.

Regulation of biases is often unwanted by the customer who feels it is a disgrace that poor Google is not allowed to offer them the good for free. Yet regulation is often necessary to make sure that the customers' own behavioral biases do not hurt them directly and, more importantly, because those biases help firms build a moat.

What Is Wrong with Firms Making Profits?

The entire objective of the capitalist system is to provide incentives for individuals to invest in firms and make profits. Inventions and new technologies may in part be the result of government expenditure, fundamental research, or even of the wartime effort—as is arguably the case with the development of nuclear energy and wireless communication—but to a large extent most technological progress comes from private investment. The demise of the planned economies in the former Soviet Union or in China proves that those centralized alternatives to the capitalist economic system are unable to create the same level of development.

The temporary market power in Schumpeter's model of creative destruction creates incentives to invest in innovation. If there is not enough innovation or the invention is a blueprint that can easily be copied, then the patent system provides the legal guarantee that the idea cannot be copied, which gives the firm enough temporary market power to recoup the investment in a successful idea. So there is nothing wrong with an innovating biotechnology firm that invents a new medicine to make temporary profits. This is precisely how a growing economy rewards risky innovation.

But things get out of hand when firms sustain excess profits for a long time. Firms continuously channel resources to maintain market power and grow to become behemoth corporations. A counterintuitive implication of market power is that those huge firms would be even larger if they had less market power. Consider the Apple iPhone. If Apple were to sell the iPhone for $400 (the total cost of production and distribution) instead of for $1,200, they would sell even more than they do today. More customers can afford to buy the phone at $400 than at $1,200.

This is another apparent contradiction of market power: if the firm that exerts market power were to price competitively, it would be even larger. But larger in what? That is the big caveat that illuminates the contradiction. What market power brings is higher prices yet lower quantities. But firms set higher prices only because that implies they can generate higher sales: they generate higher sales because the price is higher, despite the fact that they sell fewer units. And when quantities are lower, the number of workers hired is lower. Therefore, if Apple were to price the iPhone competitively at $400, the number of devices sold would go up. However, the value of sales would go down: even if Apple would sell more units, they sell them at a lower price. Most importantly, profits as well as the stock market value would decrease.

Overall, due to higher prices that are substantially above cost, some customers are priced out of the market compared to a world where market power is absent. Money is transferred from the pockets of the households to the coffers of the corporations that exert the market power. In addition, competing firms cannot get a toehold in the market. The power of these few dominant firms not only affects smaller players but also has dramatic implications for work, the most important input that those firms use in order to produce those goods and services.

In part I I have laid out the causes of market power. In the chapters in part II I analyze the implications of market power for work. Where huge gains for firms *should* lead to better lives for everyone in the workforce, the reality is exactly the opposite: the higher the profits of thriving firms and the wider their moats, the worse it is for work. That is the profit paradox, which affects not only those doing menial jobs but also the NYU graduate looking for a job or the junior programmer in Silicon Valley. First, I turn to the impact that market power has on wages.

PART II

The Harmful Consequences of Market Power

4

A Falling Tide Lowers All Boats

NICHOLAS KALDOR WAS a Hungarian-born economist who completed his undergraduate studies at the London School of Economics (LSE) in 1930 and later became a faculty member there. After serving in the British government, he went on to become a professor at Cambridge University. His research on growth and business cycles has influenced the work of a generation of economists. Incidentally, even more remarkable was his academic influence at home. Of his four daughters, two went on to become professors—Mary Kaldor, a professor of global governance at LSE, and Frances Stewart, a professor of development economics at Oxford University—at a time when there were very few women in academia.

Kaldor pointed out the remarkable regularity of a number of aggregate economic statistics, including the labor share and the capital share. For many years the Kaldor facts held up precisely, even though there had been fundamental structural change in the economy, from agriculture to manufacturing to services.

One hundred years ago, more than half of the active population in the United States worked in agriculture. Today it is less than 1 percent. Still, two-thirds of what is produced consists of the cost of labor and one-third consists of capital, as it was a century ago. We saw a sharp increase in manufacturing until the 1950s, followed by a decline in manufacturing to less than 10 percent of employment. And throughout this fundamental transformation of the economy, labor and capital shares of two-thirds and one-third did not change, at least not until the 1980s. Kaldor himself called these regularities a "stylized" view of the facts, and because of that statement the phrase "stylized facts" has made it into the economics vernacular.[1]

To refer to the constant labor share as a Kaldor fact is a recent phenomenon in economics. Earlier, Paul Samuelson, in the sixth edition of his textbook *Economics* (1964), coined the term "Bowley's law." Arthur Bowley, also at LSE and at Cambridge, had found evidence of the constancy of the wage share in the United Kingdom in the early 1920s, before Kaldor did, and he wrote about it in his book *Wages and Income in the United Kingdom since 1860* (1957).

So where does the labor share come from? Even though there are enormous differences across firms, especially the firms that have market power, let us consider the cost structure of an average firm. The typical firm spends around 20 percent of its costs on labor. At the same time, the total expenditure on labor as a percentage of gross domestic product (GDP) has historically been around two-thirds, or 66 percent. How can these numbers be compatible: Firms spend on average 20 percent on labor and the labor share in the economy is 66 percent?

The main reason for this discrepancy has to do with the intermediate inputs, all goods and services that are produced with labor at other firms. Firms hire labor to produce things, but they also buy goods and services from other firms who use labor to produce them. For example, when a biotechnology firm outsources its research experiments, it pays for some capital that those labs invest, but it also indirectly pays the salaries of the researchers in that lab. The same is true for the car manufacturer that buys the windshield wipers or the onboard computer software: workers at the supplier company have received a salary to produce the windshield wipers that the car manufacturer buys as intermediate inputs.

To account for the intermediate inputs of a firm, economists distinguish between value added and revenue. The revenue of a firm is the sum of all its sales. The value added is total revenue less intermediate inputs. The main reason to use value added is to distinguish between what a firm really produces and what it sells.

If a car dealer sells a car for $15,000 and the car manufacturer has sold it to the dealer for $12,000, we would interpret total revenue in this small economy with one dealer and one manufacturer selling one car each as being $27,000, whereas the value added of the car dealer is only $3,000 and the value added of the car manufacturer is at most $12,000, depending on how many intermediate inputs they used. As measured by how much people are willing to pay, the car dealer has created $3,000 in value to the consumer by offering a sales team and services that allow customers to make an informed decision. The value added is not the final price of $15,000. The reason to make a distinction between value added and sales is to avoid double counting, as both the manufacturer and the dealer sell part of the same car twice.

In the same vein, to construct the national accounts, the statistical authorities distinguish between gross output (GO), which is the sum of all sales, and GDP, which is the sum of all firms' value added. There are of course huge differences across firms in the share of value added out of revenue: some firms, such as wholesale firms or steel producers, use a lot of intermediate inputs and spend very little on labor; other firms, such as human resources agencies, spend the majority of their costs on labor.

Moreover, the exact measurement of GDP is not without debate; a recent book by Diane Coyle, *GDP: A Brief But Affectionate History*, talks about the history of measuring GDP and how minor changes lead to major revisions.[2] But in the national accounts, the ratio of GDP to GO is around one-half and is fairly stable over time. This means that on average, half of a firm's sales consist of intermediary goods that it buys from other firms. The remainder are the cost of labor, the cost of capital, overhead costs, and profits.

So if at an average firm around 20 percent of revenue pays for labor, with value added being one-half, the expenditure on labor is about 40 percent of value added. We are still short because we need to add self-employment and government employees. Once we add wages for self-employment and government employees, we get to Kaldor's approximate two-thirds. Of course, Kaldor's facts were never exact the way the laws of thermodynamics in physics are exact; there has always been some variation in the labor share, for example, over the business cycle between booms and recessions. But it is remarkable how Kaldor's facts have been so stable despite enormous structural change from an agrarian economy to manufacturing to a service economy.

Then came the 1980s. Something has changed fundamentally in the past four decades: the labor share has been falling substantially, from 65 percent in the 1970s to 59 percent in 2017, and the decline in the labor share is pervasive—it is observed around the world.[3] While this may appear to be a small change, the decline of six percentage points, or about 10 percent of the level in 1980, is enormous, especially because before 1980 the deviation from Kaldor's stylized facts was tiny.

This enormous decline had many economists scratching their heads because researchers did not find a convincing explanation that could explain so much of a decline. When we discovered that there has been a remarkable rise in market power, that also provided the missing piece of the puzzle.

It is precisely the role of market power that makes the declining labor share so worrisome. Market power does not simply redistribute funds from the pockets of the workers to those of the owners of the firm. Market power and the decline in the labor share destroy value in the economy. Even if we gave all of the profits to the workers they would still be worse off than under competitive markets because dominant firms sell and produce less than they could, as we will see in this chapter. And the magnitude of those losses is enormous—they are several times larger than the loss in output due to uncontrolled inflation, for example. That is why I will argue in chapter 12 that we need solutions that are extremely ambitious.

One Small Step Back for a Firm, One Giant Leap Backward for the Economy

There is a tight connection between the rise of market power and the decline of wages. First, consider an individual firm that has market power for the good it sells. If wages are set in a competitive labor market—for example, cooks in restaurants or truck drivers, where workers have many employers they can choose to work for—there is no direct effect on wages by that individual firm. That individual business will not lower the wages of its workers when it faces competition from other employers in the labor market.

But a firm with market power for the good it sells does take one fundamental step back. Because it sells at higher prices, it sells less and it produces less. Therefore, that firm reduces the number of workers it hires. If market power is widespread in the economy, and there are many dominant firms in all sectors, then the small step back becomes a giant leap backward that drives wages down in the entire economy.

If one trucking company hires fewer drivers, drivers' wages are unaffected because they can drive trucks and cars for other companies, they can work in the food industry, in security, in construction, and so on. But if there is market power in many firms in all industries, then the economy-wide demand for labor falls and, as a result, so do wages in all industries. If one locust lands and eats at the crop, there is no loss to the farmer's yield. If a swarm of locusts lands on the field, the crop disappears entirely.

This is the central thesis of the book. We tend to accept that when firms do well, the economy does well. Competing firms that make profits create jobs and work benefits. Alas, currently dominant firms exert market power and do the opposite. They generate excess profits because they face too few competitors and make consumers pay too high a price for a bottle of beer or for their grandmother's prosthetic hip. Therefore they sell fewer units, as fewer people can afford to buy. Market power now is so widespread, from tech to textiles, that it lowers production and the demand for labor. Instead of creating jobs, profitability due to market power lowers wages and destroys work. That is the profit paradox. Only a competitive marketplace where firms sell at low prices brings benefits for workers and restores a healthy economy.

In our research on market power we have shown that the fall in the labor share is due to the rise in market power. But we cannot fully understand the link between market power and the labor share if we don't understand the link with capital.

Not All Capital Is Created Equal

If firms spend less on workers as a share of GDP, to whom does the rest of GDP go? After all, GDP is the value of everything that is produced. Broadly speaking, the GDP pie is cut into labor and capital, as Kaldor pointed out. When firms have market power, the size of each piece changes: a larger piece goes to the owners of the firm, and a thinner slice goes to workers. But there is a remarkable evolution that makes the pieces of the GDP pie not add up. Not only do firms have lower expenditure on the labor cost, they also spend less on capital.[4] Then if the share of labor declines, and so does the share of capital, where does the remainder of the pie end up? The answer lies in how we define "capital."

The capital share that has declined refers to the expenditure that pays for the use and purchase of machines and buildings, for example. Instead, what is left over from sales after subtracting the cost of labor and the cost of capital expenditures is profits. Often, the cost of capital and profits are all bundled as one, but they are notably different. So really the pie has three slices: labor, capital, and profits. The confusion comes from the fact that profits are often called capital too, and to make things worse, profits and capital are often bundled as one.

Consider the following analogy. When I use my life savings of $250,000 to buy a second home that I want to rent out, I pay money to become the owner of a plot of land and the structure that is built on it. Then, given the willingness of renters to pay, I can charge a particular rent, determined by the market price based on the neighborhood and the quality of the home. There is of course variation in rents across houses, but rental markets are generally fairly competitive so I will not find a renter if I set my rental price too high.

I can, however, increase the rental income if I make an investment. For example, if I put in a new kitchen, a new heating system, and new plumbing for a total cost of $20,000, renters are willing to pay $1,000 per month instead of $700. I will make this investment only if I believe the return of $300 per month over the long run exceeds the cost of $20,000. The extent to which this higher return exceeds the amount of capital invested, everything suitably discounted, are my profits.

Investing $20,000 in the home to improve its quality—renovation—is investing in capital to generate more value. Investing $250,000 to buy the home merely changes ownership, and it does not in principle add any value to the home. Both are called investments; in both cases the amount of money I pay is called capital. Still, there is a fundamental difference: one capital investment affects the value while the other capital investment only changes hands.

There is, of course, a close relation between the two. The higher the return is on investments that change the value of a business, the higher the profits will be and the more a potential buyer is willing to pay for the business. And conversely, if a business owner is strapped for cash, she may be willing to sell part of her ownership share. For instance, she can issue shares that can be used to finance capital investment that affects the value of the business, such as buying machines.

There is no doubt that the distinction between these two types of capital is not always obvious. That said, because the two are related and the accounts have to balance, we do know from Kaldor's stylized facts in current times that labor now accounts for 59 percent of GDP and profits account for 12 percent. In the 1970s those numbers were 65 percent, and 3 percent.[5] It appears that total capital consisting of productive capital and profits has gone up, but distinguishing between productive capital and nonproductive capital (or profits) is crucial here.

When markups increase and firms sell at higher prices relative to cost, they sell fewer units of their output. And if they sell less, they produce less. Firms with market power use less labor and less capital to produce fewer units. That is why the labor and capital shares of the firms that have market power goes down, and profits go up. We know that not all firms have higher profits, but the ones that do have higher profits are the large firms with market power. The evidence shows that there are enough of those dominant firms in all sectors of the economy that there is a large impact on wages in the economy. So how does the wage of my neighbor, who works in a pet store, fall if prices in a number of sectors increase?

Why Does the Price of Beer Affect
My Neighbor's Wages?

The objective of Carlos Brito, the CEO of AB InBev (the company created after the merger of Anheuser Busch and InBev), is to maximize profits. To achieve that goal, building and exploiting market power in order to sell beer at high marked-up prices is a successful strategy, even if that means selling fewer units. Despite all the irrational behavior under the influence of alcohol, consumption decreases at higher prices, even for beer. In fact, repeated news stories point out that beer consumption is slowing down or even decreasing. Are people finally becoming sensible by starting to moderate alcohol use? No, it is not a matter of more health awareness. Beer prices have gone up, so the amount of beer consumed falls. That is simply the law of demand.

Now here is an apparent contradiction. Does the law of demand mean that AB InBev sells less beer than AB and InBev did before the merger? No. To understand this puzzle, we need to distinguish between the market demand for all beer and the individual demand for AB InBev's beer. Consider the following hypothetical example. When beer is sold at $2 a bottle, the demand for Budweiser is 2,000 bottles and the demand for Stella Artois is 3,000 bottles. As the price goes up to $3, the sales go to 1,500 bottles of Budweiser and 2,500 bottles of Stella Artois. Total demand at $2 is 5,000 bottles and at $3 is 4,000 bottles. This is the law of demand in action.

Before they merged, AB sold Budweiser and InBev sold Stella Artois. So InBev sold 3,000 bottles of Stella Artois, whereas after the merger it sold 4,000 bottles of Stella Artois and Budweiser combined. After the merger prices went up and, as a result, market demand went down. But the individual firm's demand went up, albeit under a different identity of the single firm AB InBev as opposed to the two firms AB and InBev.

Now, how does the decline in demand translate into lower wages? Higher beer prices means lower consumption, and therefore also lower production. There is no need to produce beer that no one will drink. This has consequences: beer producers buy fewer inputs (hops, grain, yeast, water, glass, barrels), they invest less capital to produce, and they hire fewer workers. Therefore the firm-level labor share declines in firms with market power. For the same reason (lower production at higher prices) there is a decline in capital.

Is market power in the beer industry important enough to affect the entire labor market in the economy? The answer is no, because beer is only a small share of consumption. But market power is prevalent across many markets in the economy, not just the beer market.

We see a pattern where an increasing number of behemoth firms dominate their market across sectors: Amazon in online retail; Walmart in physical retail; DirecTV in satellite television; Google in search engines; Coca-Cola and Pepsi in carbonated drinks; AT&T, Verizon, Sprint, and T-Mobile in wireless telecommunication; CEC Entertainment and Dave & Buster's in entertainment; Goodyear and Michelin in tires; Whirlpool, Electrolux, and General Electric in household appliances; and Compass Group, Aramark, and Sodexo in food services. Because this is the case in so many sectors, eventually we start to see the effects in the aggregate economy.

This offers a possible explanation to one of the greatest puzzles in the economics profession in recent years. Since 1980 there has been a steady decline in how much the economy spends on labor, exactly the period in which there is an increase in market power across the economy. Rising beer prices alone does not affect the economy-wide labor share, but a rise in prices in all sectors does. The remarkable rise in market power across industries can explain why the labor share has steadily declined, from 65 percent of GDP in the 1970s to 59 percent in 2016.[6]

We find ample evidence that firms with higher market power spend less on labor.[7] The higher the market power of an individual firm, the lower that firm's share of expenditure on labor. Recall that market power is measured by markups—the price relative to costs—and profits, both of which are on the rise. This is consistent with the logic of market power raising prices and lowering production.

The evidence gets even stronger once we take into account that market power is widespread across the entire economy and has increased in the last four decades. With more market power at the level of the firm, the total expenditure on labor as a share of GDP has gone down. When you consider all those decreases in the expenditure of labor of all those firms with more market power, it adds up.

It is precisely the combination of what happens at an individual firm with market power and the fact that market power has gone up so much across the entire economy over the past forty years that creates a link between the rise in market power of individual firms and the decline in the economy-wide labor share. The small step for each firm adds up to a leap backward for the economy.

Now we can go one step further. The labor share can go down for two reasons—either because firms hire fewer workers or because they pay them less, or both.[8] We now discuss each in turn.

First, firms hire fewer workers. In markets where firms raise markups because they have more market power, the total amount produced and sold is lower. And if less is produced, less labor is needed. Therefore, if wages remain constant in markets with market power, fewer workers are hired. With the rise of market power across the entire economy, the direct effect is a decline in the number of active workers in the economy, also known as the labor force participation rate.

Even if the decline in labor force participation means fewer working-age people are active, it does not mean that there is higher unemployment. Out of all people of working age, roughly 80–85 percent are active and 15–20 percent are inactive.[9] The inactive group is not the unemployed—those who are willing to work and are looking for a job. The unemployed are counted as part of the active group. And while unemployment fluctuates over the business cycle and across countries, the unemployment rate does not show a long-term trend.

In the United States in good times, the unemployment rate hovers around 5 percent—that is, out of all those who are able and willing to work, 5 percent don't have a job. When the consequences of the COVID-19 pandemic were at their worst, the unemployment rate reached 15 percent. In countries such as Spain the unemployment rate even reached 30 percent during the Great Recession. Despite those fluctuations between booms and recessions, over long periods of time the unemployment rate has not systematically increased or decreased, and it always hovers around 5 percent in good times.

As opposed to the unemployed, the inactive group are those who are not working and are not looking for a job. Those include mainly students of working age and people who voluntarily stay at home, for example because their spouse is the breadwinner or they care for children or elderly family members.

Since the mid-1990s there has been a steady decline in the share of active workers, and on the flip side therefore an increase in the share of inactive workers. Here we need to make a distinction between women and men. The inactivity rate of men has increased from 3–4 percent in the 1960s to 11 percent in 2020; back then only 3 percent of men did not work and this fraction has more than tripled.[10] This is a huge increase, and the sharpest increase occurred in the mid-1990s. Given that there is no systematic change over the long run in unemployment, the change in the share of active workers is all the more remarkable.

For women the story is different (due to the enormous increase in the number of women in the workforce), but certainly no less worrisome. In 1960, 57 percent of the women were inactive; by the year 2000 the female inactivity rate had shrunk to 22 percent.[11] The gap with men continues to be large, but those are huge gains in female labor market participation. What is disheartening is that now, just as with men, women's inactivity is on the rise again. All the gains women made in labor force participation started to erode in the mid-1990s, with the inactivity rate climbing back to 24 percent in 2019.

Why are both men and women dropping out of the labor market and more prone to stay at home? This is a major puzzle. Researchers have looked for different explanations for this long-term development. But the significant and steady rise in market power is a strong possible explanation.

The rise in market power directly leads to a decrease in the active population of workers. This is the case both for men and women. Not only is the rising tide of market power stemming the swell in women at work, it is reverting the trend. For the first time probably in history—or at least since we have been collecting data—women are dropping out of the labor force, and market power is the culprit!

Most people cannot afford to be out of work, so even if higher mark-ups lead firms to hire less labor, most workers would rather accept a lower wage than stay inactive with no earnings. This indirect effect leads to a decline in wages in the economy.

Recall that the first direct effect on labor force participation acts at the level of each firm that operates with market power. More market power leads to less hiring. This second effect of lowering wages acts indirectly through the entire economy as it brings the labor market back in equilibrium. This equilibrating force happens via an adjustment in the supply of labor to meet the lower demand, and the supply only falls when wages fall. If wages stayed the same, the same number of workers as before would continue to turn up for work, but there would not be enough jobs. Despite its subtlety, the wage effect is even more impactful.

To see how this secondary effect of market power affects wages, consider an imaginary household: Louis, a librarian, and his wife, Jane, who has a well-paying job as a college professor. They have four children. Initially, when the children were too young to go to school, Louis stayed at home with them because the cost of daycare was substantially higher than what he earned as a librarian. While he prefers to work as much as his wife, the best situation for the family is for Louis to stay at home and for Jane to go work so that they can get the higher salary. If wages for librarians were higher, Louis might choose to work instead because his salary would more than compensate for the cost of daycare.

Depending on a wide range of circumstances and family characteristics, people are more or less willing to work. Some are desperate and need a job no matter what; others work only if the job is sufficiently interesting and the pay is high enough. This sensitivity of the number of people who work to the wage is the so-called labor supply elasticity. The higher the wage, the more people will get out of bed in the morning and make it to the office.

Even though this decline in wages is an indirect *equilibrium effect* and less obvious to grasp, its impact is nonetheless devastating. In fact, the impact on wages is greatest at the bottom of the wage distribution—on those who earn least. Later in the book I will devote more attention to what happens to the top earners and to wage inequality, but let us first focus on the majority of the workers. To do so, we need to zoom in on a very simple fact that has been extensively documented in research and in media, namely that wages of the low earners have stagnated in dollar terms and have decreased as a share of GDP.[12]

Consider the wage of the median worker. Out of the roughly 160 million workers in the United States, 80 million earn more than the median worker and 80 million earn less. Because there are quite a few people who earn extremely high incomes, the wage of the median worker is a lot lower than the wage of the average worker.

Since the 1980s the weekly wage of that median worker has barely moved. Adjusted to constant 2019 dollars, it was $812 in 1980, it was $807 in 1990, and it was around $917 in 2019.[13] This is also a well-documented fact: the wages of the lowest earners have barely changed during that period. But if the weekly wage is constant, with a growing economy it must be the case that the weekly wage as a share of total output (expressed as GDP per capita) has decreased. Substantially.

Over the past forty years, GDP has nearly doubled. The median wage as a share of GDP has nearly halved.[14] The overall picture of wage stagnation of the low-income earners is therefore much more dire.

Part of the bad deal that workers got in the past four decades is masked by the increase in wage inequality. The increase in the top wages in part offsets the decline in the wages of those in the vast majority of jobs. As a result, the decline in the labor share is less pronounced than it would have been without the rise of the top wages.

The most impactful implication of the rise of market power across the economy is that wages fall. Though fewer people are active as a result of market power, those workers who cannot afford to stay at home necessarily have to accept jobs. The necessity for people to provide for their families puts downward pressure on wages. Because there is lower demand for labor by firms with market power, and market power is spread across the entire economy, the decline in wages likewise spreads across the entire economy. This is the falling tide that lowers all boats. While a lot of focus in the policy debate is on unemployment, the fact that workers massively drop out of the workforce due to low wages is the elephant in the room.

All of this sounds contradictory: workers drop out because of low salaries, yet at the same time others have to accept lower salaries. The answer is in the fact that some are not willing to work at lower wages and drop out; most cannot afford not to have earnings and reluctantly accept lower wages.

The central thesis of this book—that the effect of the tide of market power is lowering wages across the entire economy—is not commonly made by economists. In addition to this economy-wide wage effect of the tide of market power, there is a long tradition in economics arguing that individual firms suppress wages. I turn to this next, but first I make a detour to the streets of Philadelphia.

Urban Outfitters Comes to Town

On the University of Pennsylvania campus in downtown Philadelphia in 1970, the young married couple Richard Hayne and Judy Wicks co-founded the Free People's Store. Judy Wicks called it "a sixties kind of place with progressive books, houseplants, new and used clothing, and hip house wares—a sort of department store for the under-30 crowd." Two years later Judy left the marriage and the business, and she would later go on to open the White Dog Cafe on the ground floor of her house a few blocks away. Intended to be "a warm gathering place serving simple American food, where people could gather for friendship and good conversation," it became an early proponent of the local food movement using locally sourced ingredients.[15]

Meanwhile, Richard Hayne went in the opposite direction. He changed the name of the Free People's Store to Urban Outfitters. The rest is history. Urban Outfitters is now a chain of clothing retailers with four hundred stores, in the United States and around the world. Urban Outfitters made it big, and Richard Hayne is on *Forbes*'s billionaires list.[16] Judy Wick is an activist for the localist movement. Most people in town adore the White Dog Cafe, though I have heard people say: If it is so good, why isn't it a chain yet?[17]

One of the technological revolutions over the past four decades has been the rise of national chains. Each town used to have its own tailor who would produce locally and simultaneously run the store. Now most towns have an Urban Outfitters, a Gap store, and a portfolio of other national brands. This has been beneficial to the customer, who in a sense has more choice, and the competition among those retailers has increased productivity and lowered prices.

The local tailor has closed shop, and now garments are designed in headquarters in the United States, produced in Bangladesh, and sold at low prices at the standardized stores. This is another example of the role of technological innovation and globalization, where enormous investments in technology, a global supply network, and an army of cost-cutting executives distribute clothes around the country at rock-bottom costs.

These chains have driven out the local businesses that were not cost effective. The chains have market power because of the huge upfront investment to set up the distribution network together with the global supply chain, which limits entry. Moreover, even among those chains there is a hierarchy—for example, Zara is more cost effective than others due to even higher investment in technology and logistics networks. As a result, the superstar firm makes high profits while the other chains are hanging on just making the bottom line.

Prices are unambiguously lower, which is great for the customer, but because some chains are more efficient than others and because of market power, the prices of those dominant firms could have been even lower.

Those chains are in all sectors, from food and restaurants to retail and services. And some of them face competition and the threat of Schumpeterian creative destruction. In some sectors new technologies are challenging the so-called big box retail model where chains build big spaces on a huge parking lot at the edge of town: Amazon's online distribution network challenges Walmart's big box strategy, and Toys "R" Us lost its luster because it failed to latch on to online sales.

Whether you like pricey slow food from your local White Dog Cafe or a cheap cookie-cutter burger from a chain restaurant, there is space to cater to all tastes. It is clear that the customer is better off compared to a world without the chain restaurants. However, the winning chain restaurants that make it to superstars are not passing on all benefits of their cost cutting to the customer, the worker, or the economy.

The chain-restaurant revolution did bring a silver lining for work to the local labor market against the backdrop of the black cloud of rising market power. As a result of the national competition between the Gap and Urban Outfitters, the number of firms in a given local market has increased. Part of this increase is due to population growth and increased urbanization, where people desert rural towns to flock into larger urban areas. With more people in a local market, more firms enter. This shows up unambiguously in the data: the average number of establishments in a local market has increased by 50 percent.[18]

A rising population with an increase in the number of firms in a local market is of course not evidence that market power declines. What matters is at what price those firms sell their goods relative to cost and how much profit they make.

Monopsony Power

A change in the number of firms competing to sell their goods and services also means that there is a change in the number of employers competing to hire workers. This brings us to monopsony power.

Dominant firms do not only exert market power over the customer selling their products. Wherever in a small town Toyota operates a large-scale assembly line, it also pays lower wages to the workers in town. Rather than monopoly power (overcharging the customer), the practice of monopsony power consists of underpaying workers, who in this case are selling their labor. It is exactly the same logic of monopoly, only that now a single buyer (Toyota) controls the market and can pay lower prices (wages) to competing sellers of labor (workers). It is the mirror image of monopoly power, where a single seller controls the price over competing buyers. In monopsony, a single buyer controls the price over competing sellers.

The term was first used by Joan Robinson (of the London School of Economics and later Cambridge) in her book *The Economics of Imperfect*

Competition (1933), and related ideas were developed simultaneously by Edward Chamberlin of Harvard. In most cases there is limited competition from a small number of firms, not just one, in which case the appropriate term is "oligopsony."

Perhaps the most blatant example of monopsony power is the exploitation of athletes in college sports. While college athletes get tuition waivers and scholarships, as well as valuable perks in the form of access to world-class facilities and coaching, and top teaching and academic support, they do not receive any salary. Compared to what they can earn in professional leagues, the compensation of college athletes is a long distance below their market rate. Athletes generate huge amounts for revenue for their colleges, yet the athletes are not paid for their contribution. Colleges are the clear beneficiaries of this regime.

But monopsony power is not just at play in college sports. Research finds evidence that monopsony power is widespread. Firms exert power over their workers and pay them less than they would pay in a fully competitive labor market. This helps to explain why the labor share is lower than it would be without monopsony power. Firms simply pay lower wages and keep more in profits. It is important to distinguish the downward pressure on wages due to monopsony power from the falling tide that results from a lot firms' market power in the goods market. Monopsony power of a given firm *directly* affects the wages of its *own* workers. Goods market power by one firm has no effect on wages when the labor market is competitive. There is an *indirect* effect from the falling tide when there are *many* firms with goods market power: wages of *all* workers in the economy fall.

Even if the existence of monopsony is a robust finding—large firms underpay their workers substantially—there is no conclusive evidence that monopsony power has increased sharply in the past four decades.[19] The most likely reason why monopsony power has not sharply risen is that, unlike monopoly power for goods that are barely substitutable, low-skilled jobs such as drivers and security guards can easily be substituted. A large firm is never alone in town, however small the town is. There are always service jobs in other firms to cater to those working in a large firm, such as office cleaners and waiters and cooks in restaurants.

This is true especially for low-skilled workers. Instead, monopsony power appears to be higher for skilled workers who have higher education and for whom it is harder to switch jobs.[20]

Now, it is true that wages in smaller towns are lower, but we cannot take that as evidence of monopsony power. Wages in small towns are lower because the cost of living is lower. A worker is willing to accept a wage in Janesville, Wisconsin, that is 40 percent lower than in New York City because once adjusted for the cost of living, the high rents in New York, they are equally well off. The reason why wages are higher in larger cities has to do with higher productivity, driven in part by the benefits of agglomeration and dense networks of production. The wage difference between small and large cities exists without monopsony power and dominance of large firms. This phenomenon is known as the urban wage premium, which I discuss in chapter 6.

Compared to the overall effect that the tide of widespread market power has on wages economy-wide, the evidence that wages have declined because of monopsony power of large firms is thus less conclusive. People are making less mainly because the dominant firms around the country are hiring fewer workers, not because those firms are the only player in town.

Of course, the fact that monopsony power hasn't risen dramatically does not mean that it is nonexistent. There are plenty of isolated cases where workers are squeezed in wages or work conditions, often because the firm is indeed powerful and the worker or group of workers is particularly vulnerable. Migrant workers in particular are subject to monopsony power, or those who work in very specialized professions with fewer outside alternative employers.[21]

And a form of monopsony power does exist in any wage negotiation between an individual worker and a large firm due to the asymmetric balance of power. Firms and workers bargain over wages, and if workers lose bargaining power, their share of output declines. A decrease in the bargaining position is an alternative source for the decline in the labor share that affects wages directly.

Another phenomenon that affects wages directly is the recent growth in noncompete clauses—especially by the top tech firms to tie down their engineers and coders—which is an attempt to stifle competition where the dominant firm exerts monopsony power over workers. Non-compete clauses prohibit employees from joining a competitor in the same sector for a period of time after they leave the company.

Coders working for Google in Mountain View, for example, cannot join Facebook for two years after they leave the job. Currently 16 to 18 percent of all workers in the United States are subject to a noncompete clauses.[22] The origins of such clauses are often to correct a real problem where workers walk away with valuable trade secrets, but those reasons are often used as an excuse to increase the share of the firm at the detriment of the employee. The noncompete clause bestows monopsony power on the firm and lowers the wages and mobility of the workers, and it can be thought of as a form of market power by a dominant firm in a well-defined labor market.

Additionally, the absence of a sharp increase in monopsony power in local labor markets does not mean that an individual firm does not exert monopsony power over its suppliers of goods and services. Those negotiations happen at the economy-wide level, where competition is limited. Walmart, for example, squeezes its suppliers hard on prices. When Walmart buys cookies from Belgium, based on the sheer volume, they reduce the provider's margins to naught. This is not simply competition, because Walmart exploits the fact that it is a large player and that the supplier has limited alternative channels to reach such a large customer base.

Similarly, one of the greatest concerns that the business world has with Amazon is that Amazon squeezes suppliers so hard that many suppliers are no longer profitable. When those firms go bankrupt, competition suffers. To add insult to injury, through its trading platforms, Amazon collects detailed information from those suppliers, thus revealing the suppliers' strategies and proprietary information. These practices of monopsonistic squeezing of suppliers are anticompetitive and hurt entire sectors of the economy.

To finish this chapter, we reverse the roles. Could the worker have monopoly power? An important development in recent decades is the rise of licensing. It is a form of market power by workers who also tend to be part owners of the businesses in which they work. Let me introduce licensing in the sector where it is, arguably, the most prominent, and with an example that to me feels very close to home!

Licensing: Monopoly of the Worker

On a windy morning in April 2004, when my wife was past her due date for the birth of our first daughter, Emma, labor had set in. The doctor had warned us that it would take a long time for a first child and that we'd better sit it out at home as long as possible because the hospital staff would send us back home if we came in too early. And so they did when we turned up in the afternoon after some five hours of labor.

After another five hours of now more regular contractions, we returned and were admitted to the hospital. It was a Saturday evening and our doctor was off duty, but we were in the experienced hands of the gynecologist on call that weekend. The midwife told us the doctor on call was in his early sixties and had delivered thousands of babies. "He is the best," except that he was not at the hospital yet, as no other babies were urgently planning on celebrating their birthday.

So we were in the care of a group of wonderful nurses, a midwife who knew the tricks of the trade, a master anesthetist, and all of them under the command of a resident, a young doctor in training. He had started the rotation the day before and had delivered only three babies in his career. He walked in for checkups and a chat every hour or so, and he didn't lack the confidence to boss around nurses and our midwife. Despite the fact that the midwife had four thousand babies under her belt, he assertively ordered to correct her suggestions for the timing of medication and when to start the epidural.

For the firstborn the process was slow, and by 10:00 in the evening, long after my wife's water had broken, there were very frequent contractions but far too little dilation for the delivery to start. So we waited, and with the epidural, the contractions now were more bearable.

We noticed that the midwife started to get a little bit nervous. After another two hours, around midnight, the resident ignored the midwife's suggestion to call the gynecologist, who was at his home in the Philadelphia Main Line suburbs, twenty minutes away. When it was past 1:00 in the morning my wife's instinct told her the baby was on the way, and we saw that the baby was crowning. We called the midwife, who ignored the intern, called the gynecologist, and ordered everything to be prepared for action.

She told us that the doctor had insisted on the phone that the mother should not push until he had arrived. Once he was there, the delivery went very quickly and smoothly, and at 3:20 a.m. on Sunday, April 6, Emma was born.

Interestingly, after the baby was cleaned and mother and child were declared in excellent health, the gynecologist took the resident by the arm at the footboard of the bed. In front of the nurses, the midwife, and ourselves, he gave him a professional spanking. Going over the timesheet, referring to each point in time, he asked the resident what the observations were and what he had decided to do. The doctor corrected him on each of those actions. Looking down to the ground, his assertive demeanor made way for that of a dog with his tail between his legs. The nurses and midwife were smirking.

In the United States, the medical profession is the most innovative and doctors typically use more advanced techniques and have more experience in comparison to any country in the world. Yet there are so few doctors that chances are good that a baby will be delivered by a resident with no experience. The shortage of doctors in the United States is a real problem. In 2016 there were 2.5 doctors per thousand members of the population, which is substantially below the average of the twenty-seven European Union member countries (3.6 per thousand).[23] Add to that the fact that as a richer country the people of the United States demand more health care, at least those with health care coverage.

The consequence is that doctors work inhumanely long hours. Because practice makes perfect, the upside of the long hours is that American doctors do many more procedures and are extremely skilled. This argument is often used by the American Medical Association in favor of restrictions. Doctors are so good because they select only the chosen few, and they work hard to become so skilled. But as Milton Friedman pointed out,

> The American Medical Association is seldom regarded as a labor union. And it is much more than the ordinary labor union. It renders important services to its members and to the medical profession as a whole. However, it is also a labor union, and in our judgment has been one of the most successful unions in the country. For decades it kept down the number of physicians, kept up the costs of medical care, and prevented competition with "duly apprenticed and sworn" physicians by people from outside the profession—all, of course, in the name of helping the patient.[24]

Licensing of professions is as old as organized work itself. The medical profession in particular has a long history of trade restrictions. In a series of books and research papers, Morris Kleiner points out that the code of Hammurabi, a Babylonian code of law of ancient Mesopotamia dating back to 1754 BC, already stipulates fees paid for medical services and the penalties for violations and negligent treatment.[25] Of course, the code of Hammurabi is best known for rules and laws that are more brutal than medical fees, such as "an eye for an eye and a tooth for a tooth," or Lex Talionis, with the same origin as the word "retaliate." A person who caused the death of someone would have to die.

Similarly, the guilds in medieval Europe were associations of skilled artisans and merchants who in a particular town controlled the practice of their craft. They managed to operate as local monopolies, the richest of which is still exemplified in the many opulent guildhall buildings, such as the one in the city of London. At the same time they stifled competition and had detrimental effects on innovation.[26] In *The Wealth of Nations* Adam Smith denounced the inefficiencies of guilds,[27] and in France Jean-Jacques Rousseau's open criticism undermined the guilds as the leftover of a feudal society. In the years following the French Revolution, the guilds were abolished.[28]

In current times, licensing is not the exclusive privilege of doctors and dentists. Lawyers have notoriously strong restrictions on mobility across states and countries. Most states require lawyers to pass the state bar exam, supervised by the state Supreme Court, and which requires roughly three to four months of full-time work. Only members of the state's bar association are permitted to practice law.

In Europe the notary is a prestigious occupation, one that is extremely hard to join and whose services are very expensive. A restricted number of notary licenses stifles competition, and regulation that makes certification by licensed notaries mandatory ensures demand for their services. As a result, when you buy a home you are forced to spend a small percentage of the transaction price at the notary's office. He or she ensures that the contract satisfies all legal requirements. Then you pay again for the sales transaction to be written in the central register of properties, another licensed profession. When we bought our apartment in Barcelona we needed to pay a consultant to verify that there were no other outstanding debt claims on the property, that the property certificate indeed corresponded to what was written in the sales contract, and that no one else had a property claim on it. That is the economically valuable legal service, and you obtain it for a few hundred euros, a fraction of the notary fee. The licensing of notaries restricts entry of competitors and creates market power.

Licensing is not restricted to highly qualified occupations. Depending on the country or the state within the United States, a skilled worker needs a license to work as a barber, a manicurist, or a florist. In some states it takes more training and classroom hours to become a manicurist than a paramedic, or more classroom hours to become a cosmetologist than a lawyer.[29] These are clear cases where licensing serves no other purpose than to restrict entry and reduce competition.

Sadly, in most developed economies licensing is on the rise. In the United States, occupational licensing currently affects 29 percent of workers, up from 5 percent in the 1950s.[30] Research evidence shows that the monopoly power that licensing creates for insiders leads to higher wages, lower mobility of workers, and higher prices for consumers, without an increase in the quality of the service. My daughter was delivered by one of the best gynecologists in town, but due to a staff shortage she was nearly delivered by an inexperienced resident. The quality of service suffers, doctors' salaries are driven up artificially, and the cost of health care and health care insurance skyrocket.

Across sectors, wages in licensed industries are about 18 percent higher, though not for government certification, and they also limit entry and competition.[31] One study finds that for a subset of occupations with state-specific licensing exams, migration between states is 7 percent lower relative to occupations whose licensing exam is national.[32]

Whatever game one plays, playing purely by the rules pays far less than bending the rules. This is true not only for board games but also for the greater games of economic life. There are enormous incentives to create market power. Firms competing in output markets do it by reducing the number of competitors—for example, through mergers in order to achieve higher prices and a higher market share, or through innovation to create a moat.

Workers who are part owners of the businesses where they work have incentives to obtain a larger share of the output by organizing in guilds or creating licenses that restrict entry and stifle competition by outsiders. These arrangements distort the efficient functioning of the market economy and bestow market power upon a small interest group: the firm in the case of monopoly power in the output market or a group of workers in the case of licensing in the labor market. These forms of market power may be pro-business, but they are certainly not pro-market.

Sometimes the workers' motivation to create a bloc may be a reaction against the monopsony power that the firm exerts. Unions are an example. And with the demise of the union, the rebirth of guilds in the form of licensing may be an expression of this tendency to react against monopsony power of firms.

In sum, market power leads to wage stagnation and drives a wedge between the productivity of workers and the share of the pie they are paid in wages. But not all workers are created equally. In the next chapter we show how market power increases wage inequality, mainly by creating an economy of stars.

5

Economy of Stars

DURING WORLD WAR II, with most British men stationed on the front lines, in barracks, or employed in military manufacturing—and taking large numbers of casualties—England's women faced a dramatic shortage of young, able-bodied suitors. Then, following the attack on Pearl Harbor, the United States officially joined the conflict. From January 1942 through the end of the war, some three million GIs crossed the Atlantic to take up positions in Britain.[1] In a time of scarcity and hunger, these American soldiers arrived with fresh supplies of cigarettes, nylon stockings, and chocolate—and made about three times the pay as their British counterparts.

These factors made the perfect ecosystem for love affairs between young British women, fed up with the deprivations of war, and American GIs. Indeed, these relationships were widespread. And while they must have been gratifying for the participants, they touched a nerve with broader British society. Referring to these American interlopers, the Brits coined the phrase "oversexed, overpaid, and over here."[2]

The British-American dating scene during this tumultuous time helps shed light on a central aspect of wage inequality driven by market power: namely, disproportionate executive wages.

As firms grow in size, they gain market power. A rise in market power means larger firms in general, as well as a greater number of large firms in total. In vying for top talent, these growing and multiplying behemoths push up the price of poaching top executives.

To make it easier to see the parallels between wartime England and executive salaries, consider an oversimplified, heterosexual dating market. Let's say that all participants are ranked in attractiveness and that everyone in the market agrees who is more attractive than whom, male or female. In this market, all of the women prefer to date the most attractive man, and vice versa. Therefore, the most attractive woman and the most attractive man pair off. After that, the second-most attractive woman can only pair off with the second-most attractive man, and so on, until the least attractive woman finds her least attractive match.

Of course, just because the arrangement is transparent does not mean that everyone is happy. The bottom-ranked man would love to date the most attractive woman. However, were he to go after her, he would be rejected.

Real-life dating is, of course, much more complex. It depends on a wide array of factors beyond attractiveness, including serendipity, the number of opportunities in the local dating market, social pressure, and uncertainty based on limited information. But even in the real world, the outcomes we see—who dates whom—have a lot to do with the strategies of everyone else in the dating market, maybe more than those of any one actor.

The evolutionary psychologist Stephen Pinker argues that romantic love has an evolutionary origin. When a man says, "I love you" to the woman he dates, it doesn't mean he wouldn't like to date the top-ranked woman. The definition of love is that he settles for what he can get. In economic terms, love is the *equilibrium outcome* of the simplified dating market. Like it or not, every person ends up with their match. And if you know you can't do any better, you might as well take what you can get.[3]

Consider the change in the equilibrium of the wartime British dating market. While over a short period of time three million young British men were "replaced" by three million young American men with triple the income in their pockets, nothing changed on the side of the women—they were no more or less attractive or eligible than before. Yet they were all significantly better off in these new relationships. The most attractive woman would still date the most attractive man, but that man was now the most attractive American soldier. Together they would have a better lifestyle than what she would have had being with the most attractive British soldier. And this disparity repeats itself down the line. Just as the income of NBA players goes up as television revenues increase—even though the players' skill and effort remain the same—so too would the fortunes of British women rise as poor British men were substituted with rich American ones.

Now, let's apply this thinking to the realm of salaries. Clearly, executives in a job market prefer to work for the largest firm because that firm can offer the most attractive terms: salary, bonuses, and stock options, as well as prestige and career opportunities.

Let's say that given the choice, and barring any outliers, an executive looking for a CEO spot would take the helm of today's Apple over any other company. Likewise, in its search for a CEO, Apple, the most profitable company in the world, would pay whatever it takes to hire the best executive available. Certainly there is far less transparency when it comes to ranking executives in the real world. But generally speaking, we can see how executives and companies sort themselves out according to talent and size, respectively, just as participants in a dating market sort themselves out by attractiveness.

We can also see that, as firms become larger, the salaries necessary to lure each executive rises *independent of any change in their abilities*, just as an influx of well-paid American soldiers improved the lot of every woman in the British dating market.

Recent research analyzing the evolution of CEO pay draws parallels between our dating metaphor and the market for CEOs—one where firms of varying characteristics seek CEOs with different abilities. As in the case of dating, this complex world is severely simplified: firms are ranked exclusively by their size and CEOs exclusively on their ability to create value for the firm.

Because business decisions in large firms have the potential to generate large gains (or losses) for the firm, the largest firms are most eager to hire the most skilled and experienced executives. This boost in firm size makes for stiff competition for CEOs. And like the British women who had a better lifestyle with American GIs, executives in larger and more profitable firms obtain the best compensation packages.

The crux of the argument here is that the larger firm size is ultimately harmful to the stakeholders of the firm and to society at large. As American GIs' pay artificially distorted the British dating scene, so do the piles of cash on which firms with market power sit. Firms pay CEOs high salaries not only because those CEOs create more value to society, but also because those CEOs build a moat around the firm they protect. This boosts profits to the firm at the expense of customers—customers who end up paying inflated prices for goods and services.

As with dating and love, such an oversimplification must outrage people who believe that humans are driven by myriad motivating factors beyond money. Those other factors do, indeed, exist, and they no doubt contribute to the complexity of the executive market. But by reducing parts of an infinitely complex world to extremely simplified descriptions, we can better understand the workings of the underlying market mechanisms.

When I teach, I tell students that models are extremely poor representations of reality. They are like the roadmap between Amsterdam and Paris; they leave out the most beautiful willow tree near Breda, on the border between the Netherlands and Belgium, as well as the restaurant with the best escargots in Lille.

Not only does the roadmap omit such quaint details, it also magnifies objects of interest. Some maps even distort reality for the benefit of clarity. On the London tube map, for example, one mile in zone 1 appears to be much longer than a mile in zone 6. As the American doctor and cancer research pioneer Howard Skipper quipped, "A model is a lie that helps you see the truth."[4] The insight we gain from a simplified representation of the labor market for executives is this: the largest firms hire the best CEOs and pay them the most.

CEO compensation has been controversial because of its sharp rise, especially in the 1990s. During this time, company boards were fully focused on providing the right incentives—whatever it would take for CEOs to act in the best interest of the firm and its shareholders. CEOs were increasingly paid with complicated compensation schemes that depended on their performance. Stock options in particular (where the executive is paid in shares of the company) became a huge part of CEO income, the idea being that executives will do what is best for the firm if they get a share of the gains they generate. This resulted in executives being paid a load of money compared to anyone else in the company.

Soon, however, researchers discovered that these incentive schemes were delivering less than they had promised. Why? Because, in reality, there was less of an incentive problem. Stock prices depend on many factors beyond those impacted by any decision a CEO might make—factors such as oil prices and pure luck, for example.[5]

Research shows that the rise in CEO compensation is an immediate consequence of changes in market conditions. When firms become larger, compensation goes up. The rise in compensation does not result from the introduction of incentive schemes. Rather, it is simply a result of supply and demand.

In a market for executives, as firms get larger, the demand for those executives increases, even if the abilities of those executives to make profitable decisions has not changed. Because each firm typically only hires one CEO, they cannot replace one excellent executive with two mediocre ones and pay each of them half as much. You may be able to do that for a menial job, but it doesn't work with CEOs.

In a 1981 essay, the American economist and Nobel Laureate George Akerlof argued that some jobs are like dam sites: "A dam which under-utilizes a dam site, even though productive in the sense that water is usefully stored or electricity is usefully produced, will nevertheless be costly in the sense that the valuable dam site is wasted. . . . Jobs are pictured as being like dam sites and workers of different skills as being like the potential dams on the dam site. Workers of sufficiently low skills will not be able to get jobs even at zero wages, not because their output on those jobs is negative, but *because they underutilize the jobs themselves.*"[6]

Before the rise in firm size, all firms are happy with their executives. Of course, a medium-sized firm would prefer to have a top CEO, but it is simply not worth paying the salary that a large firm can pay. This is the definition of love (or equilibrium) in the market for executives.

Now, consider the thought experiment in which all firms grow a little bit. Each firm then has to pay slightly more for the same CEO in the same company.

Why? Because if you don't, then a firm that is smaller than you, but is larger than you were in the past, will find it in their ability to poach your CEO. The smaller firm has now grown and has become more productive than you were back then, and you are paying your CEO less than a scrappy smaller firm can afford to pay now. Such competitive pressure raises the compensation of all CEOs, and no firm is better off for it.

In this thought experiment, all firms still hire the same CEO as before, just at a higher level of compensation. CEOs therefore benefit from the rise in firm size, all without doing any more work or being any better at it. Simply because CEOs work for larger firms, whatever they do is more valuable than before. Increases in executive compensation are the result of both the rise in firm size and competition for scarce talent. While this rise in firm size may lead to a tremendously unjust division of the pay, it is the result of market forces and there is nothing inefficient about it.

Or is there? To answer the question of whether the rise in firm size is detrimental to society, we first need to understand why firms have become larger. With the advent of information technology, firms now do business differently and have become very large. For example, G4S—a multinational security services company headquartered in England—employs 618,000 workers worldwide in manned security services and cash handling. If you have been to a major sports or music event anywhere in the world, chances are that the security guards draped in fluorescent aprons and bibs worked for G4S. Mobile communication devices and GPS technology allow G4S to exploit scale, managing large numbers of people in a centralized manner.

But is the increase in firm size exclusively the result of new technologies? There is plenty of evidence to show that firms have grown because they have market power. Our research finds that the same market power that allows those firms to get so large also drives executive compensation. Recall that large firms compete to woo the star executive. If all firms become larger in size, they all end up paying more, and yet they do not get a better CEO for the increase in pay. The same CEO is at the helm of a larger firm, creating more value for the firm by virtue of its larger size. To keep the CEO from being poached by another growing firm, a large firm needs to pay its existing CEO more.

When the source of firm size is the rise of market power, the increase in CEO compensation is inefficient because the goods they sell are priced too high. The inefficiency stems from that fact that market power harms the consumer, even if it is beneficial for the firm. Firms with market power pay their CEOs more because the firm sets artificially high prices for the goods it sells relative to cost. The resulting higher revenues make the talented CEO more valuable to the firm with market power.

In fact, CEOs are often hired and rewarded based on their ability to create market power. Recall the message that Warren Buffett has for the dukes of the castles in which he invests: widen the moat. Even so, the same strategy that successfully generates profits for the firm—and that makes the skilled CEO so attractive—is detrimental to the customer.

The rise in CEO compensation goes hand-in-hand with the rise in market power. Firms with more market power pay their executives more. This leads us to the conclusion that executive salaries are not only high, but excessive. And it's more than just inequitable for executives to be paid hundreds of times more than the lowest-paid workers. With the evidence that market power raises executive compensation, we now know that those salaries are also inefficient. Firms with moats drive up pay in excess to get the best CEOs. This is inefficient because what those CEOs do is not in the interest of the stakeholders of those moated firms: customers pay higher prices for what the firm sells, and because of the falling tide, workers are paid lower wages.

In the absence of an economy-wide rise in market power—where a substantial fraction of firms now make significantly higher profits than they did four decades ago—executive salaries would be lower. Just like the landing of wealthy American GIs in Britain distorted the dating scene, so does the rise in market power distort executive compensation. Maybe we should redefine CEO as "chief, executive—and overpaid."

But the problem is greater than the salary of Apple's CEO. The real problem is that dominant firms are pervasive across the entire economy and in all sectors. Moreover, as a result of market power, salaries rise not only for CEOs but also for other executives, lower-level management, and just about anyone who works inside those glass-and-steel head-quarters. Because of that falling tide, workers at the bottom of the food chain, like Erin from tech support, earn lower wages and have fewer opportunities to move up the ladder.

Of course, those GIs also stormed the beaches at Normandy and were in large part to thank for the eventual end of World War II. Most British mothers-in-law would have preferred that American soldiers prepare for their landing at Normandy with a bit less pay; chances are that the landing would have been equally successful. The GI marriage market in Britain seems to indicate that CEOs would do just as good a job leading their companies to successful landings, even with less pay.

Superstars

Matthew Haag was an introverted teenager without much of a social life. Short and frail, he was no athlete. Instead he spent most of his time playing video games in his bedroom in Palos Hills, Illinois, his pale complexion bearing witness to his solitary youth. With few prospects for a successful career, his future was anything but bright. Though he eventually finished high school and completed a short business course, he had little interest in school. His first foray into the labor market was a job at McDonald's.

Haag had played video games all his life. His favorite game, *Call of Duty*, is a first-person shooter—one initially set during World War II—that has since evolved into a game based on modern warfare. By the age of thirteen he started competing. His online adversaries know him as Nadeshot—short for "grenade shot," a move in which an enemy is killed by first throwing a grenade to distract them, then following with a lethal gunshot. After playing countless hours he earned something of a reputation for being extremely good at the game. At age sixteen he went professional.

At first Haag didn't earn any money from his gaming career, only being paid for travel and expenses. But by the age of twenty-one he and his teams had won major competitions and started to pocket serious prize money. He signed publicity deals with large companies, Red Bull among them. Today he's a savvy social media star in the esports arena with a YouTube channel boasting over three million subscribers. His total earnings are over $1 million per year—orders of magnitude larger than minimum wage at McDonalds, and quite a difference from what his father makes as an experienced carpenter.[7]

In economic terms, Matthew Haag is a superstar. In a 1981 paper "The Economics of Superstars," the late Chicago economist Sherwin Rosen describes the mechanism by which a small number of people earn enormous amounts of money in a competitive market.[8] The idea is based on the same logic that helped us to understand CEO compensation, namely that the most attractive man ends up dating the most attractive woman. Rosen built on these insights and showed that, in the labor market, technological change leads to huge rewards for the few. We will see that market power further exacerbates this superstar phenomenon.

Key in Rosen's analysis is that musicians, athletes, and lawyers cannot easily be substituted by hiring more of them. Those jobs are like Akerlof's dam sites and CEO jobs. Finding the right performer for the right orchestra is again like dating. The orchestra with the largest market can attract the best violin soloist because they can offer the highest value. When the market is heavily skewed toward the very best, even small differences among performers can mean very large differences in compensation.

Rosen argued that technological change in particular has contributed to skewed market size. Before radio and television, the only way someone could hear an orchestra was to go see a concert. The best orchestra may have had access to the largest concert halls and may have toured most often, but their market size was ultimately limited to the number of tickets they could sell. Now you can stream Bach's Cello Suites by a single musician to millions of listeners instantaneously. To reach millions of customers—and generate the largest amount of revenue—you have to have the preferred cello player. And to get to number one, you need to offer payment commensurate with the revenue they'll drive. If you don't, someone else will.

As we've seen in several other ways, it's a winner-take-all market. So while superstars command enormous compensation, they are not necessarily that much better than those who follow in their wake. Small differences in ability and skills, or even in likability, lead to huge differences in compensation.

The superstar phenomenon has spread widely, from the performance arts and sports sectors to all walks of life. For example, experts in artificial intelligence (AI), whether they are academics or have made a career in coding, are in such high demand that it is not unheard of for them to earn multimillion-dollar salaries. In 2016, the British AI lab DeepMind spent an average of $345,000 on each of its four hundred employees, including nontechnical staff.[9] The same is true for specialist medical doctors. The average annual salary for orthopedic surgeons and cardiologists in the United States is close to $500,000.[10] The point about superstars, though, is not about averages, but individuals. These averages mean that some individual doctors and AI experts make salaries on par with some world-class athletes. That wasn't the case a few decades ago.

The superstar phenomenon, widespread across sectors, is not going away anytime soon.[11] Recent research shows that, economy-wide, most of the recent increase in the top 1 percent of earners is driven mainly by the increase in incomes of the top 0.01 percent. In the United States these mega-rich comprise about ten thousand households.[12]

The superstar phenomenon itself, and the fact that it is converting tiny differences in talent into huge differences in pay, cannot be understood without answering an important question: What determines who reaches the top? Why was Matthew Haag able to reach number one?

To be an expert or a top athlete you surely need some amount of knowledge and skill as well as the right physical attributes for the task at hand, be it stature for basketball or dexterity for gaming. It also requires certain personality traits, like perseverance, discipline, and grit, that allow an individual to persist when there is no light at the end of the tunnel. But a nonnegligible share of a top performer's expertise comes from having put many hours into whatever it is they do.

It's not just practice or ability or physical attributes, however. Making it to the top of the hierarchy and becoming a superstar crucially depends on two key and related aspects: opportunity and luck. Not everyone grows up in an environment that supports extreme practice, and not everyone gets the opportunity to clock the kind of hours it takes to become a professional athlete.

Part of people's stereotypical view of basketball players is that they tend to come from poor inner-city neighborhoods. And it's true: before salaries skyrocketed and the NBA became such a lucrative business, many players came from poor backgrounds.

In recent decades, however, most players have come from middle-class backgrounds, irrespective of their race. Yes, LeBron James was born to a poor teen mother in Akron, Ohio, but he is an exception. Stephen Curry (from outside Charlotte, North Carolina) and Kobe Bryant (from the Main Line outside Philadelphia) both grew up in suburban neighborhoods with middle-class families—as did two-thirds of successful NBA players.[13] When it comes to finishing school and eventually making it big in sports, one's background matters a whole lot. In fact, a person's background can be considered one of the main determinants of luck.

In the game of becoming a superstar, not everyone starts in the same place. Some are lucky enough to be born on third base, as the saying goes, while many others can score only if they hit a home run. Being born into poverty severely limits the possibilities of being successful. It doesn't just mean starting at the plate; it's also like starting down in the count.

Success depends as much on practice and opportunity as it does on ability or skill. In the long run, tiny differences in initial circumstances get blown out of proportion. And while some of that magnification is the result of technological change and globalization, as with CEOs, the pervasiveness of market power in all sectors of the economy and in all walks of life works as a catalyst. The rise of the superstar phenomenon therefore cannot be seen disconnected from the rise of market power.

Luck Is One of Your Abilities

As part of success, disentangling luck from ability is a difficult task. There is ample indirect evidence that purely random factors do significantly affect the chances of any one person becoming a superstar. For example, those born in the early months of the year are more likely to become successful professional athletes than those born in later months. By the age of six, the difference between being born in January versus December makes an enormous physical if not psychological difference. Imagine playing basketball against a child who is a few inches taller. Since birth dates and the ways schools and sports teams organize their teams are completely random, there is evidence to show that part of success is serendipitous.

And this phenomenon doesn't occur only in sports. Your chances of becoming CEO also change with your birth month. The number of CEOs born in June and July is 29 percent smaller than the number of CEOs born in other months.[14] In the United States, being born in June or July means that you are the youngest in your class—a fact that apparently puts you at a permanent disadvantage, perhaps due to lack of leadership skill development and self-confidence.

But even if we know that an outcome is caused by pure luck, we tend to trick ourselves into believing that it is due to ability. There is a Japanese saying: "Luck is one of your abilities." But there is a caveat to this nugget of wisdom: it depends on whether your luck is good or bad. Psychologists have long observed that those who are successful attribute their success to internal factors, such as skill and dexterity, and those who fail attribute their failures to external factors, such as bad luck. As the proverb says: success has many fathers, while failure is an orphan.[15] The problem is that the superstar phenomenon makes the difference between the winner who takes all and the loser who gets nothing so stark. Such polarization between outcomes makes rationalizing the idea that Mark Zuckerberg was only slightly better than another bright college student extremely difficult.

This polarization occurs all the time in sports, even within the same team. With a small number of matches and their outcomes depending on a large amount of randomness, teams and the press tend to interpret games through the lens of their results. When a team wins, it's because they played well, while losses are caused by poor performance. Manchester City coach Pep Guardiola once responded to a postgame interview question that, after a win, his team wasn't that fantastic, and during the losses, they weren't that disastrous. In a few words, the coach was implying that the difference is luck.

As Sherwin Rosen's superstar model illustrates, this polarization of the outcomes is the result of modern technology and a change in the reach of economic activity. With the development of that technology, and as these differences become greater, so has the obsession with the rationalization of those outcomes. Rather than accept that those outcomes are in part due to luck, we far more often attribute successes to ability, giving the impression that the differences in ability between those who win and those who lose are a lot larger than they actually are.

The great darts player who misses the bull's-eye gets nothing, while the one who hits it becomes a millionaire. The British-Swiss writer Alain de Botton argues that this has slipped into language. The word "loser" has become commonplace in the English language, but the original word is "unfortunate,"—a word whose root comes from Fortuna, the Roman goddess of luck.[16] "Loser" indirectly became associated with being less worthy or able, whereas "unfortunate" hints at a lack of luck.

People like to believe that the difference between the superstar and the loser is commensurate with their earnings. Had Matt Haag listened to his parents and spent more time studying than gaming, or if he had gotten hooked on *Crash Bandicoot* instead of *Call of Duty*, he might still be flipping burgers at McDonald's, gaming at night in his bedroom at his parents' house.

The same applies to cases like Lionel Messi. Messi is considered by many to be the most talented soccer player ever, but there were so many close calls that could have led to a different result. If he had given up because of any one of the challenges of his youth career—because he was too small, or because his parents wouldn't move from Argentina to Spain—he would have aspired to being a taxi driver in his home city of Rosario, earning less than $10,000 per year—a far cry from $100 million.

Recognizing that these kinds of extremely polar outcomes in earnings are the result of luck amplified by the superstar effect, it becomes important to acknowledge the value and the contribution of the losers and to appreciate them as unfortunate. The role of luck in determining these polar outcomes also has important implications for policy. When the outcomes are so extreme there is a clear motive for redistribution based on equity. Even so, the debate usually surrounds efficiency implications.

With a winner-take-all prize there are enormous incentives to enter the race and work hard. Lots of young children dream about scoring goals like Cristiano Ronaldo or Mohamed Salah. And many will play hours and hours to improve their game in the hopes of making it onto a good team. Often these players are encouraged by parents reliving their own failed dreams. A winner-take-all reward structure induces effort to win, and the higher the stakes, the more effort participants will exert. But effort can be too high, too, especially when, instead of going to school, millions of children enter soccer academies, knowing full well that only a handful will make it to the professional level.

Recent research at the University of Pennsylvania shows that entering the top income brackets is subject to a lot of randomness—and thus, luck.[17] Those in the top 1 percent, and even more, those in the top 0.1 percent, remained in that exclusive category only for one year. In other words, they got lucky. As a result, when top income earners are taxed more, there is hardly any impact on their incentives to work hard, accumulate human capital, or innovate.

Most top athletes, for example, play at the highest level for a few years. We tend to focus on the most famous players, but for every Stephen Curry there are dozens of players who play a few seasons and then disappear. And once a top athlete has made it to the top, making a few million dollars less won't make them run any slower during the game. To get there, though, the incentives to work hard are clear: you either make it and become a millionaire, or you drive a taxi if you don't.

Nonetheless, we have to be cautious before recommending high marginal tax rates on high-income earners. Doing so requires a coordinated policy among countries. Without such an effort there are other ways, besides reducing effort, to lower taxable income, leading to lost tax revenue for the government. After all, workers, and the rich in particular, are mobile.

When the French government, under former president François Hollande, increased the tax rate on individuals earning over one million euros from 48 percent to 75 percent, France's most famous film star, Gerard Depardieu, moved to Belgium to keep more of his income and France got nothing. And his is not an isolated case. Research has shown that top soccer players choose where to play in response to a country's tax rates. Lower taxes attract better players, which also means that more foreign players displace locals.[18]

Short stints of superstardom and their associated luck are everywhere. For instance, Ron Johnson was once the darling of corporate America. The master retail mind behind the Apple Store, he replaced the old cluttered racks at checkout stations with a new shopping experience—one with a minimalist design and homey pine wooden tables that invite the customer to explore and ultimately to buy a MacBook or an iPhone. Even tedious tasks like troubleshooting software and repairing hardware transformed into enjoyable experiences at the Genius Bar. Once the Apple Store was declared a success, Johnson jumped from a senior vice president position at Apple to Target, which he revamped into the modern, hip retailer it has become. His repeated success eventually landed him the job as CEO at J. C. Penney, one of the largest retailers in the United States.

Unfortunately for him (and for shareholders), he didn't find the same success at J. C. Penney, his tenure lasting a mere fourteen months. Brought in to modernize the company and attract new customers, he changed the brand's strategy, shifting it from a discount and mark-down outlet to a retailer selling designer products at transparent prices without psychological gimmicks to trick people into buying more.

He argued that customers could see through the fake prices as markdowns of artificially set higher prices (my father used to dislike sales offers, saying "they charge you half of double"). Instead, Johnson introduced lower prices from the outset. And, as he did with the Apple Store, he hoped to turn J. C. Penney into a place people enjoyed hanging out—into an experience.

What Johnson failed to appreciate was that the typical J. C. Penney customer is a retired bargain hunter who loves the game of finding the markdown—whose shopping success is measured by the amount of savings at the cashier, not necessarily how much they actually pay.

At the same time, it seemed no amount of remodeling would go far enough to attract young buyers—buyers who wouldn't be caught dead shopping alongside older people paying with coupons. Add to that Johnson's inflated sense of self-confidence and an abrasive management style, all in an established company that he knew very little about, and the result was a business disaster. When sales dropped 32 percent in the fourth quarter of 2012, the press called it the "worst quarter in retail history."[19] In early 2013, when J. C. Penney's share price had fallen 51 percent, Johnson was fired.[20]

Rather than the exception, Ron Johnson's experience is the rule. Most CEOs, like most top athletes, get one shot. This is to a large extent due to the component of luck. Randomness in the economic environment (for example, an oil price shock for an airline executive) has nothing to do with performance or management. It is simply luck—an external factor that affects a firm's performance.

Research shows that, with compensation in the form of stock options, a large component of CEO salaries can be attributed to luck.[21] If oil prices go up, the profits and share price of oil companies goes up, irrespective of the dexterity of the CEO. As a result, incentive schemes like stock options have very little effect on executive performance.

In addition to the uncertainty of market conditions, the true ability of the CEO is unknown, implying that the superstar phenomenon has some error in assigning the best CEO to the largest, most productive firm.[22] Executives who are at the helm of an important company but turn out to be the wrong person for the job make decisions that affect their firms negatively, both in the short and the long run.

Despite their bad performances, their companies still end up forking over substantial salaries. When J. C. Penney's share price reached its low point in 2012, Johnson received a mere $1.9 million—but he still made $53 million in 2011, when he was in the midst of making decisions that would do the most damage.[23]

The rise in recent decades of the superstar phenomenon, with such enormous polarization in corporate America and around the world, is amplified by market power. As with CEOs, market power increases returns, giving the largest firms the ability to bid for the best workers, whether they be the finest AI minds in Silicon Valley or the sharpest consultants in Boston. Beyond superstars are those who generate the most extreme of the extreme incomes—individuals whose success is due exclusively to the rise of corporate power, mainly in financial markets.

Megastars

So far we have talked about CEOs and star athletes, but the real high-income earners can't be found on the front pages of glossy magazines. A sizable number of people make a lot more money than the superstars, and they can still go out to dinner at any restaurant without having to pose for selfies and sign autographs, as anonymously as you or I can. These people tend to be financial managers and owners of private equity firms. Let us call these financial managers "megastars," to distinguish them from the superstars.

In 2004, Eddie Lampert became the first Wall Street manager to make more than $1 billion in one year. He had started his career at Goldman Sachs before setting up ESL Investments. With ESL he invests in public equity and hedging markets, typically taking a small number of large financial positions that he holds for a long time.

While Lampert is surely a very talented manager, he has had his share of luck, too. Financial managers who have been lucky to amass large amounts of money because they continue to invest. Not all continue to be lucky, but a few, like Eddie Lampert, become extremely rich. One way to think of the streak of luck he had in 2004 is as if they played a variation of *Who Wants to Be a Millionaire?*, but for billionaires.

The game goes as follows. A room has 1,024 financial managers who each have $1 million. They randomly meet in 512 pairs, toss a coin, and the winner gets $2 million while the loser gets nothing and leaves. Now there are 512 managers with $2 million each. They randomly meet, toss a coin, and the winner gets $4 million while the loser—or rather, the unfortunate—gets nothing and leaves. The remaining 256 managers randomly meet again, toss a coin, and now 128 are left. This goes on for nine rounds, until there are only two managers left, each with $512 million. They toss a coin, and one of them gets $1.024 billion. And the winner is . . . Eddie Lampert.

That was 2004. He continued to invest after that. Within ten years he had assets that reached nearly $4 billion. One of those financial positions was with the retail giant Sears. As a majority shareholder, when Sears ran into financial difficulties he became the CEO in 2013. Eddie Lampert is now better known for being the CEO who ran Sears into the ground, filing for bankruptcy in 2018. In the process, being the activist investor that he was, he put up a substantial amount of his own funds. By 2017, even before the bankruptcy, his private net worth was down to one-third of what it was at its highest, a mere $1.69 billion.

The outlandish salaries of the megastars are to a large extent a return on capital and a huge component of luck—much less compensation for their skill. Or as Warren Buffett has said, "Investing is not a game where the guy with the 160 IQ beats the guy with the 130 IQ. . . . Once you have ordinary intelligence, what you need is the temperament to control the urges that get other people into trouble."[24]

Buffet still attributes success to some kind of emotional skill ("temperament"), but the main point is that investors are not workers, and they cannot forever outperform the market. Eventually, if an outcome, such as $1 billion in income, is driven by randomness, there will be reversion to the mean. To explain the concept of mean reversion, let's go back nearly two centuries to the wood-paneled university chambers of Victorian England.

Studying hereditary traits, the statistician and social scientist Sir Francis Galton (Charles Darwin's half-cousin) was intrigued by the way that offspring inherit certain characteristics, even though population characteristics remain stable. For example, in a stable population, the sons and daughters of tall parents tend to be shorter, on average, than their parents. For offspring of short parents, the reverse is true. He proposed a theoretical model with randomness—that the answer could be found in the notion of regression to the mean, a term that eventually entered into regression analysis and statistics in general.

Galton was a prodigy. In a time with very little formal knowledge of statistics, he also came up with the idea that the average predictions of a large group of people are much more precise than those of individuals— a notion that, following James Surowiecki's book of the same name, became known as "the wisdom of crowds."[25] His idea of regression to the mean is important in nearly any data analysis. If there was no regression to the mean (or mean reversion), with a random component to hereditary height, eventually, it stands to reason, some people would grow taller than redwood trees.

In evolutionary biology, regression to the mean is a force toward stability in a population. It is also a force toward stability in finance. The good shocks and good luck can be so extraordinary that they result in exceptionally high returns on financial investments, but eventually bad shocks hit. Eddie Lampert's portfolio hit extreme returns, but he could not beat the market forever. Today he is the poster child of mean reversion—and that luck is the dominant driver of megastardom. There is a bit of irony in the fact that, originally, Galton called his idea of regression to the mean "regression to mediocrity."

For every superstar and for every megastar, there are thousands of other rich people earning high incomes without any kind of stardom. With a labor force of approximately 160 million in the United States, there are 1.6 million people in the so-called top 1 percent. To make it into that club, an individual needs to earn at least $520,000 per year in labor and capital income. Moreover, the *average* income in the top 1 percent is a lot higher and stands at $1.5 million.[26] The increase in the average total income of the top 1 percent between 1980 and 2018 is 217 percent. During that same period, wages of the median worker (fiftieth percentile) have stagnated.

Many of those in the top 1 percent are fortunate to make such a good living, but they are also hardworking. Still, they owe at least part of their earnings to investment, not just ability and skill. If a doctor or a dentist sets up a practice that hires technicians, nurses, and possibly other doctors, then the doctor's earnings are a mix between her human capital— time spent treating patients—and the return on her investment in building the practice. In other words, wages and profits are mixed.

In the United States in particular, because of a loophole in the tax code, many professionals (doctors, lawyers, and dentists) tend to register as a corporation, the so-called S-corporation, a company that is taxed under Subchapter S of chapter 1 of the Internal Revenue Code. This is also the case with business owners who actively manage their firms. The loophole allows those professionals to pay less in taxes than they would if they were to be paid as employees.

In some sense, this is the polar opposite of what Alfred Chandler describes in his Pulitzer Prize–winning book *The Visible Hand*—the idea that the rise of modern capitalism a century ago is a transition from owner-managed firms to large firms run by a class of professional managers who do not own them.[27]

It would be tempting to interpret the pervasiveness of the S-corporation as evidence of a return to a nineteenth-century model of entrepreneurship. But the S-corporation's pervasiveness is due neither to a shift in economic forces nor technological advances. It is for purely fiscal reasons. S-corporations are not subject to corporate income tax, and shareholder income is taxed as profits on their individual tax return, meaning sizable tax savings compared to drawing a salary (though the owner/manager must draw a minimum salary to satisfy Social Security requirements).[28] This is called pass-through business income. A recent study shows that over 69 percent of the top 1 percent, and 84 percent of the top 0.1 percent, earn some income from pass-through business income. Some of it is return on capital, but a large portion of it is salary income.[29]

The highest incomes in the economy result from superstar effects—from small differences in ability becoming enormously magnified. There is a role for luck, to be sure, especially in financial markets. But the magnitude of the polarization, as well as its pervasiveness across all walks of the economy, is due to market power. There are more tournaments to cultivate superstars, and because of market power the winner now takes more than ever.

Market power and superstardom even stretches into the Ivy League's ivory towers. Next, we turn to the college of stars.

6

Unequal We Stand

Superstars in the Ivies

The Ivy League is definitely a different league than the Premier League, the top soccer league in England, but there are quite a few superstars among academics. The outliers there are the medical doctors at university hospitals, many of whom also hold positions as professors at the university. Top researchers in many fields require multimillion-dollar labs with expensive equipment and large teams of scientists. They obviously obtain funding from agencies, but it is not unheard of for a university to invest $5 million to move a researcher and their team from a competing university and start a new laboratory.

Anyone who has attended one of the top schools as an undergraduate student knows that professors are not hired only for their teaching skill. Professors are there because they are the top researchers. After all, the reputation of the university hinges entirely on whether it can show that it has experts in research. Students want to study at the institutions where the best researchers are, even if those researchers are not star teachers or even if they do not teach at all and classes are given by adjunct professors and doctoral students.

So the race is on to attract the superstar researchers. Part of the expense is to set up the lab and part is for the salary of the principal investigator. And in all fields, the rise of academic salaries at the top institutions has been extraordinary. Even junior professors fresh out of PhD programs now command a total compensation package that is three times what it was twenty years ago; top senior researchers earn salaries that are on par with those of some professional athletes. These are of course not the average salaries for professors—they are the salaries for the superstars.

What drives the rise in salaries? Economists like to argue that it is the option of working outside academia. There is some truth to that. The high salaries for medical doctors in hospitals mean that for universities to have a chance to attract doctors to research and teach at the university, they have to offer competitive salaries. The same is true for computer scientists specialized in machine learning who are offered the most enviable compensation packages at the top tech companies, or finance experts who are lured by high-paying jobs in finance or even independently starting their own hedge funds.

In the late 1990s, Sandy Grossman, a superstar academic, made the decision to jump ship from an academic job at the Wharton School at the University of Pennsylvania to set up his own hedge fund. This illustrates that for some academics there are extremely lucrative alternative jobs out there. As an aside, apparently being rich is not all that matters, as Grossman quipped: "When I was an academic, people in finance asked, 'If you are so smart, why ain't you rich?' Now that I have made money with a hedge fund, the academics ask, 'If you are so rich, why ain't you smart anymore?'"[1]

But of the many professors in all fields, only a few, such as Grossman, have access to those well-paying jobs outside the ivory tower of the university. Most academics are so specialized—and potentially so innately peculiar that they chose to be academics in the first place—that there are hardly any outside jobs available, let alone those that pay well. Still, wages of all academics have gone up, especially for those who are the best in their fields.

The underlying force for this rise in compensation is very similar to the force that has given rise to the increase in CEO compensation. Recall that CEOs in a superstar market are paid more because firms have become larger and have increased their market power. And due to the rise of such market power, this rise in compensation is excessive because the prices of the goods and services they sell are artificially high.

Market power also plays a role in the rise of Ivy League compensation. Top universities have market power, and the cost of attending college is remarkably similar across institutions, which raises some suspicion of collusion in price fixing. Not surprisingly, given the excess demand to enter those elite institutions, tuition fees are very high. But given the number of applicants, Harvard could charge ten times as much and still fill each freshman class (in fact, they do "invite" millions of dollars in donations to a select group of rich alumni whose offspring do not make the grade for traditional admission in exchange for a spot in the incoming class).

Yet, the university's strategy is not necessarily to maximize revenue from student tuition. Building a diverse incoming class, giving generous grants to gifted students from humble backgrounds, and turning away many applicants who are willing to pay full tuition does not strike me as a revenue-maximizing strategy—unless we take a very long view, of students who become alumni that do well.

Today most university endowment money comes from donations. Former alumni and friends of the university give enormous amounts of money for buildings, labs, and sports facilities, and to finance chaired professorships in the various departments. These donations, much more than tuition fees, explain why the endowments, and hence the economic size of the elite universities, have grown measurably. Alumni who can donate do so because they have become very wealthy and often attribute their success to their college experience. The superstars and megastars who made it in financial markets willingly give some of their stardust back to their alma mater. They donate to do good or because they have a need to be recognized on benches in the park, on the named chairs of professors, or on the entrances of buildings.

Market power that lavishly feeds the bank accounts of executives and financiers in turn feeds the endowments of universities. Those who have done well are now able to do some good. That is why Harvard's endowment has now reached nearly $40 billion.[2] In exchange, the university has to make sure that its campus offers the best educational experience possible, but above all, the school must maintain its reputation as a top-notch research institution.

The only thing a university can do to stay at the top of the rankings is to buy respected researchers. Similar to firms with market power that sit on cash from charging high prices, which in turn artificially increases the compensation for superstar executives, Ivy League schools sit on cash from donors and drive up the salaries of their researchers. If one top researcher was paid 25 percent less than what other schools offered, they would leave and go to any of the other top schools. Competition among schools thus drives up salaries. But if all researchers were paid half, I bet that most researchers—both superstars and mortals—would continue in the job. The job is pretty rewarding, even without the stardust money!

A Digression: Doing Good

Universities and the arts are an attractive channel for giving back, though donors each have their own story. For over forty years the Sackler brothers (Mortimer, Arthur, and Raymond) have had their own addiction—they have donated generously. They have established their legacies via donations linked to the most precious pieces of Egyptian art in the Metropolitan Museum in New York, Michelangelo's *Taddei Tondo* at the Royal Academy in London, Asian art at the Smithsonian Institution in Washington, DC, and the remains of Persian king Darius I at the Louvre. Their generous donations have also chiseled the Sackler name in the stones of numerous prestigious university institutions and the wooden chairs dedicated to professorships, especially those related to biomedical science, at NYU, Tufts, Cambridge, Tel Aviv, Yale, Harvard, MIT, and so on. At nearly every donation ceremony you hear about how so-and-so has done well in life and in business, and now they are doing good by giving back. That is exactly what the Sacklers did.

As Jewish immigrants in New York, the three brothers trained as medical doctors, specializing in psychiatry. But the Sacklers did not make their money from seeing patients. They became one of the wealthiest families in the United States, with an estimated joint net worth of $16 billion, because they owned numerous companies, one of which discovered OxyContin.

OxyContin is an opioid that was a breakthrough in pain medication because the active ingredient is released gradually. As a result, a patient can receive pain relief for twelve hours from taking one pill. Previously such cases required an intravenous drip of morphine. The opioid was an immediate success and quickly made the Sacklers billionaires. But their discovery also contributed to the opioid epidemic, with an estimated 72,000 overdose deaths in 2017 in the United States alone.[3] OxyContin is particularly lethal because by grinding the pill, the active ingredient designed to be administered gradually is released instantaneously. The effect is multiple times stronger than heroin and therefore also proportionately as addictive.

Of course, there are many other opioid products that have also contributed to the epidemic. But the Sacklers' contribution was the art of marketing pain medication. Their campaigns seduced doctors into prescribing the medicine, and their lobbying convinced the authorities to approve their medicine with the argument that the drug was a safe and nonaddictive panacea for pain management. They managed to obtain FDA approval without clinical studies on the effect of addiction of the drug or the propensity for abuse. Their marketing techniques knowingly hid the addictive effects and played down the potency of the drug.[4] As a result they sold OxyContin to all kinds of patients with a large range of pain issues, and they sold extremely high doses.

The Sacklers' company, Purdue Pharma, is now owned by descendants of the Sacklers. The firm also produces and sells other opioid blockbusters such as fentanyl, codeine, and hydrocodone. As a privately held company there are few publication requirements, and the Sackler family's involvement has always remained hard to ascertain. The Sackler name is very visibly linked to their philanthropy, but until recently it was virtually absent from opioids and opioid research, the source of their fortune. They might prefer that people not know that in order for them to do good, they had to do bad in the first place. Or, as Mario Puzo wrote in the epigraph to his 1969 best seller *The Godfather*, "Behind every great fortune there is a crime." The same sentiment was voiced by Teddy Roosevelt, who said of John D. Rockefeller when he was denied by Congress to set up a national charitable foundation to channel his wealth and that of his fellow captains of industry: "No amount of charity in spending such fortunes can compensate in any way for the misconduct in acquiring them."[5]

Of course, many current-day fortunes are the result of success stories that epitomize the American dream. It is hard to see what Mark Zuckerberg or Bill Gates did wrong except for being successful at a very young age and being extremely generous soon afterward. Charitable giving is such a quintessential American story, where it accounts for about 2 percent of GDP.[6] No other country gives more to charity than the United States. Donations are in part stimulated by generous tax incentives—any gift is fully deductible—which means that the incentives for charity are highest for those paying the highest tax rates. And with the exception of donations to religion, the lion's share of charity is directed at educational institutions. People love to give back to their alma mater and donors love to be associated with the noble objectives of education and research.

People increasingly utter concerns about the nobility of philanthropy, however, including those who have obtained the money in an honest manner or those who do not use philanthropy to dissociate their names from the unfavorable origins of their wealth.[7] One of charitable giving's greatest shortcomings is that donations do not really target the poor or reduce inequality. Harvard and Stanford are laudable institutions, but with endowments of $39 billion and $25 billion, it is a tough case to make that an additional dollar does more good on their well-endowed campuses than at inner-city public schools. Elite universities admit fewer than two thousand or so undergraduate students per year, so a limit remains to how many economically disadvantaged students they can target.

From a libertarian viewpoint, the argument goes that the voluntary nature of charity allows donors to direct their gifts to be spent on a project of their choice, as opposed to taxes spent on a government-mandated program. What is wrong with that? While recipient universities work hard to build reputations that gifts are unconditional and cannot be earmarked, which college presidents in their right minds are going to turn down $30 million if the donor insists it is spent on funding an unnecessary project? And large projects are what most donors want: architectural jewels, new state-of-the-art research labs, and plenty of high-capacity sports facilities.

Few donors are interested in giving money to inner-city schools with problems of drugs and violence. Based on who they give to, they seem to prefer not to have their name in gold-plated letters at the school entrance above a metal detector. The result is that donations, however well intended and generous, often fail to target those in society who need it most. But most importantly, donations are not free: the $1 million donation to Harvard costs the taxpayer $350,000 if the donor pays a 35 percent marginal tax rate. The total amount of foregone tax income is in the order of $50 billion per year.

When the source of the fortune is market power, then the real cost to society is how these fortunes raise consumer prices, how they depress wages, how they lower labor force participation, and how they create excessive wage inequality. This is even more costly than the tax revenue foregone. On top of it all, the donations to universities create even more inequality by pushing up academic salaries. After all, educational institutions are among the largest beneficiaries of philanthropy, and no academic will ever complain when their salary increases.

Mini-stars: The College Premium

Superstar pay is of course extreme, and most people do not earn those top salaries. Unfortunately, and despite rapid technological progress, we cannot bring a larger share of people into the top 1 percent. But even for those who are not members of this select club earning over $520,000,[8] for the 99 percent remaining a lot has changed in the past four decades. In particular, the difference between the compensation of those with a college degree and those without a degree, called the college premium, has grown steadily.

In 1980, the average income of a college graduate in the United States was 46 percent higher than the average salary of those without college degrees.[9] In 2012 that premium has increased to 96 percent, an increase by 50 percentage points. No wonder parents are desperate to get their children accepted into college and students are willing to incur enormous debt to pay for ever-increasing tuition. The typical worker with a college degree is not a superstar—very few reach this celestial level—but with an average salary premium of 96 percent, college graduates can be categorized as mini-stars. This rise in the college premium is not exclusive to the United States; in most advanced countries this increase has occurred as well.

Not surprisingly, the number of mini-stars is on the rise. With such an increasing return on a college degree, enrollment and graduation numbers have increased substantially. Because parents realize the enormous differences between the earnings of college graduates and noncollege graduates, they send their children en masse to study on campuses around the country, despite the enormous cost. In 1980, around 18 percent of the US adult population had a college degree from any college, including state colleges and Ivy League institutions; in 2019 it is 39 percent.[10] What is striking is that despite the enormous increase in college enrollment, the college premium has nonetheless continued to increase. This is the big puzzle of the mini-stars phenomenon.

Simple supply-and-demand logic tells us that if the supply of college-educated workers goes up and the supply of noncollege graduates goes down, the relative price—or the college premium—should drop. This is especially the case because the supply of college graduates has nearly doubled. But in spite of the large increase in the number of college graduates in the United States, their wage relative to nongraduates has failed to decline and instead has risen substantially.

Of course, not every college graduate ends up in a job that is commensurate with their academic achievement. That was the case of Erin, the senior technical advisor at the tech support company in New Mexico, for example. Still, with more than twice as many college graduates vying for those jobs, we would expect their wages to go down and not up.

How can we explain this rise in the college premium? In the late 1980s and early 1990s, Larry Katz from Harvard and Kevin Murphy from the University of Chicago proposed a simple and appealing explanation—that technology has changed in favor of college graduates.[11] This is often called skill-biased technological change. In order to produce output, firms need both skilled (college graduates) and unskilled workers, two groups that are not interchangeable.

To run a fast-food franchise, one needs managers and burger flippers. The manager can step in when a burger flipper does not show up, but ultimately there is only so much substitution possible, so the firm needs to hire both skilled and unskilled workers. Since what and how firms produce today is different from several decades ago, so is the need for firms to hire workers. The economy has moved from predominantly manufacturing firms that demanded low-skilled manual workers toward a knowledge and service economy with a high demand for skilled, college-educated workers. Knowledge workers with college degrees have become more productive.

People who write computer code, for example, generate much more revenue for a company than if they were cleaning or working in the office cafeteria. With this change in the technology and a higher productivity of college workers, firms bid up the wages for those workers. The reader may sense Adam Smith's "invisible hand." Firms don't want to pay higher wages, but if they don't, workers find jobs elsewhere. No such pressure exists on the low-skill wage earners because many tasks that were previously done by low-skill workers have been automated. A simplistic way of seeing this shift is that robots have reduced the demand for low-skilled work, and in order to build and program those robots, there has been an increase in demand for high-skilled work by college graduates.

Later research extended the logic of skill-biased technological change by showing that most of the productivity difference between college graduates and those without degrees is driven by capital investment. Computers make the college graduates exceptionally more productive, and computer prices have dropped dramatically. As a result, cheap investment in information technology (IT) boosts college workers' productivity much more than that of the noncollege workers, which in turn drives up their wages and therefore the college premium.[12]

The increase in the college premium is large, but so is the response. The number of college-educated workers has doubled, all of them competing for those college jobs. This puts enormous downward pressure on the college premium. Imagine what the college premium would have been had we not seen such a large increase in the number of college graduates. This shows that the implied technological change is even greater than what the college premium reveals. Such a fundamental change may be too good to be true, even during the internet revolution.

The rise in the college premium is also driven by the rise in market power. Just as the superstar phenomenon and the resulting sharp rise in CEO wages is driven by the rise in market power, so too is the rise in the college premium driven by the rise in market power.

The best way to think about low-skilled work is that the number of workers needed is fairly proportional to how much the firm produces. A fast-food franchise that opens half as many restaurants needs half as many people to wait tables and work in the kitchens. Because market power and higher prices suppress the amount of meals sold, fewer low-skilled workers need to be hired.

The proportionality between workers and output is not so stark for college graduates. When a firm has market power it grows larger, and it spends relatively more resources hiring skilled workers. This higher demand for skilled workers increases the wage, and hence the college premium. Part of the rise in the college premium is due to the rise of market power and the remainder is due to technological change that makes college workers more productive. Firms with market power reduce production and disproportionately decrease their demand for workers without a college education. Instead, the skilled workers build and maintain the moat, and the resulting higher prices of what is sold leave the unskilled workers with very little to do.

To be clear, there are enormous differences even within the group of people with college degrees and within the group without college degrees. Quite a few people without college degrees earn substantially more than people with them. Those differences within each group may be due to luck or other abilities that are not necessarily captured by a college education. After all, Bill Gates and Mark Zuckerberg are college dropouts, and Erin, the senior technical advisor, has multiple college degrees and her salary is even lower than that of the average high school graduate.

Not everything that students learn in college is valued by the market. The pool of workers who are accepted into college may be different from and more productive than those who are not accepted. If all of the smart kids in high school go to college and they end up securing higher-paying jobs, college is a selection device.

This would mean that a college degree doesn't *make* you more productive, but it reveals that you likely are. One could ask why it is necessary to go to college in the first place and pay high tuition if there is no added value. But if firms do not know who the smart kids are, the only way for a smart kid to show this intelligence is to take college exams and do well academically. The students do not become more productive—the tests just signal to employers that they are smart, a phenomenon known as the signaling theory of education.

While an appealing explanation, Joe Altonji and Charles Pierret find that the signaling component of the college premium is limited.[13] After all, firms would be able to identify the smart kids based on other characteristics that are observable fairly early in a way that is a lot cheaper than college education. Basically, the firm would do the job of the admissions officer in college in selecting the brightest students. They use information on their high school grades, their extracurricular activities, whether they have held summer jobs, or whether they were the captains of athletics teams.

Similarly, auto insurance companies discriminate risky from less risky drivers based on a wide range of characteristics of both the driver and the car. The insurance premium for a red car that is identical to any other color car is higher. Red cars are not more dangerous vehicles, but people who choose to drive red cars tend to be more prone to having accidents.

As an aside, a major revolution in auto insurance happened in the 1990s when insurance companies discovered that the credit ratings of individuals are a very precise predictor of accidents. Why on earth would better credit make you a better driver? That is the wrong question. What the data shows is that there are certain personality traits—usually referred to as noncognitive skills, which are not acquired through study but are either innate or are acquired by early childhood—that simultaneously affect a person's frugality, their ability to pay their bills on time, and their solvency, as well as their driving skills.

In sum, earnings of the college educated have gone up considerably more, turning college graduates into mini-stars. Technological change has contributed to this development, but the dramatic rise in the college premium is also driven by market power. Dominant firms with market power increase the demand for high-skilled workers who help protect the moat. In firms with market power, high-skilled workers contribute to making the firm more profitable, and therefore they reap a share of the profits. Instead, in firms that face fierce competition there are no profits to be shared.

The evolution of the college premium tells us about what happens to inequality within the entire economy. Now we zoom in closer at the firm level and ask how much of the rise in inequality we see economy-wide originates within the firms.

Inequality within the Firm: A Tale of Outsourcing

The rise in the college premium (mini-stars) and the superstar phenomenon have a lot to say about the increase in inequality in the overall economy. And if there is an increase in inequality economy-wide, it would only be natural that inequality within the firms must increase as well. If the top 1 percent wages have grown much faster than the median wages in the economy, then the wages of the top earners within the firm must have grown much faster than the wages of the median worker in the same firm. The salaries of the executives must now be multiple times higher than the salaries of the workers whose pay is ranked in the middle of the pack within the firm. But that is wrong! As it turns out, growing wage inequality within the firm is another myth about work.

Let's take a look at a very common phenomenon from the last few decades: the outsourcing of services, such as the staffing of the reception desk at a large consulting firm in the Brussels office. Meet Nancy, in her forties and with a professional and businesslike appearance. When I meet her around 11:30 a.m., she fills me in on her day, which starts at 7:30 a.m. and runs until 1:30 p.m., three days a week; her colleague works from 10:30 a.m. until 6:30 p.m. As soon as Nancy arrives early in the morning, she starts printing badges for scheduled visitors. She is also responsible for managing the meeting rooms and ordering catering for meetings. Telephone traffic is a minor part of her daily job. Most external callers call people directly. But with a thousand people on site, on average five hundred of whom are permanently present, the job is hectic, especially early in the mornings when she is alone.

Nancy's job does not differ that much from any other receptionist's job, except that she is not employed by the consulting firm. Like the cleaning team or certain IT services, companies buy her services from an outside company, Eligio in this case. Eligio has about 180 receptionists on its payroll, all of whom are working at companies in Belgium, mostly in the Brussels area. The contract between the consulting firm and Eligio specifies when and by how many people the desk is staffed, and Eligio guarantees the coverage and the quality of the service. Nancy is employed by Eligio, even though she spends virtually all her time at the consulting firm. When asked who felt like her employer, she responded adamantly that it is Eligio. If instead she was employed in-house, the terms would be similar with an annual gross salary of around 15,000 euros for nineteen hours per week. The major difference is that she feels a stronger sense of job security and flexibility at Eligio.

Eligio offers Nancy job security. If the host firm were to relocate to an area not convenient for her commute, then Eligio would find another client closer to her home. In fact, since she started with Eligio in 2012 she has been with three different companies as a receptionist—the US corporation General Electric, the French utility company Fabricom GDF Suez, and now in consulting.

As Nancy mentioned, Eligio also offers her more flexibility. She began her career at a medium-sized lawyers' office where she had worked as a student intern, and she was promoted to become the personal assistant of one of the partners. Ten years into the same firm, and after the birth of her second son, who needs special attention, she decided to leave the job to stay at home. After another ten years as a stay-at-home mom she wanted to go back to work, albeit as a part-timer.

Is the Eligio business model also cost effective compared to the host firm doing in-house hiring? Taking into account holidays, illness, and other reasons for being absent, an average full-time employee is absent on thirty-two occasions, which can be painful for the employer, especially when the worker is absent due to illness or a family emergency. In the case of a visible job like a receptionist, an absence will not go unnoticed: visitors cannot enter the building, meeting schedules are disrupted, and catering is not ordered. Dealing with staffing is not the consulting firm's core business, whereas Eligio, with 180 receptionists on the payroll, can efficiently organize the permanent staffing and emergency substitutions. Eligio argues that it can offer all these advantages at a cost that is 10 percent lower than under self-management.

Outsourcing of goods and services is not new, of course. For years firms that had their own trucks switched to specialized logistics and transportation companies. Most cleaning jobs are now done by workers employed by a specialized cleaning company. The division of labor is the central theme in Adam Smith's *The Wealth of Nations*, written two and a half centuries ago, in preindustrial times.

Before the advent of the large firm, most economic production was organized around individual artisans or at most a small group of workers often consisting of family members. Unskilled workers specialized in producing food and agricultural products. Skilled workers, like blacksmiths, bakers, and milliners, specialized in producing goods and some services. Even the division of labor in the eighteenth century was not entirely new. The first division of labor within the household in prehistoric times was a division of services of some sort, such as the nursing of offspring and foraging.

As Smith forcefully argued, division of labor is limited by the extent of the market. Bakers and locksmiths did not need receptionists one hundred years ago, but large service firms today do. Though there are differences between the division of labor in service jobs as opposed to manufacturing, key is the scale and the fact that today it happens between large firms, keeping in mind that the typical client of Eligio has three hundred employees, with some having as many as three thousand. There is no doubt that those large firms need a receptionist. Eligio itself and its competitors did not exist ten years ago. Interestingly, they do not employ a receptionist to sit at the front desk. Though they are a 180-person-strong firm, with only three people on site, their office is too small.

Nancy's experience exemplifies how outsourcing benefits everyone: the cost of providing the service is lower for the consulting firm and it offers more flexibility to the worker. But another reason firms opt for outsourcing is to decrease wages, which obviously does not benefit the worker. Deborah Goldschmidt and Johannes Schmieder at Boston University have looked at the effect on wages caused by outsourcing. Following German workers in the cleaning, security, logistics, and food services sectors, there has been a huge increase since the 1990s in the number of jobs that are being outsourced rather than produced in-house.

The researchers also looked at workers initially employed in a particular area of a given firm—for example, in the cafeteria—and followed them to see what happened as they continued to work in the same cafeteria but now as employees of an outside food services firm instead. As a result of the outsourcing, wages for similar jobs gradually decreased and they were about 10 percent lower after ten years compared to those that were not outsourced. At the same time, there are hardly any changes in the employment status and other indicators, including hours worked.[14]

This wage decrease indicates that firms can obtain the same or similar services at lower wages delivered from outside the firm. Even if wages do not decrease, outsourcing can reduce the labor cost because benefits are lower, especially at companies that offer generous health and other benefits to lure highly valuable workers. If a tech company offers free day care to its programmers or a university offers tuition waivers to the children of the faculty, those organizations may be forced to offer those benefits to the janitors as well. When janitors are employed by an outside firm, there is no such pressure to offer those benefits.

The outsourcing of services also points to the reasons why Erin, the senior technical advisor working for a mobile phone manufacturer, is not employed by the parent company. Working in high tech is not synonymous with earning high wages. Large tech firms outsource all activities that are not at the core of their businesses, including customer support, implementation of software, and the help desk. This implies that the Silicon Valley designers work on high-value projects and earn high wages, while those doing the outsourced services work in lower-value, lower-wage firms.

Those outsourced service firms are highly competitive and have little or no market power, in large part because the outsourcing firms are so dominant that they can set up different sourcing firms to compete against each other. Within the tech sector, as in nearly all other sectors, firms increasingly polarize into high-paying, high-profit firms coexisting with low-paying, low-profit firms. Moreover, the profile of workers hired within each of these two types of firms looks increasingly similar, with high-skilled superstars in the central office and low-skilled workers in the firm that sources the services.

This observed rise in polarization is often called assortative matching, or sorting. High-skilled, high-paid workers tend to work in firms with more high-skilled workers, and low-skilled, low-paid workers tend to work in firms with more low-skilled workers. This is largely driven by technological change with increased division of labor in a service economy away from manufacturing. In current times, one firm predominantly employs engineers, or consultants, and other firms predominantly hire technicians, or receptionists, as in the case of Eligio.

Less of this sorting existed in the 1970s, when the factory had engineers, technicians, and janitors on the same payroll. As a result, all firms looked fairly similar in composition. All firms had workers of all skills and all pay levels. Even today, a large part of the wage differentials are between workers with different experience levels, between juniors and seniors. In the glass-and-steel buildings in Silicon Valley, AI programmers with star salaries share the floor with juniors who have nice but not quite star salaries. At the consulting firm, the partners earn quite a lot more than the junior associates.

What has changed is that in the 1970s virtually all inequality was within the firm, with partners, receptionists, and janitors all on the same payroll. Now the payroll of the host firm is predominantly populated by consultants—in the case of Eligio, by receptionists. This increase in sorting is a driving force behind one of the most robust stylized facts across countries, with evidence found in the United States, Sweden, France, and Germany.[15] Four decades ago nearly all of the wage inequality in the economy was due to inequality within firms. In terms of wage inequality, firms were representative of the economy as a whole. Now inequality within firms accounts for only two-thirds of economy-wide inequality. The sharp rise in earnings inequality that we experienced over the past four decades was mostly due to an increase in inequality between firms. Within firms, inequality has barely increased.[16]

There is a parallel with evolutionary biology. The Stanford biologist Luigi Cavalli-Sforza has disproven the conceived wisdom that there are significant genetic differences between subpopulations of humans. Nearly all of the variation in the gene pool among individuals throughout the world is due to the variation within any subpopulation. As a result, the variation in the gene pool of, say, the Zulus in Africa is nearly identical to that of the Sámi people at the Arctic Circle in northern Scandinavia. All of the variation is within populations—hardly any variation is between populations.[17] The implication of this finding is that race does not have a distinctively genetic meaning.

Now let us make the parallel with wage inequality in firms. Four decades ago firms were like the genetics of a subpopulation of humans. The lion's share of the wage inequality in the population is due to differences within firms, not between firms. Instead, in current times, about two-thirds of the increase in wage inequality is due to inequality between firms and one-third is due to inequality within firms. Now firms are a lot more different in terms of the wage composition. Some firms have mainly high earners, and other firms have predominantly low earners.

The increase in inequality is in large part due to firms externalizing the inequality, as is the case with outsourcing. There is evidence that the reason for this development toward more specialization within firms is often driven by technological change. Firms that adopt new technologies, such as information and communications technology (ICT) or robots, tend to upgrade the skill composition by hiring more skilled workers and paying higher wages. The firms that do not adopt new technologies increasingly absorb the low-wage workers.[18]

Trade liberalization and globalization is yet another force toward the same end, an increase in wage inequality between firms and more sorting of skills within firms. In an analysis of the impact of globalization on the labor market in Denmark, researchers found that occupational reallocation is a key determinant in crowning the winners and losers of trade liberalization and globalization, confirming that globalization is another expression of technological progress, among others, through decreasing transportation and communication costs.[19]

Of course, outsourcing is also a matter of scale. Adam Smith's concept of the extent of the market helps explain that only if there are enough firms that need the services of a receptionist will it be profitable for a firm to enter the market and specialize in running the business for receptionists, exploiting the gains from specialization. And if receptionists work at different sites for different firms, outsourcing increasingly is done by one firm that is the unique client of the sourcing company. Erin's help-desk company has only one client, the mobile phone manufacturer.

Why would mobile phone manufacturers outsource the customer service that is exclusive to its own business? The answer is market power. With a large scale of production the firm can let different providers of customer services compete against each other. As long as the producer can obtain an input of its production process—in this case the technical support—at a competitive price, the head office cannot do better producing it in-house at the same competitive cost.

Firms with market power understand the benefit of competitive markets and make extensive use of this principle of competition when dealing with their providers. In the same way, AB InBev does not get involved in the hops or glass bottle production as long as those markets remain competitive. Sometimes a large buyer of those inputs (goods or services) can use their size to exert monopsony power the way that large firms lower wages in small towns.

The motto of the firm with market power is to outsource anything as long as there is an input sector that can deliver competitively. CEOs like large moats around their own castles, but they only buy from castles that have no moats.

If outsourcing and technological change has increased the inequality between firms, next I will argue that between countries, the opposite is happening. When it comes to inequality, countries are looking increasingly like each other. At the same time, inequality within countries has increased. Through the process of globalization, countries import inequality.

Importing Inequality and Simpson's Paradox

In an obscure article published in a reputed statistics journal in 1951, Edward Simpson described an apparent paradox.[20] Though he studied statistics in Cambridge after the World War II, Simpson never became an academic statistician. Barely twenty years old, during the war Simpson had worked at Bletchley Park, where he was introduced to statistics and cryptanalysis. Bletchley Park, an estate in Buckinghamshire built at the end of the nineteenth century by the English financier Sir Herbert Samuel Leon, served as the central codebreaking site for the Allies during World War II. From 1942 until 1945, Simpson saw mathematical and statistical geniuses like Alan Turing work to decipher the Enigma code and penetrate the secret communications of the German command.

After the war Simpson studied statistics, and in 1951 he came up with a paradox using a medical trial as an example to illustrate it. Since then, the paradox has appeared frequently in research studies. A simplified description of the paradox based on a fictitious example goes as follows. A study follows one thousand smokers and one thousand nonsmokers over twenty years and measures the number of deaths. In the sample of smokers, three hundred (or 30 percent) die; in the sample of nonsmokers, 360 (or 36 percent) die. Maybe we should encourage smoking and get the Marlboro cowboy back? Hold on.

When we look at the mortality rate by age in table 1, the nonsmokers have a lower mortality rate than the smokers for all ages (20 percent versus 25 percent for those aged fifty to seventy, and 40 percent versus 50 percent for those aged seventy to ninety). The problem with the two

TABLE 1. Simpson's Paradox: A fictitious example of
death rates of smokers and nonsmokers.

	Smokers	Nonsmokers
Age 50–70	200/800 (25%)	40/200 (20%)
Age 70–90	100/200 (50%)	320/800 (40%)
Age 50–90	300/1,000 (30%)	360/1,000 (36%)

sample populations in this fictitious example is that the smokers have many more young patients (eight hundred versus two hundred). In other words, the populations of smokers and nonsmokers are not equally balanced. Because the young have lower mortality rates, that also translates into an overall lower mortality rate of 30 percent rather than 36 percent.

What does Simpon's paradox have to do with work or inequality? Consider first income inequality within countries. With a few exceptions, within-country income inequality has increased in most countries around the world since the 1970s. Measures of labor inequality are typically labor income, but there are also other measures of inequality such as wealth or capital income that have increased.

At the same time, when we consider the world income distribution—and treat the incomes of individuals anywhere in the world as one distribution—we note that there is a decline in inequality. From a historical perspective, the decline in global inequality is a relatively new phenomenon. From the early nineteenth century onward, there has been a continuous increase in world inequality. Most notably, a number of countries, mainly in North America and Western Europe, grew rapidly, creating a gap with many developing countries in Asia, Africa, and Latin America. By the 1970s this evolution had generated a world income distribution with two humps: the group of rich countries with high average income and relatively moderate inequality within each country, and the poor countries with low average income and again relatively low within-country income inequality.

Since the late 1970s, this double-hump pattern has given way to a single-hump pattern of income.[21] The main reason is that large poor countries such as India and China have grown rapidly—their average income has gone up—and these countries have started to catch up to the rich countries. As a result, there is no longer a group of poor countries (the first hump) that lags far behind the group of rich countries (the second hump) but a lot of middle-income countries, so the distribution of income now has a single hump.

Despite the decline in inequality worldwide, income inequality *within* each of these groups of countries has increased. This is reminiscent of Simpson's paradox, now at the country level and extended to allow for inequality. As we compare groups (smokers/nonsmokers and rich/poor countries) with different compositions, once we bundle them together, those compositions change over the total population.

In the 1970s, the group of countries that included India and China not only had lower average income but also lower inequality. By the 2000s, average incomes in India and China had picked up, which allowed for convergence between their average incomes and those of the countries in the West. Still, within each country there has been an increase in inequality. At the same time, income inequality within Western countries went up as well. Still, because incomes have gone up across the board in China, the poorest Chinese are now closer to the richest Americans than they were in the past. Hence there is a decline in the worldwide inequality despite the rising inequality within China and within the United States.

The reason for much of the convergence of the poorer countries is globalization, the increased integration of distant economies. Today, firms can easily design an electronic device in Silicon Valley and produce it in Guangzhou, China. The end product has a large percentage of its value that is generated abroad. This integration of the labor market increases the demand for low-wage workers in Mexico and China, thus driving up their wages and allowing China to catch up to the United States.

At the same time, within the United States and China, global competition increases the inequality within both countries as a divergence exists in the demand for skilled and unskilled labor, an example of the mini-star phenomenon.[22] With the increased geographical integration of production, the economies of China and India look increasingly similar to the Western economies. But the Western economies have evolved to look more like China and India, too.

What has been the result? More inequality within our own economies at home and in adjacent neighborhoods, and less inequality between economies far away. In the process of importing huge amounts
of goods and services, countries have come to import the inequality that
used to be far away. Globalization and trade has transformed inequality;
inequality between countries has morphed into inequality within
countries.

The silver lining is the decline in inequality worldwide, but the dark
cloud is the inequality within countries. Globalization is just another
form of technological change, and market power is enhanced by rapid
technological change and globalization. The rise of within-country inequality is therefore due in part to the rise in market power, which can
only be addressed by scaling down the hegemony of dominant firms.

Urban Inequality: City of Stars

Part of the inequality in wages that we observe is geographical, within
each country. Jobs in small towns in rural communities pay substantially
lower wages than those same jobs in large cities. In fact, wages are systematically higher the larger the size of a city—not just between rural
areas and cities—a concept known as the urban wage premium. The
average weekly wage in the New York metropolitan area, with twenty
million inhabitants, is $1,284, or 41 percent higher than the average wage
of $908 in Janesville, Wisconsin, with a population of 163,000.[23] This
difference is not specific to these two cities. As the population doubles,
wages go up on average by about 4.2 percent.[24] And this difference holds
up even after we account for so-called amenities such as weather, services, transportation, and congestion.

The difference in wages shows how much more productive workers
are when they are surrounded by more people. These statistics tell us
that benefits of agglomeration into densely populated areas are sizable.
Unfortunately, we still have little understanding of what drives those
agglomeration effects. There are plenty of theories and potential
explanations—scale and network effects, labor market spillovers,
knowledge spillovers, learning—but little direct evidence supports of

any of those theories. Analyzing these agglomeration benefits is a notoriously hard problem—one of the major open questions in economics—and economic researchers have yet to find a definitive way to solve it.

The one thing on which all students and researchers of urban economics agree is that the agglomeration benefits exist, that they can be measured, and that the resulting urban wage premium is large. But those wage differences are meaningless without taking into account the cost of living. If the cost of living in Janesville was the same as in New York, only a few die-hard Janesvilleans would remain. All others would move to New York, opt for the higher wage, and pay no extra cost. But that, unfortunately, is not the case.

The cost of living in New York is a lot higher than in Janesville. Per square meter/foot, the housing cost—whether owning or renting—is more than double. Therefore, even though people have higher incomes in New York, they live in smaller apartments and they still spend more on housing than Janesvillians. In fact, researchers have discovered a remarkable regularity: on average, households spend a constant fraction of their income on housing, about one-quarter of their pretax income or one-third of their after-tax income.[25] This regularity is irrespective of where they live. The New Yorker household with a 41 percent higher income spends 41 percent more on housing and gets a smaller apartment as a bonus.[26] As a result, the urban-wage premium is offset by the cost of living. Now there is an economic reason to live in a small town despite the lower wages.

Still, even if we account for the cost of living, larger cities may have higher average wages because there are more high-skilled workers. Most people will gladly accept the premise that larger cities indeed attract the more skilled, possibly inspired by Sinatra's version of New York: "If I can make it there, I can make it anywhere." But the facts tell us a different story. The average skill is the same across cities of different sizes, and it is not systematically higher in larger cities than in smaller cities.[27] The urban-wage premium is not driven by selection: average wages are not higher because the average worker in large cities is more skilled.

But that does not mean that there are no systematic differences in the skill *composition* across cities. To the contrary, there is evidence of spatial sorting, the fact that the composition of skilled workers does change across cities of different sizes even if the average does not. Big cities systematically *do* have more high-skilled workers.

So there is some truth in Sinatra's claim. The fundamental caveat is that big cities like New York also have disproportionately more low-skilled workers. What's left for smaller cities? As we'll see, they have more medium-skilled workers. Even if the average skill is constant across cities, big cities have a more unequal composition of skills than small cities. And since higher-skilled workers earn higher wages, the inequality in skills translates into inequality in wages. In sum, large cities have more income inequality than small cities.

What drives this pattern of spatial sorting of skilled workers and the resulting wage inequality? Doctors and lawyers are attracted to large cities because of the agglomeration effects. The best cancer researchers are at Memorial Sloan Kettering in New York, the best actors and movie professionals are in Los Angeles, and the best programmers are in Silicon Valley. Once you have that concentration of high-skilled workers (mini-stars) or even superstars, they need other, less-star-studded workers around them. Those urban professionals demand services, low-skilled services in particular.

In the hospital, doctors need people to clean the operating theater, but above all, busy professionals need low-skilled domestic help—people who prepare their food, look after their children, and clean their apartments. The agglomeration effects of the big city attract the high-skilled workforce, which in turn attracts the low-skilled workforce. In comparison, small cities rarely, if ever, attract the superstars, and hence there is less demand for those low-skilled services, too.

While the inequality and spatial sorting exists at all ages,[28] an additional contributor to the higher wage inequality in large cities stems from uncertainty about labor market success. For young workers, the large city also acts as a laboratory for experimentation. The young without much experience move to the big city to try their luck. They have barely accumulated any skills and are poorly paid. As time progresses, those who are successful settle in the city and end up making a career with corresponding high wages. Those who are unlucky and do not make enough money to live comfortably in the big city return to smaller, more affordable places (often where they are from originally). This selection leads to a pattern of spatial sorting with a disproportionate presence of young, low-skilled workers in big cities who try their luck and a disproportionate number of successful winners who stay around. The smaller cities therefore have more medium earners, many of whom have returned from the big city to be a bigger fish in a small pond.[29]

This spatial sorting of skilled workers and the resulting wage inequality has been on the rise. In fact, in the 1970s there was no systematic difference in wage inequality across different-size cities.[30] Income inequality in large cities has started to rise since 1980. This is when market power began to rise, as seen in chapter 1, figure 2.

There is evidence that markups are higher in large cities than in small cities. This can be concluded directly from where firms are located,[31] as well as from where products are sold.[32] While more research is needed, this evidence suggests that market power is the driver of the increase in the inequality across cities. As market power is larger in large cities, this contributes to the rise in urban inequality in larger cities and cities of rising (and falling) stars.

The Disappearing Middle: Job Polarization

The last piece of the puzzle that completes the picture of how wages and wage inequality have evolved is the phenomenon of job polarization. Since the late 1970s there has been an increase in the number of people employed both in the highest- and the lowest-wage occupations, and a decrease in the number of people employed in the middle-wage occupations.

At the bottom of the wage distribution, we see increasing numbers of people as security guards and shop assistants, and fewer people working in manufacturing plants, while at the top we see more people moving away from such medium-pay occupations as bank tellers and toward work as well-paid programmers or consultants. This polarization in the number of people employed in these extreme occupations naturally leads to an increase in wage inequality. There are more low-wage earners and more high-wage earners. The job polarization phenomenon was first documented for data from Britain, and it has been confirmed in a wide range of developed countries, including the United States.[33]

The main driver of job polarization is technological change that is biased against routine tasks. Computers and robots have become effective at replacing tasks that involve a lot of routine acts.[34] Manufacturing jobs, such as machine tool operators, assemblers, and precision and handicraft workers are now executed by robots, and the tasks in service jobs such as office clerks, secretarial staff, and customer service workers have to a large extent been replaced by computers.

These middle-paying occupations all have a high content of routine activity. With the demand for routine activity decreasing, there has been an increase in the demand for nonroutine tasks. This works in two directions: First, upward, toward more productive tasks that require more thinking and creativity, such as computer coding or supervision and teaching. These tasks have a high cognitive component—people like programmers and supervisors have to think and solve problems. Programmers and supervisors now take the place of the routine jobs of clerks and bank tellers. Second, there is substitution of routine tasks downward. Within the group of tasks that have a higher manual component and a lower cognitive component, routine tasks in manufacturing, for example, are making way for jobs that are manual but nonroutine, including sales personnel, security guards, and health care workers. These jobs cannot easily be automated, yet they are predominantly manual and at the bottom of the pay scale. It is precisely the common force up and down and away from routine tasks that causes a movement away from the middle jobs. Nonroutine tasks that require one's brain more than one's hands move up the job ladder, and those that require just one's hands move down the job ladder. The result is job polarization, with more high- and low-paid jobs, and fewer middle-class jobs. The disappearing middle.

Research shows that the main driving force of job polarization is the advent of ICT as well as globalization. As I have argued previously, globalization is just another form of technological change, as transportation and communication becomes easier and above all cheaper. But more than globalization, recent research for different countries shows that industries with faster ICT change see a greater shift of demand of jobs away from middle-educated workers to highly educated ones.[35]

Tying things together, let's go back to the college green. Like the increase in the college premium—that the average wage of those with a college degree has increased substantially, the mini-stars—the job polarization phenomenon is predominantly a labor demand force. Labor supply—the amount and type of training that workers receive, as well as the experience they accumulate—adjusts, but technology mainly pushes work away from routine tasks, which drives job polarization. The routine hypothesis affects the college educated positively, as the nonroutine jobs with more cognitive content are better paid, and it affects the noncollege educated negatively as the nonroutine manual jobs are paid worse. The routinization hypothesis therefore helps explain the rise in the college premium.[36]

Does market power have anything to do with job polarization? As far as I know, there is no research showing that market power is responsible for job polarization, and I do not insinuate that market power is the cause. Instead, I hypothesize that market power and job polarization are both caused by a common force, namely routinization. That is, the routinization hypothesis not only drives job polarization, but it also allows firms to exert market power.

While the rise of market power is not exclusive to the IT sector, information technology is a key determinant in the rise of those large firms, especially those that have gained market power by means of rapid technological change, whether Amazon in retail or Zara in textiles. These companies are much more productive than their competitors precisely because they invested more in labor-saving technology and automation than their competitors could ever dream.

For example, the Kiva robots used in the Amazon fulfillment centers have turned warehouse logistics on its head. Before, even in automatized warehouses, goods would be stored on static shelves and human operators would go to the shelves and pick the goods to be shipped. Now static shelves are substituted for mobile units that are moved by Kiva robots, square automated guided vehicles about sixteen inches tall that move underneath mobile shelves and lift them with a corkscrew movement. The robots then carry the shelves to a human operator, who packs the item and prepares it for shipment. This development further exemplifies how technology replaces routine jobs. At the same time, when executed at a large scale, routinization lowers costs and creates market power because no other competitor can generate cost reduction at such a large scale.

As a caveat to job polarization, the Kiva example also illustrates that dominant firms use technology simultaneously in multiple ways to gain market power. In 2012, when they realized the strategic importance of the robots, Amazon acquired Kiva Systems to create Amazon Robotics, which now caters exclusively to Amazon and does not sell its robots to other clients. By avoiding sales to competitors and suppressing the diffusion of this robotics technology, Amazon is widening the moat, making it harder for other firms to catch up.

In sum, market power has contributed to the current economy of stars and a galaxy of different stars. Wage inequality is in part driven by the power that firms exert in the market for the goods they sell, which leads to overpaid CEOs and superstars and helps explain why college graduates are mini-stars. Dominant firms tend to outsource much of their work, which explains why most inequality growth is not within firms but between firms, with highly paid, skilled designers in headquarters and low-paid technicians employed by service firms. With goods and services, globalization also imports wage inequality. We also tend to see more inequality in our cities, and due to automation the middle-income jobs are disappearing.

In addition to the decline in wages for those at the bottom of the wage ladder as a result of the rise of market power and wage inequality, market power also has effects beyond the wages paid. In the next chapter we turn to the effect that market power has on the decline in job mobility.

7

The Gold Watch Myth

CHANCES ARE THAT one of your grandparents or someone in your extended circle of friends and family received a watch from their employer when they retired. A gold watch was often the reward for the loyal employee who entered the company out of school and retired from the same company forty-odd years later. This image is associated with a different era of work.

Instead, in current times, in an ailing job market with few attractive jobs and low pay, one would expect that workers are not very attached to a job. As a result, workers today switch frequently between jobs. A worker at a fast-food chain that pays low wages might take a week off and look for a new job, since there is not much lost from not working. After all, the pay is low anyway.

People tend to perceive current times as uncertain. Today jobs are unstable, whereas one or two generations ago jobs were secure and lasted forever, or at least until the gold watch, right?

The data overwhelmingly shows that the opposite is true: average job duration today is actually about one year longer than it was three decades ago. The average job today lasts 4.2 years, whereas it lasted 3.2 years in the early 1990s.[1] And since job duration is longer today, it must be the case that the likelihood of a worker switching jobs has gone down. That is simply the other side of the same coin: if the likelihood to switch a job is constant at 10 percent each month, then on average the duration of a job is ten months. Instead, if the likelihood of switching is 20 percent, then the average duration is five months. Consistent with the increased duration of jobs, we find indeed that the likelihood of switching has decreased from 3.8 percent in the mid-1990s to 2.9 percent today.[2]

If workers switch jobs less frequently, then firms renew their work-force at a slower rate. This is the decline in business dynamism that has been observed since 1980. Back then, firms changed 35 percent of their workforce annually. Currently, firms only change 25 percent of their workers.[3]

But why is it that people do not switch jobs as fast as they used to? This is one of the most intriguing research questions for economists and experts studying labor market dynamism and how firms adjust their workforce in response to changing economic conditions. For more than a decade now, researchers have documented this decline in labor market dynamism, the fact that firms adjust their labor force less frequently than they did four decades ago. And if firms adjust their workforce less often, worker job duration increases.

An immediate explanation could be that the decline in dynamism is simply technological progress. A century ago, workers would turn up at the port and be hired as longshoremen on a daily basis. With the advent of container freight, those jobs became obsolete. Now, the logic goes, workers have more long-term employment relations with long-term contracts. The problem with this explanation is that this phenomenon of the decrease in labor market dynamism started relatively recently.

Researchers have also proposed other explanations for the decline in labor market dynamism, from the demographic changes such as an aging population or the increase in skilled workers, to the advent of li-censing legislation that protects jobs and stifles job mobility. However, the evidence shows that these explanations cannot account for the ma-jority of the increase in job duration and the corresponding decrease in labor market dynamism.[4]

At the same time there are other developments, such as the decline in unionization coverage or the rise in service jobs (which are of longer average duration than manufacturing jobs). Unionized jobs are more protected and tend to pay higher wages, and they are therefore longer-lasting jobs. With fewer union jobs the prediction would be the oppo-site: jobs would be of shorter duration, not longer.

Why Does the Price of Beer Affect
My Neighbor's Promotion?

There is another, more immediate explanation for the decline in labor market dynamism. But to get to that, we need to get into the shoes of the owner of a gas station. Consider Sunoco and Exxon gas stations at two corners of an intersection. Say they sell gas at $2 a gallon and that reflects the cost, including nonexcessive profits as compensation for risky capital investment. At that price customers are indifferent and the two firms split the market equally. If crude oil prices drop and total cost goes down by 10 percent, then at any price at or above the economic cost of $1.80 the firms will make no losses and stay in business.

Suppose Exxon keeps the price at $2. Then Sunoco can capture the entire market by lowering its price by a little, say to $1.95. Sunoco will capture nearly the entire market, selling double the amount and still making an even greater profit than selling at $2 while splitting the market with Exxon. The much higher volume compensates for the slightly lower price. Since changing prices is a matter of pressing a button that changes the electronic awning and not repainting the board, it can be done immediately and at no cost.

Exxon will not sit still and lose its entire market share, so in turn Exxon will respond by lowering its price below $1.95. Eventually, the only outcome is that both set a price equal to the cost. In a competitive market, when the cost of the good sold becomes cheaper, prices fall. In fact, prices fall by the same amount as the decrease in cost. Economists call this *complete pass-through*. Faced with competition, firms pass on all gains from lower costs to the customer—not because Sunoco loves the customer, but because the competitive pressure forces them. If Sunoco keeps prices high, it will sell nothing.

Things are different when there is only one gas station at the intersection. In a less-competitive environment, pass-through is incomplete. If the next gas station is far away, the firm has market power. With a drop in the price of crude oil, Sunoco does not lose too many customers keeping its price at $2. Many drivers may not be aware of the fall in costs, and even those that are aware might not find it profitable to drive to the next town where prices are lower. Eventually Sunoco will lower the price to the point where it can ensure enough customers while keeping the price high enough to make profits, for example to $1.90. When firms have market power, pass-through is incomplete and the firm passes on only part of the cost savings to the customer.

Economists typically measure pass-through with the impact of exchange rate fluctuation on prices of importers (or exporters). Those cost fluctuations are easy to measure and affect all importers equally. Research finds that as an OECD average, around 46 percent of the cost savings are passed on to the customer immediately, and 64 percent over a longer horizon. That means that only around half of the cost savings are passed on to the customers. For the United States, pass-through is even lower—23 percent immediately and 42 percent over a longer horizon.[5] This seems to indicate that on average, markets are not exactly operating under the idealized tenet of perfect competition and that there is evidence of market power.

Because the knife cuts both ways, cost increases are also (incompletely) passed on to the customer. Therefore, fluctuations in cost imply fluctuations in prices. The main insight is that the same cost fluctuations lead to larger fluctuations in prices under competition than under market power. Like a bike with highly pressurized tires, a competitive market translates any pothole as a shock to your body. Instead, market power is more like a motorbike or a car with comfortable shock absorbers; your body feels some movement, but most of the shock is absorbed by the coil near your wheel.

The fluctuations of prices also go hand-in-hand with fluctuations in quantities sold, only in the opposite direction. As the price of gas doubles, people drive less and therefore buy less gas. As prices go down they buy more. Therefore, under fierce competition, sharp fluctuations in price translate in sharp fluctuations in quantity, whereas under market power the modest fluctuations in prices translate in modest fluctuations in how much is sold. This implies that market power leads to far less volatility of how much is produced.

Why does this matter for jobs? Firms adjust how many workers they hire in response to how much they produce. This is most apparent when

we look at seasonal variation. H&R Block, the largest retail tax preparation company in the United States, hires heavily during tax season. They
have only about 2,700 full-time employees but reach over 90,000 employees, including the temporary ones, in the months before the filing
deadline of April 15.[6] Likewise, restaurants near the beach hire only during the summer, and strawberry farmers during harvesting season. That
is why many statistics are seasonally adjusted. The seasonal fluctuations
are systematic (they occur at the same time each year) and they are
predictable.

Most firms have very little seasonal variation, but they adjust employment as they adjust their production. With high crude oil prices, gas
stations sell less. And when white Stan Smith tennis shoes are in fashion
again thirty years after they were first produced, Adidas hires more
people to produce and sell them. These nonseasonal fluctuations are
driven by a plethora of factors, both on the demand side and on the
supply side, from fashion to new technologies.

These fluctuations translate into how much is produced and therefore into how many people are hired. Because of the incomplete pass-
through, the extent to which those fluctuations in demand, technology,
and costs are translated into the number of workers hired depends on
the market power that firms have. When there is fierce competition,
every little bump in the demand or in the costs is passed on to prices,
prices pass it on to quantities, and quantities pass it on to the number
of workers. Instead, when market power is high, those changes in demand or technology are only partially transmitted into price changes
and the shocks are absorbed. For the same shocks, dampened changes
in the quantities sold lead to dampened changes in how many people
are hired to produce and sell the goods.

There is ample evidence that the shocks have not changed. Firms are
not experiencing higher fluctuations in their demand or their costs now
compared to the 1980s. What has changed is the response to those
shocks. Research shows that due to market power, workers switch jobs
less frequently and the duration of the jobs is longer. This is the Gold
Watch myth. Workers now stay in their jobs longer than they used to a
couple of generations ago. And the effects are large, as we saw earlier.

While in the 1980s 3.8 percent of workers switched every month, now that share has gone down to 2.9 percent.[7] In current times workers are about two-thirds as likely to switch jobs.

From Labor Mobility to Migration

It may appear that there is no connection, but the rate at which firms adjust their workforce also has implications for the rate at which families migrate between cities and states, and internationally between countries. One of the main reasons why households relocate is because of job opportunities and promotions. While most of us dream of moving to places where the weather is pleasant, the air is pure, and the views are spectacular, the main reason for people at working age to relocate is another job.

Firms offer those job opportunities because they are adjusting their production needs. If there is a sudden spike in output to be produced, hiring increases. Now we know that when firms have market power, they translate those spikes less into output, because with more market power, the shocks are absorbed. While some job changes are within the same city, sometimes the best job opportunities are out of town, which requires relocation to a different city. As a result, firms with more market power adjust their workforce less frequently, leading to a decreased need to move between cities. People stay in their jobs longer, and therefore families are more likely to stay in the same town. The rise in market power therefore leads to a decline in migration.

This is indeed what the data on migration reveal, and the facts are striking. In 1980, the migration rate between states was 3 percent per year. By 2016, that rate was 1.5 percent.[8] In less than four decades, the relocation rate of households has halved. This is a dramatic change, with many factors other than market power contributing to this decline. Perhaps we do not need to relocate, but it is easier to commute. And researchers have proposed other explanations, such as an aging population or the advent of new technologies that reduce the misallocation of people to places, and as a result there is a decline in the need to relocate workers. But without the rise of market power, those explanations cannot fully account for the sharp decline in migration rates.

What is most striking is that we see this decline at a time when the cost of migration is lower than ever. A century ago the cost of migrating was much greater, both nationally and internationally. My great-grandparents had five children and lived on a shoestring budget in the three decades covering the two world wars. They were modest farmers in a rural village, keeping a few animals and growing chicory. But with the onset of World War I, life was tough.

When the children started to get married and were having children of their own, the family felt the pressure at the table. There was scarcity of land to work on and an abundance of mouths to feed. Three of my great-uncles decided to leave, all of them at different times. Saving every Belgian franc they could earn, they each bought a third-class ticket on the Red Star Line transatlantic service from Antwerp straight to Ellis Island, where they passed the medical exam and were added to the Ellis Island registry of immigrants.[9]

Two of them made it immediately to Detroit, where they ended up working at the Ford factory. The other brother ended up as a farmer in Montana after a spell in Canada. One of my great-uncles went twice—first to settle and find work, and later to bring over his wife and his children. One of his children, Suzanne, became a bit of celebrity in her birthplace when she came back to Belgium in the fall of 1944 during the liberation by the Allied troops. She had joined the US Army as a nurse and eventually rose to the rank of lieutenant colonel. When she walked into her paternal village, the family members were in awe to see that all American soldiers would stand at attention and salute her wherever she walked.

There is a world of difference between migration then and now. Moving long distances then was akin to the trip of an explorer to unknown continents. Even as late as the early twentieth century, moving west within the United States meant moving to towns and land that were barely settled, let alone developed. Add to that the high cost and inconvenience of slow and costly transportation by rail or horse-drawn cart, and the fact that people, who were a lot poorer without access to any funds or credit, faced enormous risks.

Things became a lot easier in the decades following World War II with the development of the highway networks, faster trains, and air travel. The 1960s was the epoch of massive migration in Europe, within countries in terms of urbanization, and between countries, mainly from the Mediterranean to Germany, France, and Belgium. In the United States it was not uncommon for families to move every few years between states. So with cheap flights and extensive travel options, we would expect to see much more movement.

And we do, of course, see a lot more travel. According to the United Nations World Tourism Organization, the total number of arrivals in any location around the world is estimated to be 1.3 billion, up threefold in the past twenty-five years.[10] Most of this is for leisure and to visit friends and relatives, and a small portion is for business and professional activities. Yet, with such cheap and convenient travel and relocation options, one would expect that it is now a lot easier to relocate and move house. All of that has of course changed dramatically with the COVID-19 pandemic, and it remains to be seen whether the change in travel is temporary or whether we will return to the frequencies of travel seen before the pandemic.

The decline in the cost of travel has not led to an increase in people relocating. Even though we travel much more frequently than our parents' generation, it is a myth that we move homes more frequently: we move less because we change jobs less, the Gold Watch myth fueled by market power.

International migration is of course very different. For a start, there is typically no free mobility of people across countries. This generates potentially large differences in economic opportunities. Instead, when there is free mobility between cities within a country, those differences in economic opportunities disappear because people move—the so-called principle of *arbitrage*. Wages may be higher in New York than in Janesville, Wisconsin, but so is the cost of living. People will move to where they are best off, given wages and housing prices. As a result, in theory people must generally be indifferent when it comes to choosing a location. That is not the case between countries because there is no free mobility. In medieval times there was no free mobility between cities either because only documented citizens had access to enter the gates. This generated similar economic differences that made some cities more attractive than others or made living in cities more appealing than living in the countryside.

The greater the economic differences, the greater the sacrifices people will make to move. Anyone who visited Israel in the late 1990s and early 2000s and rode in a taxi may have had a good chance to encounter a driver who was a reputable concert pianist, a professor of mathematics, or a top-notch nuclear physicist.

With the value of education strongly embedded in Jewish culture, many of the Russian Jews had completed many years of schooling and obtained important positions in education, research, and culture. An Israeli colleague who is the son of Russian Jewish immigrants told me the going joke among immigrants: "How do you know a Russian Jew in Israel is not a concert pianist? If they carry a violin case."

When they arrived in Israel, the new immigrants faced three barriers that affected their job prospects and hence their earnings. The first is that many did not speak Hebrew fluently. This put them at a disadvantage for jobs such as teaching, for example. Second, the poor performance of the economy before the collapse of the Soviet Union had left them with little savings, so they needed to get a job quickly to feed their families and rent places to live. But third, and most importantly, they all came with extremely good credentials, both in terms of their education and past work experience, for the best jobs and for high-ranking positions. As a result, the largest competitors of Russian Jews arriving in Israel in the 1990s were the other Russian Jews living in Israel. With this excess supply of nuclear physicists and concert pianists, you could hire the best at a low salary, and most ended up switching to all kinds of jobs where they could make no use of their excellent qualifications.

Is the Decline in Labor Market Dynamics Bad?

The fact that people change jobs less frequently, and the fact that households are less likely to switch towns, is great for stability. Children do not have to switch school and leave their friends behind, and spouses do not have to find new opportunities because their wives have careers that require them to relocate frequently. Job stability is the objective of many costly social policies. As a result of market power, job stability comes for free. But does it?

While the job stability is desirable, we should not forget that the reasons for the decline in job switching is an increase in market power. Firms are pricing their goods too high, and as a result customers are paying too much for what they buy. With the same income they can buy fewer things (i.e., the real wage is lower). In addition, wages decline due to the decline in the demand for labor. Are workers willing to accept a lower income to gain job security? Only if the price is right.

With the efficiency loss from high prices, it is unlikely that the job security gains outweigh the costs. And the loss does not end there. Job security is great if all workers have the same job and don't care about promotions, or for those who are lucky and sit at the top of the job hierarchy. But job security is much more damaging if it reduces the speed of promotions and if it prevents workers from upward mobility for those at the bottom of the job ladder.

For reasons independent of market power (mainly labor regulation), most of Europe, and in particular the Mediterranean countries, are notorious for low job mobility with slow promotions and strong job security. A Spanish friend of mine had worked for years in the financial sector in London while his wife stayed in Barcelona. When they started a family he decided to return to Barcelona and found a job at one of the large Spanish banks. Locally it is considered the Rolls-Royce of jobs: plenty of benefits, infinite job security, and a decent compensation. But soon after he started, he realized that the opportunities for promotion were exclusively linked to the retirement of his older colleagues. He came from a dynamic work environment in London where people moved on constantly to new opportunities both inside and outside the bank, which in turn created promotions inside. He had moved up through the ranks very quickly. Instead, at the bank in Barcelona, promotions were rare. The great Paul Samuelson, a Nobel Laureate in economics, said the following about scientific progress around a table with economics professors, but I guess it can be paraphrased around the table of any human resource meeting in a Spanish company: promotion happens funeral by funeral by funeral.

At face value, the decline in mobility may become desirable because decline brings job security, but it also reduces opportunities. When mobility goes down, workers have fewer chances for promotion and their wages stagnate. Market power may appear to bring job security and stability, but more than anything else, it stifles the American dream.

Market power has tangible effects on wages and labor mobility, as we have seen in chapters 4–6. In the next chapter we turn to analyzing consequences beyond the labor market. Market power also has an impact on the social fabric, health outcomes, wealth, startups, and interest rates.

8

Rich Suburbanite, Poor Suburbanite

IN THE WELL-OFF SUBURBS of Mercer County, New Jersey, a profound transformation is happening. In 2017 I was on sabbatical in Princeton, New Jersey, a college town of about sixteen thousand inhabitants. Jobs in town are dominated by the university and the pharmaceutical industry around it, but it is close enough to New York to attract the high-earning commuters who look for good schools. It is a wealthy suburb, especially considering what life is like a few miles away in downtown Trenton.

Walking my dog along the streets behind Princeton High School, I would often say hi to our neighbor Joe and his wife Betty, who lived a couple of blocks down the road. During times of good weather they were always sitting outside their house, with their agitated dog, attached to a long leash, charging toward us. Their house was a typical model from the 1960s or 1970s, a sprawling, single-story dwelling with a wide facade, a low-pitched roof, and a front-facing garage. These houses were originally built with the advent of the car culture between World War II and the 1970s, when houses could be built farther apart on larger plots of land. Even though the lawn was immaculate, no major work had been done to the house since it was originally built. In the driveway, Joe and Betty parked their Mercury Grand Marquis from the Ford Motor Company. Production of the car stopped in 2011 so there were no new vintages around, and theirs must have been more than fifteen years old. We never talked about our professional lives, but it appeared that they were both either at the end of their careers or recently retired.

On my own street, there was a newly built suburban house. The developer bought an older house in the style of Joe and Betty's, tore it down, and built a new one. Not quite a "McMansion," but built after its image and quite imposing with three floors, cathedral ceilings, a fully finished basement, and a two-car garage. The whole transformation from ranch house to mini-McMansion was done in six months. Those moving in were scientists working at different pharmaceutical companies. Wei and Li Min were born and educated in China, and each had a PhD from an American university. They were in their thirties and had two children under the age of five. Their parents from China lived with them and looked after the children. The two cars on the driveway were a Tesla model 3 and a Volvo X90. Wei and Li Min were not the exception: those moving into the neighborhood and into the newly built houses were highly educated, high-earning professionals, many of them born outside the United States.

My guess is that Joe and Betty's last household annual income was among the lowest in the neighborhood, and even below the country-wide average. That of Wei and Jing Li is probably well over $400,000. They are most likely in the top 1 percent of the household income distribution. Even though the two families live in the same neighborhood, their land has similar value, and their property taxes are equally expensive, their lives could not be more different: their houses, their cars, and, of course, their careers underscore how salaries have distinctly changed since the neighborhood was first established.

The older generation who were at the top of the ladder when they moved into the neighborhood can now barely afford to live there anymore, with skyrocketing property taxes and moderate incomes or pensions. More importantly, the children of families like Joe and Betty's cannot afford to live in the neighborhood and have to move to less-affluent neighborhoods. Income and social inequality is further reinforced by spatial segregation and ultimately ghettoization.[1]

As the economy changes, so do workers and what they do. In the first half of the twentieth century, new technologies drove workers en masse from farms to factories, and in recent decades again from factories to service jobs. But these changes do not occur at the same rate for everyone. More importantly, they happen by generation. When economic opportunities run out on the farm, the younger generation moves to find work but the older generation stays, often earning an impossibly low income. With farming communities disappearing in the middle of the twentieth century, nostalgia lingered for the good old times on the farm and how factories destroyed the good life. Now there is nostalgia for those factory jobs. New technologies lead to structural change in the economy, and that happens to different generations at a different pace.

When I studied for my PhD at the London School of Economics, a classmate's father was a shepherd in a remote mountain village in Spain. Even in the 1990s sheepherding had already become a rare occupation. Joe and Betty are today's shepherds, left behind in their old house with an old-model car in the driveway. Economic progress has costly transitions, and those are not borne equally. Those bearing most of the cost are often aging workers because making the transition from the old-technology economy to the new-technology economy is too costly for them. It requires starting afresh at the bottom of the job ladder and, with limited active labor life left, the investment does not pay off. Beyond a certain age, making this professional transition is not an option. Many older workers therefore choose to wait it out, and they end up with low salaries and even precarious living standards relative to what those standards were when they started out.

There is evidence that the brunt of innovation falls disproportionately on older workers, with younger workers even being overpaid, especially in information technology (IT) jobs. Because older workers tend to be less IT savvy, there is shortage of IT-literate workers, which drives up the salaries for young IT workers.[2] This is one of the great contradictions of economic progress: while technological change offers amazing opportunities and social mobility for the younger generations, it leaves behind shepherds and retirees living month-to-month. The big challenge is to minimize the damage to those left behind without damaging the prospects of technological progress. I will return to this challenge in the next chapter.

In addition to technological change, there is another reason why the older generation in the beginning of the twenty-first century has drawn the short straw. Joe and Betty's generation is hit a second time in their career paths because they are baby boomers. In the United States, in the post–World War II period of rapid economic growth, there was a sharp rise in the birth rate to over 25 births per 1,000 inhabitants for several years. By the early 1970s, however, the birth rate had fallen back to its prewar levels of as low as 12 births per 1,000 inhabitants.[3] Being born in a population cohort that is twice as populous as other cohorts has substantial effects on the labor market. Being a baby boomer must have felt like taking a bus during peak hours. Most people experience the bus as very busy. Half of the time the bus is empty, but since few people are there when it is empty, few people experience it as empty.[4] Taking a bus during peak hours is exactly what happens to the baby boomers: it always feels busy.

The reason why the baby boom matters for work is that it determines people's job prospects. The composition of workers in a firm typically consists of a mix of the young and inexperienced and the old and experienced. When young, a worker gets on the bottom rungs of the job ladder to gradually climb and make it to the top as a supervisor or a manager when old. With their experience, the old workers act as teachers, mentors, and supervisors. Now, for the sake of argument, suppose we need young and old workers in equal proportions. Then a baby boom really throws a wrench in the wheel of the boomers and bestows a windfall on everyone else.

When the boomers were young workers in the 1970s and 1980s, for every experienced worker there were two inexperienced workers. The labor market balances these numbers in different ways. The obvious but least relevant one is that half of the boomers stay out of work. More important is the effect it has on wages. With an excess of inexperienced young workers, those young baby boomers were hired at lower wages. If a baby boomer didn't want to work at low wages, someone else would be willing to do so for less. With a glut of young boomers, there were plenty. Even the positive effects it may have are a curse in disguise. Some of the brightest young workers might have been promoted early because there were too few supervisors, but those were paid low wages anyway because they had little experience.

If things were bad when the boomers were young, they became worse when they got older and more experienced. In the 1990s and early 2000s, the new cohorts were born at a rate of 15 per 1,000 inhabitants; therefore there are now too few young workers and too many old, experienced workers. The result is that they are underpaid again, now as experienced workers.

Rapid technological change and the baby boom have affected the current older generation the most. But the rise of market power has also contributed to the growing gap the baby boomers have experienced with other cohorts. Market power slows down social mobility overall, making the transition toward new technologies harder and more costly and increasing polarization across generations, especially for older workers. It also drives a wedge between the haves and the have-nots, right in the hearts of our communities. Inequality is inevitable and will always exist, but in a competitive economy the disparities are much smaller and far less persistent across generations. A competitive economy makes for similar lifestyles throughout the town.

There has always been inequality across locations, from wealthy neighborhoods to poorer, inner-city neighborhoods. But the evolving geographical segregation within the better neighborhoods leads to cultural alienation, especially by the middle class that didn't make it in the superstar economy. Much of this alienation is driven by property prices and the absence of affordable housing for normal working people. Even those who sell their valuable suburban property are forced to move out. The proceeds of cashing out may get them through retirement, but it irreversibly diminishes the family fortune permanently.

More importantly, the forced abandonment of the neighborhood severs their connection to the centers of the economic gravity where superstars are made, economically marginalizing their families. The superstar economy that gives rise to this suburban schism is artificially propped up by megafirms that concentrate wealth in the hands of a few workers and entrepreneurs. The only thing that can address this polarization is restoring competition to the marketplace—something that requires the novel antitrust policies that I will discuss later.

Health Outcomes

Sadly, a now-standard narrative on some anti-immigration cable television channels is that older white males are angry not only because they have lower wages but because immigration and globalization are taking the well-paying jobs. In addition, immigrants of different cultures who do not care about family values or Christian religion are supposedly destroying the social fabric of society. They have children out of wedlock, they abuse alcohol and opioids, and their incarceration rates are through the roof.

The reality is much more nuanced. Opioid addiction has shattered families in left-behind areas, including in rural America and in the Rust Belt. The cohesive family with children born within wedlock, with grandparents looking after them, and with a social community for support, is that of Wei and Li Min. Older white males who experience opioid addiction in their families now often have to cope with the fact that their neighbors are richer and are part of a much more cohesive social fabric, which makes them much happier. Not only the superstar immigrants enjoy a more privileged social environment; many of the lower-income Latino and Asian migrants, who are even poorer than Joe and Betty, have a much richer social network. Joe ended his career at the bottom of the job ladder, and he is now also on the lower rungs of the social ladder. And this has an effect on health.

Ever since it has been measured, human life expectancy has been increasing. That is one of the major achievements of technological and economic progress. We have access to better food and a more regular intake of abundant calories, we have better information about unhealthy lifestyles, and health care technology has made enormous advances. Yet, for one particular subpopulation in the United States, this trend has been reversed.

In their book *Deaths of Despair*, Anne Case and Angus Deaton show that starting in the late 1990s, the mortality rate of white Americans aged forty-five to fifty-four has started to increase again, where for all other subpopulations it is decreasing further. This rise in midlife mortality is observed for both men and women and for all education groups, though the most marked increase is in those with less education. This phenomenon is specific to the United States, as in all other developed countries mortality rates for this subpopulation have continued to decline.[5] In the late 1990s, those middle-aged white Americans were the baby boomers; today they are the children of the baby boomers.

Case and Deaton's research shows that the cause of the rise in mortality of middle-aged white Americans is mainly poisoning, suicide, and chronic liver diseases. This is not entirely new, but what this research calls attention to is the fact that drug and alcohol deaths are large enough to revert the downward trend in mortality. Case and Deaton hint at the fact that economic factors may explain the rise in mortality of this demographic group. Inequality started to increase when this generation became adults, and they were the first generation where most were no better off than their parents.

It is true that many of the developments in inequality are also there in other countries where there is no such increase in mortality. But the rise of inequality in the United States is also more pronounced. As a result of this rise in inequality, a substantial number of people of this generation are worse off than their parents due to stagnant wages and rising inequality. Since the rise of market power leads to a rise in inequality, and inequality leads to the rise in mortality due to suicide and drug abuse, it is not implausible that market power has a hand in the rise in mortality of this generation.

In addition, inequality in life expectancy is growing. The richest men (the top 1 percent of household income) in America live fifteen years longer than the poorest (the ninety-ninth percentile of household income). For women the difference is ten years.[6] The gap increased by more than three years between 2001 and 2014. The differences are driven not only by economic outcomes, such as unemployment differences, residential segregation, income inequality, or unemployment rates, but also by differences in behavior, such as smoking, obesity, and exercise. There is a positive effect on life expectancy in areas with more immigrants, higher housing prices (big cities), and more college graduates.[7]

Economic outcomes, and inequality in particular, affect people's health. What we have seen throughout this book is that market power increases the income gap between the rich and the poor. The rise of market power is therefore a prime candidate to explain the rise in inequality of health outcomes. The rise of dominant firms and lack of competition affect not only the wages common workers are paid for their labor, but it also affects their physical health.

We have seen throughout that market power also negatively affects the health of the economy. Yet, despite the negative economic impact, next we'll see that the stock market thrives. The dichotomy between the real economy and the stock market is at the crux of the profit paradox.

High on Stocks, Low on Economic Health

The stock market is a roller coaster. Who knows what will have happened to the stock market between the time I write these lines and you read them? Even if, as a result of a big shock, the stock market falls dramatically—as it did with the outbreak of the COVID-19 pandemic in 2020 or the Great Recession in 2008—the major stock market indexes recover within a few years (within months in the case of COVID-19). If we take the long view and focus on the evolution of stocks since World War II, without obfuscating the long-term view with these sharp short-term fluctuations, we see something different.

In November 2020, the Dow Jones reached the 30,000 mark. While the index always has its ups and downs, since the 1980s the Dow, adjusted for inflation, has been growing at an average rate of about 6.2 percent per year. It wasn't always like that. In 1981 the inflation-adjusted index was at the same level as it was after World War II in 1946, or zero real growth over that thirty-five year period.[8]

This shows that since 1980, big- and not-so-big business has thrived. The US company Mylan, for example, the producer of the anti-allergy device EpiPen, which we discussed in chapter 2, has consistently reported impressive profits in recent years and, as a result, an excellent stock market performance. There are plenty of companies of all sizes with thriving stock market valuations. Most of the large companies that we all know and love have had unprecedented stock market success in recent years: Apple, Visa, Johnson & Johnson, Alphabet, and so on.

As you would expect, the firms with the highest stock valuations are also those with the most market power: there are fewer firms in the market, and each firm commands a larger market share. This cozy situation with less competition allows firms to make more profits. This is not a phenomenon exclusive to the giants in the tech industry. Market power is spread across all industries, from tech to textiles.

It is not surprising that our economy is high on stocks. Investors are always on the lookout for firms with market power. No one in recent history has been more successful than Warren Buffett at picking out which castles have the biggest moats—stocks of companies that have and grow market power. When market power enables Mylan to increase the price of EpiPens, its stock price rises because investors believe that this will increase the firm's profits. And if profits increase, investors are willing to pay more for the company's stock. But too often, a high in the stock market is taken as a sign of the economy's good health. It is not, because in a competitive economy, markets where firms make high profits attract new entrants who see an opportunity to grab a share of those profits. Even if you improve your technology to stay ahead, competitors will follow suit and innovate. Competition inevitably reduces market power and lowers prices, and low market power reduces a company's stock price.

In the data we find a direct relationship between the stock market valuation of a firm and its market power. As we would expect, individual firms with higher market power have higher stock values.[9] We measure the firm's stock market performance as the ratio of its stock market valuation to its sales. We find that across all listed firms, the average of this ratio has increased from less than 0.5 in 1980 to over 1.5 now. This increase by a factor of three is enormous, and it has risen most for those firms that have the most market power. This rise reflects that investors expect to receive an increase in future dividends. After all, the stock market valuation of a firm is an indicator of its future profitability.

Never has this been more manifest than during the COVID-19 crisis. While unemployment was at historical highs of 14 percent and gross domestic product (GDP) dropped by nearly 10 percent, the stock market quickly recovered. Listed firms making on average 15 percent less in sales, but their profits did not suffer because they commensurately reduced costs. And because these companies continued to face a lack of competition, their profits are expected to go up further, even despite a reduction in sales. Competition for the dominant firms on the stock market may drop even more as small, unlisted firms declare bankruptcy.

Now, don't get me wrong: stock prices adequately reflect the value of the companies, but with current levels of market power, stock market valuation is a bad indicator of economic health. This gets to the heart of the profit paradox. Stocks have grown exceptionally in the past three and a half decades, yet the economy has gradually become sicker, with high prices, low output growth, and low wages. Unfortunately, the losses of an unhealthy economy outweigh the gains from high stocks. As the growth of output slows down, eventually even Warren Buffett will feel it in his portfolio.

I have already made the case that market power hits working people particularly hard. Because market power is endemic across the economy, it has profound implications for work. Market power means higher prices, and lower quantities sold, which in turn lowers the demand for labor and therefore wages. The typical worker is hit twice: her wages are lower due to lower labor demand, and what she consumes is sold at monopolistic prices, further lowering her purchasing power. And if this is not enough, the worker is hit a third time because she holds no stocks and therefore forgoes the financial gains of market power.

But for now, many enjoy the high of stocks and they barely suffer the ailments of the unhealthy economy. If you are reading this, chances are you own stock in a pension fund and you hold a decent position on the job ladder, so you are most likely a net beneficiary of market power. Maybe the only cost you pay is an overpriced EpiPen for your child with allergies.

To make things worse, even in the massive economic downturns of the COVID-19 pandemic in 2020 or the Great Recession in 2008, policy interventions to resuscitate the economy disproportionately favor stockholders of large companies. In no recession does anyone anticipate a large drop in demand for, say, air travel. But does the taxpayer need to bail out the airlines, thus giving a huge payout to the shareholders? Those shareholders decided to take a risk, with an upside and a downside. With bailouts there is only an upside risk, financed by taxes mainly on work.

The greatest concern is for households who do not hold stocks and lose out on the gains from market power. This generates an increasingly distorted distribution of wealth. Not only is income increasingly unequally distributed, but so is wealth. Many of those with little wealth and who fully suffer the symptoms of the unhealthy economy are left uninformed. But also many of our own children will be among the losers. Young people now have lower-paying jobs and hold substantially less wealth than those a generation ago, and as a result, they buy homes at later ages than their parents did. Even if you are a net winner, your capital gains do not outweigh all the losses of those around you.

Government policy currently tilts the scale pro-business, away from pro-market, which creates an increasing gap in wealth between those with stocks and those without (we will return to that policy in chapter 12). Fighting market power raises output, and it will inevitably lead to redistribution with lower prices, higher wages, and lower returns on stocks. In the current political environment, with the winners high on stocks and the losers sedated by cable television, there is no imminent danger to your pension fund yet (if you have one). Like the opioid epidemic, this epidemic will take time to cure, and it will be extremely costly for those who currently own stocks when they see their wealth decimated if firms lose their market power and those hefty profits. But if ever the cure starts and the patient fully recovers with competitive markets as we knew them in the 1980s, be prepared for a Dow Jones below 10,000 instead of at 30,000. That sign will be vital of good economic health. The profit paradox again.

The Startup Myth

The ebullient stock market reflects the profitability of the dominant firms, but it also hides the struggles of most other firms. Recall that more than half of the firms show lower markups now than in the 1980s, and only the very top firms have extremely high market power. Since the stock market disproportionately reflects the dominant firms, we cannot hail the stock market success as a victory for all firms, including ones that are privately held. In addition to adversely affecting work and those households that do not hold any wealth in stock, the rise of market power also affects most nondominant firms. The current economic climate is certainly not pro-market. Now we see that it is not even pro-business because the majority of the businesses, especially the small- and medium-sized enterprises, are having harder times than ever. The current climate is pro–*big* business.

So how does that square with our general perception that in this time of technological innovation, this is a better climate than ever for new startups? In the past two to three decades we have seen an enormous growth of new startups in tech. Some of these startups, such as Google, Amazon, and Facebook, have grown in nearly no time to become the largest companies in the world. But it is not just these giants—there are also a large number of smaller or less well-known startups that have been successful. And then there are a number of startups that never made it, such as pets.com or govWorks.com, which was immortalized in the movie *Startup.com*. The failure of startups is, of course, part of the risky investment.

It may be our general perception that this is an epoch of new startups, but it is a myth. The facts are unambiguous. Just before 1980, the startup rate—the fraction of firms in the economy that were founded less than one year ago—was 14 percent, and by 2018 it was 8 percent.[10] People's misperception that there are more startups today may have to do with the fact that we only see the tip of the iceberg of startups. And with those giant tech firms like Google, Facebook, and Amazon, the successful startups are very salient. Of course, we are talking about many small startups, most of which fail relatively early on. In addition, startups are in all sectors, not just in the technology sector—for example, a newly founded small restaurant or bar, a small accounting firm catering to local businesses, or a biotechnology firm that grows out of a patent at a university.

Those are all startups, and there are a lot fewer of them. And if there are fewer startups, fewer firms make it big. Not surprisingly and as a result, the number of initial public offerings (IPOs)—firms that list on the stock market—are dwindling. The average number of IPOs per year fell from 409 in the 1990s to 117 in the 2010s, and to 112 in 2019.[11]

The mechanism behind the decline in startups is complex. Above we discussed how profits have grown so much and yet fewer firms enter the market. Dominant firms have managed to widen the moats around their castles. This is against the basic tenet of capitalism: If other firms generate excess profits, anyone with some capital can step in, produce a similar product, and compete for the profitable firm's customers by offering lower prices. Such price competition gives the entrant firm a share of the profits.

Why does this not happen today? The reason is the rise of market power. First, the decrease in startups is both the consequence and the cause of market power. The latter is a tempting explanation: if fewer firms enter, there is less competition and therefore incumbent firms have more market power. But startup activity or entry of firms is, as economists call it, an equilibrium outcome. That means that whether firms enter into a market or not is determined simultaneously with how much market power there is in that market.

The falling startup rate is indeed the consequence of the rise in market power, once one takes into account why there is market power in the first place. As we discussed in chapter 3, explaining the lopsided technological progress of companies like Amazon, firms invest heavily in becoming more productive, either by producing at lower cost or by producing better and higher-quality goods. When such investment coincides with economies of scale, the firm that moves first has both the necessary scale and the low cost to compete against any competitors who have a small market share (if at all) and low profits. The scale and efficiency gives Amazon a cost advantage to sell at rock-bottom prices.

If incumbents can barely compete, then new entrants can compete even less. The only way a new entrant can enter the market and be profitable is if it manages to generate the same cost efficiency and the same scale. This requires enormous investment and is the reason why the incumbent firm has market power in the first place. The resulting market power, therefore, makes it harder for new firms to get a toehold in the market and lowers the startup rate.

The presence of dominant firms that are on the lookout to take over competitors may be a good enough reason to start a new company. It is the dream of any entrepreneur in their parents' garage to build a company like YouTube or Instagram that eventually will be taken over by one of the tech giants. It doesn't make a difference whether the company makes it to the stock market independently or whether it is taken over—in either case, the founder is a young billionaire.

Again, these examples are the tip of the iceberg. Google and Facebook are not throwing money at startups just because they have loads of it. They also have the in-house expertise and the resources to start up such firms with similar technologies. If the startup has no significant advantage technologically, and most importantly, if it does not have the economies of scale that platforms like YouTube and Instagram have, there is no need to offer money for a competitor whose technology can easily be copied. Again, with more market power there is no reason to start up a firm with the hope of being taken over.

Like an overvalued stock market, anemic startup rates are a sign of an unhealthy economy, sickened by the rise of market power. I will now turn to a last sign of bad health of the economy—the lack of inflation. This is a consequence of market power that makes policymakers at the highest echelons slightly nervous.

Inflation and Falling Interest Rates

Arguably the most successful influence that academic economists have had on policy is stabilizing inflation. By now, most developed countries have set up independent central banks that, in the spirit of independent judiciaries, are not directly susceptible to political whims and electoral cycles.

Politicians may be tempted to make their administration look success-ful in creating economic growth by stimulating the economy with extra spending, resulting in better economic performance without raising taxes. They can do this by increasing the government debt, but a much more effective way, which draws little attention, is by printing money. The injec-tion of money may have a short-term stimulus effect, but it eventually haunts the economy later on when price levels rise and households suffer from higher prices and hence lower purchasing power.

The view of many economists is that inflation per se is not harmful, but rather that unexpected variation in inflation is, because the value of people's future incomes becomes unpredictable. The objective of an independent central bank is therefore to see to it that inflation is stable, usually around 2 percent per year.

Historically, inflation levels have been very low, close to zero. Of course, the concern with inflation has been acknowledged ever since the introduction of money as a medium of exchange, whether in the form of paper money, which came into use in the Song dynasty in China as early as the eleventh century, or in the form of coins during the Span-ish Price Revolution in the second half of the fifteenth century, during which the inflow of gold and silver from the Spanish Empire led to an average inflation of 1 to 1.5 percent per annum.[12] This is low by modern standards, but there was virtually no paper money then, and most im-portantly, it was the result of an uncontrolled influx of gold and silver from South America rather than a purposeful policy.

Since then, politicians have discovered the benefits of exploiting the seigniorage, or windfall gain, that the government obtains from printing valueless pieces of paper that it issues in return for real goods and ser-vices. The holder of the paper pays for that seigniorage through inflation because over time inflation lowers the purchasing power of the same amount of money. Inflation has been a convenient tool to finance exces-sive amounts of debt, for example during wars, without raising taxes on labor. This ends in an escalating spiral that leads to hyperinflation, where increasingly higher inflation is needed to sustain the same level of government spending, as many dictators have experienced. While inflation can be a beneficial tool to finance government expenditure, the

consensus now is that low and predictable inflation is desirable to ensure a safe environment for investment by firms and households.
Around the world, an independent central bank has proven to be the
best way to achieve that objective of price stability.

But in recent years, central bankers are facing new challenges. Surprisingly, one of those challenges is that inflation is too low. With low
inflation, central banks find that monetary policy responds very little to
the stimulus of low interest rates. And this is where the shoe pinches.
The risk-free rate—the rate of return on an investment without any risk
of a loss—has fallen steadily since the early 1980s and is now at rock
bottom. Investors use the ten-year US Treasury bond return as a bench-
mark for the risk-free rate because it is a fairly safe investment. This US
Treasury bond return shows a sharp decline since the early 1980s.

Of course, we need to adjust for inflation, which was a whopping
12.5 percent in 1980. Even after adjusting for inflation, though, this measure for the risk-free rate has been declining since 1980 from around
3 percent to just over 1 percent currently.[13] The problem with a low,
risk-free interest rate is that there is little room for monetary policy to
stimulate the economy once the interest rate is so low and close to zero.
In addition to the risk-free rate, inflation is currently very low, and there
is little rise in inflation in response to expansionary monetary policy.

This is why central bankers are so puzzled by the rise of market
power. The rise of market power means that prices have been rising too
much. When firms build market power over time, they sell their goods
at a price that is higher each year. As a result, if there had been no rise
of market power and markups had stayed constant on average instead
of rising from 1.21 to 1.54,[14] then inflation would have been lower, at the
rate of roughly 1 percent per year between 1980 and today. Even lower?
Central bankers have such a hard time increasing inflation! To understand this, let us simplify a bit.

With technological progress, the cost of producing goods becomes
cheaper, and as a result so does the price, at least if the market is competitive. Consider, for example, the extreme case where the only thing
we consume is computers. According to Moore's law, the number of
transistors per square centimeter in an integrated circuit doubles every

two years, and this exponential growth leads to an exponential decline in prices. Then, in our computer economy, we'd see dramatically falling inflation. Yes, we still only use one computer, but the computer now is a lot faster and not more expensive than it was a few decades ago. Thus, once adjusted for quality, the price of computing power has fallen. This implies that we can certainly imagine a world with negative inflation rather than positive inflation.

Of course, we consume a lot more than computers; other goods see rising prices with economic development. Land is scarce, and the price of housing has been growing at a fairly constant rate ever since data on housing prices has been collected. Still, overall there has been a fall in the prices for a substantial portion of our consumption basket, most notably manufactured goods, agricultural goods and food, and transportation. Prices fall because, over time, the cost of production has fallen as a result of technological progress.

Now, how can the Federal Reserve keep the inflation rate at 2 percent if a substantial share of our consumption is becoming cheaper? Money, like computers and food, can be interpreted as just another good that we value. By injecting more money into the economy, money becomes more abundant and hence cheaper. The same amount of goods and services are now exchanged against a larger amount of money, and as a result prices of all those other goods go up and the value of money goes down. That is inflation. Therefore, even if rapid technological progress leads to decreasing prices, the central bank—whether it is the US Federal Reserve, the European Central Bank (ECB), or the central bank of any other country—can increase the amount of money in the economy to fabricate a rise in inflation. Then the inflation target of 2 percent can be achieved even if technological change leads to falling prices.

With steadily rising markups since the 1980s due to the rise of market power, the central bank did not have to inject as much money into the economy as it would have injected when there was no market power and markets were competitive. The key insight here is that technological progress affects the cost of production, whereas market power affects the ratio of the price to the cost. So we can have both declining costs (from technological progress) and increasing markups (from market power). With rapid technological progress we can still have declining prices and increasing markups. For example, if there is market power in the computer industry, prices of quality-adjusted machines decrease due to rapid technological progress, but not as much as they would under perfect competition because markups go up.

Since the Federal Reserve or the ECB adjusts the money supply in order to attain the inflation target of 2 percent, market power does not affect inflation, even if prices are higher under market power than under perfect competition. The central bank injects less money in the economy under rising market power than under competitive markets in order to keep its 2 percent inflation target.

A more worrisome implication of the rise of market power than the effect on inflation is the effect on the risk-free interest rate. The determining factors of interest rates are highly complex, in particular because central bank monetary policy interferes with the interest rate. But let us focus on the most fundamental drivers of supply and demand.

In the language of economists, the interest rate is the price that equilibrates the supply and demand for capital over a period of time. With bread, bakers supply loaves and households buy them. If there is a shortage the price goes up, and if there is an abundance the price goes down. Likewise with capital: If there is a shortage in the supply of capital the interest rate increases, and if there is an abundance the interest rate decreases.

Now, what is the effect of market power on the supply and demand for capital? When firms sell at higher prices, they sell less quantity. This implies that to produce a smaller quantity, less capital investment is needed. If Apple sold the most recent iPhone model at $400 instead of $1,200, they would sell more units and would need to invest more in production, so market power decreases the demand for capital. Indeed, research finds that the investment in capital (by those who buy capital by paying interest and in turn investing it) has gone down.[15]

What has happened to the supply of capital? The supply of capital comes from the savings of households and the funds that firms have available after investment—in other words, profits. The savings rate of households has fallen somewhat, from around 11 percent in 1980 to

8 percent today.[16] But most importantly, there has been a sharp increase in the economy-wide profit rate as a share of GDP, from 5 percent in 1980 to 12 percent in 2019[17] (and for the publicly traded firms, the profit rate has shot up from around 3 percent of value added in the early 1980s to around 15 percent in recent years[18]). That is a sharp increase in the supply of capital, and it is much larger than the decline in the savings rate. With the demand for capital decreasing and the total supply increasing, we expect to see a drop in the interest rate, and this is exactly what has happened over the past four decades. The risk-free interest rate has fallen from around 3 percent to 1 percent.[19]

Observe the crucial distinction between spending money as an investment in capital and capital spent on an asset that returns a profit. In chapter 4 I made a distinction between buying a house and renting it out in its existing condition versus spending additional money to renovate the house to increase its rental income. Market power increases profits, money that will be used to buy more capital, and it decreases investment and hence the demand for capital.

The low risk-free rates, basically as a result of an excess amount of cash held by firms with market power, causes problems for central bankers. With rock-bottom rates, the economy is already stimulated to the maximum. And with market power there are not many interesting projects to invest in. The result is that the monetary authorities lose their ability to stimulate the economy. The problem that market power causes for monetary policy is not low inflation rates; the problem is low interest rates.

In part II we have discussed all the dire consequences—for work and beyond—of an economy on market power steroids. Not only is inequality higher, and wages and labor mobility lower; market power affects people's health and it distorts the stock market and the success of small business startups. It drives a schism through society that can only be remedied by restoring competition to the marketplace—something that requires novel antitrust policies. Before we get to how, I want to point out that not all is grim.

PART III

The Future of Work and Finding Solutions

9

Plenty of Reasons to Be Optimistic

WHILE RAPID TECHNOLOGICAL CHANGE is, to a large extent, what allows firms to build market power, we cannot make the mistake of throwing the baby out with the bath water. The rise of market power should not be an excuse to resurrect the Luddites, the mid-nineteenth-century English displaced workers who destroyed the labor-saving weaving machines. In the long run, technological change is the unique driver of progress. We cannot afford to mute innovation.

Work in modern times now shares similarities with work a century ago, but overall we are in a much better place now than we were a hundred years ago. Transitions are costly—there are always winners and losers—but in the long run technological change and globalization increase the standard of living and make people unambiguously better off. Even Joe and Betty, and the many left behind by rapid economic progress, are worse off only relative to Wei and Li Min. Most would say they are better off than the shepherd, one of the "losers" of a generation ago.

In economic terms, the standard of living for nearly everyone is higher now than when they were children, only now their house is no longer the fanciest one on the block. And while Erin, our senior technical advisor from chapter 1, has drawn the shortest economic stick, her overall quality of life is significantly higher than that of those who were at the bottom of the ladder a century ago; she has a much greater life expectancy, she consumes an abundance of calories, she has much more free time, and she has access to cheap transportation and travel. Moreover, she can be cured from many illnesses, and vaccines help us to avoid many deadly illnesses. Even the COVID-19 pandemic now is much less deadly than it would have been only half a century ago because of the development of a vaccine.

The effect of technological progress is striking. We may forget how infectious diseases that are curable now were still deadly until fairly recently. George Orwell could not recover from tuberculosis in 1950 at University College Hospital—arguably one of the best medical centers in Great Britain—because he did not get the proper antibiotics treatment, despite the fact that he had connections to help him obtain scarce medicine and money in the bank from the royalties of his best-selling novel *Animal Farm*.[1] He died because the treatment was still in its early stages of development.

Technological progress increases consumption and raises well-being, all through lower relative prices. The best example of this is the cost of food. Households in most Western countries now spend on average 12 percent of their income on food,[2] and all the food is produced by less than 1 percent of the population employed in agriculture. A century ago, expenditure on food for most households was by far the largest item and constituted nearly the entire budget. The concept known as Engel's law captures the relation between expenditure and income: with economic progress we consume more food, but as a share of our income we spend less on it. Due to technological progress, fewer people are needed to produce the same output, and as a result prices fall.

Trade and globalization are just other manifestations of technological progress and increasing economic specialization. According to the World Bank, in China alone 800 million people were lifted out of poverty in the last four decades. The poverty rate (defined as the percentage of the population living on $3.20 or less) in China dropped from 90 percent in the early 1990s to 5 percent in 2016.[3] And even if, as a result of growth in China and India, inequality has gone up, as we discussed in chapter 6, inequality measured globally has gone down sharply. Trade has an amazing effect on overall economic development and poverty reduction.

One of the most striking aspects of technological progress is that it democratizes overall well-being. At the bottom of the ladder, life is surprisingly comfortable compared to times when families had numerous children, several of them dying within the first year, and when the entire family was exposed to malnutrition and health. But it is not only those at the bottom of the ladder who had a lower quality of life. At least until the eighteenth century, the vast majority of people was living in extreme poverty,[4] and the average life expectancy around the world was barely thirty years. Even in 1900, at the height of the Second Industrial Revolution, life expectancy was only thirty-two years, or some fifty years less than what it is in developed countries today.[5] Only a few were privileged enough to have a comfortable and wealthy lifestyle.

However, going back in time before the First Industrial Revolution in the eighteenth century, even those at the top of the ladder didn't have the quality of life that now even poor people enjoy. Economists sometimes refer to the Mansa Musa, an emperor of the Islamic Empire of Mali during the fourteenth century. He expanded his empire and was one of the largest producers of gold at a time when there was enormous demand. Though it is hard to value his worth, historians are in agreement that he was possibly the richest person ever and multiple times richer than today's richest person, Jeff Bezos, whose net worth is estimated at more than $185 billion.[6] Still, life for Mansa Musa was no walk in the park. Though he lived much longer than average for those times, he died at fifty-six, twenty-five years younger than the average person now. And in the absence of eyeglasses he probably could barely see, he was susceptible to die from tooth decay and other common health problems that are easily curable now, and it would have taken him months to visit cities in his empire in a trip that now takes a few hours.

Today, someone at the bottom of the ladder on average works less than forty hours, communicates instantaneously with a mobile phone, expects to live until eighty, has heating and air conditioning, and lives in a secure shelter. The quality of their lives is in many ways superior to that of Mansa Musa, the richest person in history.

Despite all the misgivings about where the economy of work is going, it is too easy to forget that we are a lot better off now than even a few generations ago. Technological innovation is the driver of all the economic progress, and we should be careful not to come up with a cure that is worse than the disease.

A lot is misperception. Hans Rosling, the late scientist and facilitator of clear communication and representation of facts and statistics, used surveys of common people to show the discrepancy between popular opinion and facts, and in particular who was at the source of the misconceptions. He asked people a number of specific questions about facts related to quality of life and progress, such as child mortality, poverty, and economic well-being.[7]

It turns out that people are very pessimistic about progress. Given four options, only 9 percent answered that we are a lot better off now than past generations, where the correct answer is that indeed we are a lot better off, so 100 percent of the respondents should have given the answer that we are a lot better off on all metrics he asked about. Rosling would quip that even monkeys do better because they cannot grasp the question and would randomize rather than respond based on biases, as most people did.

What is worrisome, however, is that even experts such as academics and policymakers don't do better—only 8 percent of them consider us substantially better off. Most disheartening of all, though, is the fact that among journalists, only 2 percent think that we are substantially better off now. Rosling argues that those who are creating the opinions of the population at large are the worst informed.

It is not just about progress in general; there are also some persistent misperceptions about work. The lump of labor fallacy is the main one.

Lump of Labor and Growth

The total value of what we produce as measured by real gross domestic product (GDP) per capita in the United States and measured in constant 2012 dollars was $6,000 in 1900, and it is $58,000 today, an increase by a factor of ten.[8] And countries like China and India that remained behind until the 1990s are now quickly catching up; they have managed to lift millions out of poverty, a feat that international institutions like the World Bank had not managed to do in the second half of the twentieth century despite good intentions and spending billions. Of course, GDP is not necessarily a good measure of well-being or of happiness, but other broader objective measures also show that we are a lot better off.

The only reason why we are better off is because now we can produce more valuable goods and services with the same amount of work. Such labor-saving technological progress is the sole engine of economic growth. A century ago more than half the population was still doing hard manual labor in agriculture, and most of the remaining population was working long, repetitive hours on assembly lines in manufacturing.

Now, less than 1 percent of the workforce in advanced economies can produce enough food to feed the entire population, and only 8 percent of the workforce is active in manufacturing.[9] Those jobs in agriculture and manufacturing have been replaced by new jobs. I don't think the backbreaking manual work on the farm or standing on the assembly line doing repetitive work for hours on end are jobs that anyone wants back.

Yet, as jobs are destroyed in the process of technological progress, there is a romantic yearning for those jobs in manufacturing or even in agriculture. The argument goes that the jobs that are destroyed are never replaced, and if they are replaced, the new jobs are of worse quality and are paid less. But there is limited evidence for that, especially over long periods of time. The reality is that a hundred years ago, tunnels and canals were dug by people, but now those backbreaking jobs are performed by machines.

This romanticism goes back the Luddites. Around 1800, a movement began in the textile mills in Nottingham, England, and spread through the entire region. The Second Industrial Revolution was about to start. While initially the Luddite movement was an early day labor movement demanding better work conditions, it came to symbolize the resistance against automatization. The working conditions following the Napoleonic Wars were dismal, wages were low, and prices for food and other basic necessities fluctuated widely. Machinery for producing textiles, such as the stocking frame for mechanical knitting, the lacemaking machine, or the Jacquard loom with flying shuttle were introduced and increased productivity with less labor. This came at the detriment of workers, who were either laid off or forced to do less-skilled work at lower wages. In order to protect their jobs and their livelihoods, the Luddites destroyed the new machines. The idea was that this would force the industrialists to continue working with the old machines and stop further investment in technology.

Most technological innovation is labor saving. If the owner of a parking lot installs a ticket vending machine with an automatic barrier, they save on the labor cost of the attendant and substitute the cost of the machine. Innovation need not be robotization or the introduction of new machines; it can be the introduction of new ideas that are saving labor cost, such as IKEA's flat-packed furniture, which down on the cost of transportation. Furniture is shipped to the stores at lower cost, and the customer doesn't need to hire a transportation service to get the furniture home. And when Norwegian, the Scandinavian airline based in a country with the highest labor cost in Europe, hires pilots from Thailand and stewards from Spain and Portugal, it gets a cost advantage over its direct competitor, SAS, the traditional Scandinavian airline operator that hires predominantly local, high-wage employees. But these low-cost airlines do not only use labor mobility and international migration to lower costs—they also streamline the entire operation. In 2016 Norwegian was particularly efficient doing just that: they transported an average of 5,055 passengers per worker employed for the entire year, compared to SAS, which transported an average of 2,745 passengers per worker.[10] These cost savings surely affect the quality of service, but enough customers are willing to put up with that in exchange for lower ticket prices. To generate these gains, Norwegian does not use a robot or automation in the strict sense, but it engages in labor-saving innovation processes. Rather than a machine, the novelty is an idea that leads to the reorganization of production.

It is clear that the incentives to innovate accrue to the firm because the innovating firm gains new customers as it sells at lower prices and temporarily increases its profits. IKEA makes profits by selling furniture at a substantially lower cost than a competitor who sells the same furniture but requires a transportation service. Norwegian is profitable because it can deliver a flight between Oslo and Lisbon at a substantially lower cost than SAS. And the eighteenth-century textiles producer can make cloth and knitted goods at a lower cost, giving them a higher profit.

All these firms are also obtaining a higher market share because they sell at lower prices and therefore they attract more customers. If goods are sold in a competitive market, then technological innovation and cost gains are all passed on to the customer. If IKEA can produce flat-packed furniture then anyone else can too, at least once patents run out after fifteen years. Competition eventually leads to lower prices and dissipating profits.

The firm that fails to innovate and keep up with the advancing technology stays behind. This is the whole idea of Schumpeter's notion of creative destruction. But as mentioned earlier, there are also other losers in the process, especially in the transition. The displaced worker at the firm that goes bankrupt or at the firm that innovates and sheds jobs is either out of a job or earns a lower wage if they have to perform lower-skilled tasks in order to hang on to a job at the same firm. This tension between the innovating entrepreneur as the winner and the worker as the loser gives rise to the popular support for the Luddite argument even today, especially if in the transition the innovating entrepreneur makes profits. The immediate effect of robots and automation is to make workers poorer and firms richer.

The key piece of the argument is that in a market economy with competition, in the wake of labor-saving technological innovations, prices drop. That was the case for eighteenth-century textiles, as it is for airfares from Oslo to Lisbon and flat-packed furniture. If it makes sense for one firm to produce cheaper textiles with labor-saving technology, other firms will soon follow suit. Now the innovating firms can hang on for a limited time only to its higher profits as well as their grown market share.

Once the competitors have adopted the new technology, all firms will produce at a lower cost and compete for customers, which eventually lowers prices. In a competitive economy the gains from innovation are passed on to the consumer. A worker with the same income can now buy the same goods (adjusted for the change in quality) at a lower price and therefore sees an increase in their real income. This is the crux of why there is a Luddite fallacy. Labor-saving technology allows workers to buy the goods produced at a lower cost as long as firms operate in a competitive market. A few centuries on, that means that the average family in America today spends less than 13 percent of their income on food, compared to 43 percent in 1901.[11]

What about the displaced worker? George Orwell argued that when comparing capitalism to socialism, capitalism gives rise to "dole queues."[12] While it is true that recessions, and the Great Depression in the early 1930s in particular, have been periods of high unemployment, we have not seen a permanent rise in unemployment in the wake of technological progress in a capitalist economy. This itself hinges on another, intimately related fallacy, that there is a "lump of labor," meaning the amount of work available is fixed and predetermined. The parking lot attendant whose job is replaced by an automated barrier and ticket machine will never again perform that job. But that does not mean that they cannot perform another job. More importantly, that does not mean they will take someone else's job when they do find a new one.

Not all workers affected by technological change are equally well off, nor are all winners. Some groups of workers in certain locations, with certain skills and of certain ages, will be more affected than others, in particular if they are not able to adjust by retraining or relocating. Most miners near the Appalachian coal mines will find few job prospects without relocating and learning new skills, and the last cattle herder at the age of fifty-five might have to give up on the hope of doing a job anywhere related to cattle herding when agribusiness takes over. Technological innovation is disruptive for workers and requires costly adjustment.

Ultimately there is as much work as there are people willing to enter the labor market. Yes, there is unemployment, but that results from the less-than-perfect process of matching the supply to the demand for labor. That imperfect matching process is even more heavily distorted in recessions. But in the long run, what matters is whether an able-bodied individual is capable of finding a job, and that depends on the wage they are willing to accept to do the work. If a spouse of a highly paid executive decides that it is better to stay at home to look after the children rather than earn $11 an hour, then he is not unemployed but inactive. The main difference is that the unemployed want to work at a given wage but do not find a job; the inactive *choose* not to work at a given wage.

The problem for the workers displaced due to technological progress therefore is not so much that they cannot find a job or that there are dole queues, but rather that displaced workers face new job opportunities at lower wages. Mines now become highly robotized.[13] While the mine's output has increased due to this technological innovation, the number of employees has dropped. Those workers who have been retained to operate the robots typically see a wage increase; others have been laid off, and they are likely to see a wage drop when changing occupations. The skilled miner who becomes an Uber driver or a security guard is likely to earn only a few dollars more than minimum wage. Even if they start a new, skilled occupation with promising career prospects, they need to enter at the bottom of the job ladder before they can climb up to higher-paying jobs in that occupation.

The number of jobs is not fixed, and technological progress does not lead to massive unemployment. There is no given lump of labor. If there were, unemployment would be over 99 percent today. Recall that only a few generations ago nearly the entire population was active in agriculture, and today that number is less than 1 percent. What happens in the long run is that displaced workers become active in other, newly created jobs. In the process, we have to take care of older, displaced workers with few job prospects, but that is how innovation and creative destruction works.

This continuous innovation and job creation is unique to humankind and sets it apart from other species. Yet, perhaps inspired by Malthusianism, people are tempted to compare workers to animals for whom the scarcity of resources leads to poverty and eventually death. But as Henry George, in his critique of Malthusianism, points out: "There is a difference between the animal and the man. Both the [hawk] and the man eat chickens, but the more [hawks] the fewer chickens, while the more men the more chickens."[14] Just as the amount of food for humans is not fixed, neither is the number of jobs. If more people want to work, more is produced.

If one believes there is a lump of labor, one could claim that the massive rise in women taking up jobs gives rise to unemployment. The number of working women has increased, and we haven't seen a rise in unemployment in good times. Nor have the early retirement policies in several European countries led to a decline in unemployment. Teachers, bank tellers, and postal service workers were all sent into mandatory retirement at ages as young as fifty years old in an attempt to create more jobs. We have seen no decrease in unemployment, only an increase in the number of workers who were forced to remain inactive.

The populist idea that immigrants take away jobs is another example of the lump of labor fallacy. The French extremist Front National used to campaign on the famous slogan "Two million unemployed is two million immigrants too many." To be consistent, with the sharp increase in female labor force participation, Marine Le Pen, the current leader of the National Rally political party, should say that "two million unemployed is two million women too many." This simply shows how wrong the lump of labor argument is.

In the second half of the twentieth century, female labor force participation doubled in most Western economies (in the United States it increased from around 43 percent in 1962 to 76 percent in 2019[15]). During that time unemployment has continued to fluctuate around 5–10 percent. If more people work, more of them earn income and will eventually spend it. As a result, there is more demand for goods and services, which in turn requires more labor. And it is not just the number of people who work, it is also how much each of them does. The thirty-five-hour week introduced by then–French prime minister Lionel Jospin in 2000 has not induced firms to hire more workers, and consequently we haven't seen a decrease in unemployment.

The amount of work is simply not fixed. Over the history of time, work has moved out of the production of food toward other jobs: the production of knowledge and designing machines that save labor in agriculture and manufacturing, coding translators that run on artificial intelligence, driving Uber cars, and working as security guards and tourist guides. The key insight is that technological progress, even though it displaces workers, raises the real income of all workers. Even if some workers' nominal income drops, with those lower wages they can buy more because the cost of goods has gone down. Technological progress is to the benefit of everyone.

There is, however, one important caveat, which goes to the heart of the central theme of this book. This only works well if markets are competitive. That is the profit paradox. When firms have market power, labor-saving technological innovations lower the cost of the firm but not the price of the goods they produce. Firms can keep out entrants who would otherwise compete for market shares and who thus lower consumer prices. In addition, the tide of market power economy-wide lowers wages, further decreasing the purchasing power of workers.

In Europe, for example, labor-saving innovations by airlines like Norwegian, EasyJet, and Ryanair have resulted in substantially cheaper travel. However, in the US market the same innovations have not led to the same decrease in prices. A *Washington Post* investigation finds that comparable flights in the United States are twice as expensive as in Europe.[16] Many factors are at play, but with the four dominant airlines commanding over 70 percent of the US market share there is much less competition, in large part due to the lack of pro-competitive regulation in recent years. Fewer firms can enter, and that creates market power for the incumbents, which allows them to charge higher prices. The labor-saving technological progress has led to higher profits, not to lower prices.

With higher prices, the gains from technological progress are no longer unambiguous. Under perfect competition, firms can gain an edge on their competitors only temporarily, and in the long run profits will be competed away. That is the whole idea behind pro-competitive capitalism: new technology allows a firm to obtain a temporary advantage and profits, which will quickly be adopted by competitors, and that in turn will water down the profits of the first mover. In light of this, the actions of the Luddites may be understood as a reaction against the market power of the owners and as a demand for better working conditions for workers. When a Gen Z-er calls a person who is reluctant to use mobile technology and social media a Luddite, they focus only on one aspect of the machine-destroying actions of the historical group. Those Gen Z-ers ignore the Luddites' demands for higher wages and better working conditions that had deteriorated from the market power that new technology bestowed on the innovating firms.

More than a technology-averse individual, today's equivalent of the people that the Luddite represented is Erin, the senior technical advisor whose wage is stagnating because of rising market power. Firms innovating in new technologies in particular have managed to build moats, which has resulted in an economy-wide lowering tide of wages. We definitely do not want to break today's looms and derail technological progress, but Erin has good reasons to demand that the economy infested with market power be fixed so that wages rise across the board. Today's Luddites would also come up for the rights of Joe and Betty and the left-behind Rust Belt workers in Ohio. Because of the disruptive transformation of the economy, older workers bear a disproportionate cost of the transition. The reason is because switching occupations is costly.[17]

Career choices are long-term decisions. Most of the career building is done while learning on the job and climbing the job ladder. Reaching a gratifying job with expertise and responsibility can easily take ten to fifteen years, not counting formal education. Therefore the transition cost is not so much of switching jobs but of switching occupations.

A secretary in a trucking company needs the same skills and abilities as a secretary in a health insurance company. When new technologies make the trucking industry jobs disappear, the secretary can easily switch to a secretarial job with a health provider. The problem is when they switch occupations, say from administrative work to becoming a nurse. The new job might require training but, most importantly, the new job requires starting at the bottom of the job ladder. Before a worker gets back to the level of wages where they were before leaving, they need to climb the whole ladder again. And the lower rungs of the ladder are slippery—workers who try a new occupation are more likely to drop out and try another occupation[18]—and switching occupations leads to lower wages. When technology speeds up, those affected bear a disproportionate cost. As we have seen, they are often older workers.

Despite the costly transitions and the fact that technological progress can be distortionary over a short horizon, it suffices to look at the long-term picture to see the enormous gains from innovation and trade. These gains can be explained almost entirely by the ongoing process of the division of labor.

Division of Labor, Specialization, Innovation: Rinse and Repeat

In the Pleistocene epoch that ended about 12,000 years ago, the hunter-gatherer society started the division of labor within the household, specializing in hunting versus caring for offspring. This early division of labor is not exclusive to humans and extends to many other species, but humans in particular need to care intensively for their offspring.

When the first predecessor of *homo sapiens* started to walk upright, their waist grew tighter. At the same time they were evolving into a species with a greater mental capacity, a larger brain, and therefore a larger head. The smaller waist and the larger head means humans are born prematurely. Most mammals walk moments after birth, while humans take one year. Even though evolution changes many things, according to simple logic, a full pregnancy should be twenty-one months. A twelve-month premature birth therefore requires special care for the offspring, which has made the need for cooperation within the household crucial for survival. Without cooperation, both parents could care for the children half of the time and look for food half of the time, but the division of labor creates gains for all when there is specialization.

Consider, for example, the case where the father can obtain sufficient food for the family by foraging for nine hours, and the mother can do it in eight hours; the father can care for the offspring in seven hours and the mother in four hours. If both spend half the time foraging and half the time caring for the offspring, the father works eight hours and the mother six hours, for a total of fourteen hours. Instead, if they focus on their comparative advantage—foraging for the father and nursing for the mother—then they obtain the same amount of food and care with nine hours by the father and four hours by the mother, thirteen hours in total. There is an efficiency gain for the whole family of one hour. This stems from the comparative advantage in this example of the mother at nursing and the father at foraging.

Two things are worth observing about comparative advantage and the division of labor. First, even though the mother is better at both activities (she has an absolute advantage), she only performs the activity at which she is relatively more productive, nursing in this example. Second, the household as a whole gains, but that does not necessarily imply that each individual is better off. The father ends up working one more hour, and all the gains are for the mother, who gets the benefit of two hours. Of course, he could work the same hours as before with the mother doing all the nursing and some foraging. Division of labor and specialization is efficiency improving in the aggregate, but the gains are not necessarily positive for everyone.

The division of labor also has a major impact in the long run. Now with an extra hour available, the household can engage in other activities to improve their quality of life. That could mean doing more foraging and nursing or improving and learning, but it could also mean doing different activities. For example, with the extra hour the household can raise an animal or make a tool—that is, make a capital investment.

This capital investment in turn increases future productivity, which will make foraging less time intensive. Specialization also increases experience; practice makes perfect. With twice the amount of time spent on foraging by the father and twice the amount spent on nursing by the mother, each can get more done in less time. This is where technological progress comes in. Through division of labor and specialization, labor becomes more productive both by itself (more experience) and with the help of tools (capital investment).

Once the exchange goes beyond the narrow household and reaches the extended family, and then the local community of several households in a settlement, we are off to an exchange or barter economy. Next, workers go beyond their own settlement and meet at places to exchange goods, the precursor of the marketplace. These developments in prehistoric times should make clear that division of labor, specialization, and technological progress are not synonymous with capitalism, whatever the meaning of that is. Even in the communist Soviet Union trade and exchange followed from the division of labor, specialization, and technological progress. And it is not exclusive to humans, either; other animals cooperate as well, but in different ways. Bees are notoriously cooperative, and birds fly in a "V" pattern to minimize the effort. Specialization is a universal force that leads to optimized resources. The division of labor of humans is a cooperative endeavor and requires trust.

Trust is central because the division of labor typically involves trade over time. Even if there is barter, where goods are exchanged simultaneously, much of the effort and investment to bring the goods to the market are made up front. When a machine is produced or a drug is invented, a company hires scientists years in advance, before any customer buys the good. Crucially, there is uncertainty about the investment. Division of labor requires both specialization and limited risk to ensure that future exchange opportunities are predictable. An environment with limited exposure to risk provides incentives for workers to do highly specific tasks now that will be paid for in the future.

Eventually, anything that is traded embodies the work of many individuals. Specialization is so extensive that we have no way of knowing the exact detailed contribution. It is clear that a car has thousands of hardware pieces, most of which have been produced by different firms and hence different individuals. In addition, there are millions of lines of code written by thousands of programmers. Some of those include standard algorithms that are licensed and were produced by programmers who have nothing to do with the car manufacturers.

It is impossible to track the source of time and work of each component in a car. But even a service like a haircut or a massage, which appears to be a straightforward service provided by one person, involves an intractable number of contributions by different individuals. Who built the shopping mall where the barbershop is housed, and who manufactured the chair and the scissors? Each involves a large number of components. Some of those were transported and delivered, which brings us back to the countless people who have contributed to producing a car.

Detailed specialization is only beneficial if there is a large enough market for the specialized good or service that is produced. As Adam Smith pointed out, the division of labor is limited by the extent of the market.[19] Specialization will thrive only if it pays sufficiently, and equally importantly, if it justifies the investment in education or tools in order to perform the task. Well-functioning economic institutions that facilitate the exchange of goods and services ensure a maximal degree of specialization and division of labor. A firm that ships goods should have the guarantee that there are laws and enforcement to minimize the risk of the goods not being delivered. Institutions build trust. And a factory that invests in infrastructure should have a good prediction of inflation to calculate as accurately as possible the return on investment. Central banks provide institutional security and minimize exposure to aggregate risk.

This hugely specialized system is extremely valuable. We can produce goods and services of enormous value at a remarkably low cost. Unless it is a hobby, it clearly does not pay to have a small vegetable garden in your backyard in order to be self-reliant on food. The cost in terms of hours worked, evaluated at the wage rate you command doing your regular job, is so high that it is multiple times cheaper to buy vegetables in the supermarket or even a farmers' market. The price of agricultural products relative to housing, for example, is much smaller, and as a result the share of expenditure on food is now a lot lower than it was a few generations ago. This is captured by Engel's law, which we described earlier. Overall, the price of manufactured goods becomes relatively cheaper. When I first went skiing in the 1980s, to rent ski equipment for a week was about as expensive as a weekly ski pass. Now it is one-half or one-third the cost of the ski pass.

As the economy produces more with less labor, one might expect that the share of value that can be attributed to labor diminishes. Less than 10 percent of the workforce today produces all agricultural and manufactured goods, compared to over 90 percent a century ago. It seems a reasonable (but wrong) conjecture that the share of output attributed to labor declines.

But we know from the Kaldor facts (discussed in chapter 4) that labor accounts for roughly two-thirds of value created in the economy. Yes, that share has been declining due to the rise of market power, but it is remarkable that labor continues to have such a large share of output. This is evidence that in the face of technological progress, there is no such thing as a lump of labor. Freed-up labor is employed in other productive activities.

Eventually, all value is attributable to labor. That is, the one-third that is attributed to capital was produced with labor in the past. A machine built last year using labor and capital and sold this year appears as a capital good, but it embodies past labor. So even the capital share is a measure of labor, but it is labor that was used to build machines and structures that make workers more productive.

That is the essence of Adam Smith's observation two centuries ago: "Labor was the first price, the original purchase—money that was paid for all things. It was not by gold or by silver, but by labor, that all wealth of the world was originally purchased."[20] But the gains from technological change do not always accrue to today's labor. Ownership of capital—built with past labor—obtains a compensation for making the investment in capital.

In a healthy economy, the force that keeps the right compensation of capital in check is free entry of competing firms.

Free Entry

A moat around a firm's castle is what enables the firm to build and maintain market power; free entry is the force that ensures that competitors can overcome the moat and gain access to the castle. If a firm can make generous profits, anyone with some capital and know-how to spare will want to enter the market and grab some of those profits. Just as in evolutionary biology, environmental pressures such as the availability of food and the presence of other competitors (predators and competing animals from the same species) leads to the fittest species, in economics the threat of free entry ensures the lowest prices and the maximal share of output to labor. Free entry ensures that capital is adequately compensated, but no more than needed.

To see how strong this force is, consider the example of Bongo. Back in early 2000, during the peak of the dot-com boom, Bruno Spaas and Mark Verhagen, two recent university graduates with a few years of experience working in tech and advertising, had an idea. They wanted to offer weekend activities and short holidays that were unique—a distant reality from the canned trips that cookie-cutter operators were offering.

Their main innovation was to offer unique activities such as rafting, a balloon ride, or an exceptional small hotel on the English chalk cliffs with real-time updated availability. Back then, twenty years ago, it was entirely novel that a balloonist could update their availability via the web portal (no smartphones yet). The consumer could book instantaneously with up-to-date availability. Moreover, they had a no-nonsense approach with fixed all-in prices without hidden costs and a range of options for locations and activities. Those who used it, both the vendors and the customers, loved it, and it attracted a heavy amount of traffic to their website. The problem was that sales were limited. In a saturated world of tour operators and despite heavy advertising, back then customers were reluctant to pay with credit cards online and they preferred to call the hotel directly. The internet was providing valuable information and was a useful tool for the hotel owners to manage reservations, but it did not generate sales.

After a year of investment and experimenting with many different offers and activities, the founders and owners were continuing to incur losses and decided to try something new in the run-up to Christmas. They figured that people may want to give holidays as a present and that they might want to book a balloon ride or a gastronomic weekend for the next summer, to give to family and friends. Initially, those gifts materialized merely in a printout of the confirmation number, which is somewhat of a lame present. A few years later the gift vouchers evolved into Bongo. Bongo was explicitly marketed as a gift, presented in a box with glossy photographs and with different options of different activities to choose from. You could give a menu with a balloon ride, a romantic dinner, or a weekend trip somewhere nice, one of which would surely make the receiver happy. It was an instant success, and in the days leading up to Christmas they could hardly keep up with the demand. Moreover, the stylish boxes were also distributed at travel agencies and later on in supermarkets and newspaper outlets, where people picked them up as last-minute gifts, and those stores begged for more supplies. The Bongo boxes sold like hotcakes.

The basic principle of the invention, a gift card, was of course not new. But there was something about the presentation, the application to holidays and experiences, and the appeal of the message in the gift that made it desirable. If I give a bungee jump to my nephew, it is a lot cooler than if I give a 50-euro voucher. But the success was not only in the demand. There were two unintended side effects of the business model that also turned this popular success into an unprecedented financial success. The first side effect was that people tend to buy a Bongo in December, and the nephew bungee jumps in August. The average time that elapses between purchase and use is nine months because at the time of purchase the customer pays for the Bongo, but Bongo only pays the provider (the bungee jump operator) at the time of service, nine months later. As a result, Bongo was sitting on cash for nine months. Not only did this resolve any cash flow problems the company might have to run its operations or improve the services, they had three-quarters of the annual revenue available as capital on which they could obtain a financial return, either from depositing it in the bank or from investing.

The second unexpected side effect was that a small fraction of the Bongos were never converted. For hotel stays and gastronomic weekends, the no-take-up fraction was tiny, but for bungee jumps it was huge. For some activities, less than half of the Bongos were converted. After all, a bungee jump is exciting and cool to give, especially for the giver, but it takes a bit more courage to make the jump. There is a good chance that the nephew has a fear of heights or that his mom is not convinced that Uncle Ken's present was so great after all, and the Bongo mysteriously disappears. To avoid this, an Adventure Bongo was offered with a broad set of choices, including alternative activities that were less intimidating. Still, the Bongo with the adventure theme had a significantly lower take-up rate. The implication of a 95 percent take-up rate is that a Bongo sold for 100 euros only cost the company 95 euros on average—a nice 5 percent windfall margin that is pure profit.

The combination of the windfall margin and the return on nine months' cash effectively turned the company into a financial entity more than a travel agency. With the huge demand and the enormous financial returns, Bongo became an instant startup success. Initially active in Belgium, the Netherlands, and Luxembourg, they soon extended operations to nine countries in Europe, and by 2007 the company had total revenues of over 150 million euros.

If many customers knew about Bongo, so did other investors and entrepreneurs who were looking for investment opportunities. Bongo's extraordinary profits acted on entry like a red flag on a bull. Bongo had some intellectual property on the name and the format of the gift box, but they could not patent the idea. Initially the company could hold off some of the competition, but they increasingly faced new competitors threatening to enter their market and eat away at the profits. In the summer of 2007 a French company with the backing of a private equity fund offered to buy the company. The French firm thought they could generate even higher profits, possibly by even further reducing the take-up rate. By the end of 2007 the takeover was completed, and Bruno and Mark sold their Bongo company. Just in time.

Just in time, because it was shortly before the fall of Lehman Brothers and the start of the Great Recession, and there was still ample money going around for inflated takeovers and merger and acquisition activity. But more importantly, it was just in time because of entry in the market. Only a few years later, Bongo (later renamed to Smart Box) was still the market leader but now there were numerous competitors, many of them locally active only in one country and often owned by a large tour operator with a retail network. With competitive pressure, Smart Box had to lower prices to avoid customers buying from the new entrants. Prices even fell below the cost to the bungee jump provider, eating away at the margin from the no take-up.

The Bongo story is a poster-child example of Schumpeterian creative destruction. Innovation leads to a new way of doing business with excessive profit margins and replacing older, more traditional ways. But the new way of doing business itself is temporary and short lived, as entry of competitors leads to price competition, which eventually erodes the early profits. Entry puts discipline on the reward for capital and results in profits that are high enough to induce firms to enter but no higher than needed to compensate for the investment. The beneficiary is the customer, who can buy goods and services at the lowest prices possible, as well as the worker. As we discussed in chapter 3, lower prices economy-wide and adequately priced capital eventually lift the tide of wages and raises the labor share.

Technological progress and the resulting division of labor and increased specialization do not imply that the freed-up labor is used exclusively to produce more goods and services; the freed-up time and labor can also be used for more leisure time. Next, we zoom in on the effect that technological progress has on hours worked.

Is Leisure the End of Labor?

The story goes that on a white sandy beach somewhere in Africa, a fisherman sits under a palm tree grilling a fish he caught that morning. A Westerner walks by and they have a chat about life. The Westerner asks the fisherman why he doesn't use his boat in the afternoon; he can sell the extra fish he catches in the afternoon at the market and save some money. With that money he can buy a second boat, hire some employees, and double the catch. Eventually he can grow his business and own an entire fleet of boats, hire fishermen, and make money without having to go out to sea himself. The fisherman asks the Westerner what he should do once he has all that money. The Westerner suggests that he can retire, go to a beautiful beach, and relax under a palm tree. The fisherman looks at him incredulously: "Why should I wait until I retire to relax under a palm tree on a beautiful beach? What do you think I am doing right now?"

There is a commonly held belief that times were much better in less-developed societies and that our modern society, with technological progress, international trade, and growth has turned our lives into a rat race where we run fast to stay in place. Today we are forced to work longer hours. And indeed, there are plenty of professionals who work long hours with little salary to show for it, especially early on in their careers. Consultants at McKinsey, associates at law firms, brokers on Wall Street and in the City of London, and medical doctors all notoriously work extremely long hours, arriving at work before dawn, coming home late at night, and eating three meals at their desks. While they tend to have very nice salaries, clocking eighty-plus hours per week, the hourly pay is often not much better than that of a fast-food worker.

There are also plenty of people with more common, modestly paid jobs who work long hours these days. Those in the gig economy in particular have the freedom to work as much as they want, which often means working long days in order to make ends meet. How many times have I stepped into an Uber where the driver works extra hours during evenings, on weekends, and on holidays? I recall a high school mathematics teacher who told me about the beauty of teaching mathematics and getting boys and girls excited by it. Yet, it was July and he told me he'd rather work for Uber than earn a pittance teaching a summer school math program.

While there are plenty of people working long hours, there are even more people who work short hours. There has always been a wide dispersion in hours worked. When people give examples of long hours, invariably they tend to focus on one of those professions with extreme hours, as I did before. But not only is there a difference across professions, there are huge differences across population groups by age and gender as well as by income. Still, those extremes and the fact that some groups work long hours are not representative of what is going on in the economy overall.

Workers around the world now clock remarkably fewer hours than decades and centuries ago. Recent research finds that since the Second Industrial Revolution, working hours have been falling by 0.3 percent per year, or seven minutes per week. That might seem like peanuts, but over a long period of time those minutes add up. Average weekly working hours in the United States have fallen from seventy hours in 1830 to forty in 2015, meaning that now we work only about half as much.[21]

In 1930, John Maynard Keynes wrote an essay predicting that by the year 2000 we would work fifteen hours per week.[22] While he got the exact numbers completely wrong—in particular how rapid the decline in hours would be—he did get the prediction right that gradually we would work less and less. If hours keep declining at the rate they have shrunk in the last 150 years, then it will not be until well past 2200 that the average workweek will be fifteen hours.[23] That prediction for the future of course assumes that there is no decline in productivity growth and that there is no change in the desire for households to trade off leisure activities against earning more money.

Of course, over the very long run a lot has changed in the economy. When the majority of workers were employed on the farm or in factories, hours were brutally long: six- or seven-day weeks, starting early and finishing late. Now most service jobs require fewer than forty hours. Mostly, though, people work shorter hours because we have become richer. Because of Engel's law, we spend less of our income on food and other necessities, and we can spend it on other goods and services.

It is not immediately clear that with higher wages we would choose to work less. On the one hand it is more beneficial to work, as one hour generates more income (this is known as the substitution effect). On the other hand, once we have enough consumption we prefer to spend more time on leisure activities (this is known as the income effect). The evidence supports the fact that over time with higher productivity of labor and thus higher wages, households spend more hours on leisure activities, from attending sporting events, to traveling, to outdoor activities, to watching movies. We have more time, and leisure activities have become much cheaper. For Norwegians it is cheaper to go "Suden"—freely translated as "heading south," which means to take a low-cost Norwegian Airlines flight from Oslo to Mallorca for a short holiday—than it is to go drinking and eat out at home given the high prices of everything, and of alcohol in particular.

Aristotle had the following to say about leisure: "Happiness is thought to depend on leisure; for we are busy that we may have leisure, and make war that we may live in peace."[24] Perhaps we can generously interpret Aristotle's quotation "for we are busy that we may have leisure" as "the end of labor is to gain leisure." Over time, our work and techno-logical progress seems to achieve exactly that.

We now turn to another aspect of work where hours worked and leisure morph into one, the gig economy.

The Gig Economy

Like robots and other labor-saving technologies, the gig economy is a threat to work. There are already too few jobs, and now new technolo-gies make it even easier for anyone with a car, a smartphone, and a few hours to spare to steal work from licensed taxi drivers. One of those job thieves is Eutychios.

When Eutychios, after a full career as a teacher and principal in a Boston school, reached retirement age and had to leave his job in 2002, he wanted to continue to work but couldn't find a job. He applied for all kinds of jobs but seldom received an response. His favorite of those job prospects was being a substitute teacher, but he thinks that his age was a major reason that he was not hired, though no employer would ever tell him as much.

Eutychios says he became so desperate that he was willing to take almost any job, as long as it was legal. But he also understood why em-ployers did not want to hire him. Why should they invest in you if you will be able to work only a few years and you might get sick more often than a younger worker? He admits that his inability to find a job was not only due to his age, of course. Eutychios has been asking for flexibility to travel, in particular to be able to take one month off every three or four months. He did get some offers and even ended up doing some short-lived jobs. At Papa Gino's he was offered a job as a delivery driver, but the condition was no facial hair. He had sported a beard all of his adult life and was not willing to get a makeover at his age. He did deliver briefly for Pizza Hut, but once he came back after his first month off, someone else had taken his job and he was not hired again.

When Eutychios first thought of working for a popular ridesharing company, he was concerned that he was stealing the taxi drivers' jobs. Eventually it had become clear to him that he had no other option. In

October 2015, at the age of seventy-nine, he began working as an Uber driver, and he immediately loved it. He is never late. He has no supervisor. He is not dealing with money. He likes the security and information he and the customers have about each other. The only problem is where to go to the bathroom because there is nowhere to park in Boston. He loves it so much that he works ten hours a day, seven days a week. Now he has an Uber credit card that pays for his gas from his account, so whatever he takes in is net of costs, except of course the maintenance, repairs, and depreciation of the car. His daily goal is to make twenty trips, which gives him an income of about $150, or about $4,500 per month.

Eutychios is married with six grown children, and he has a pension and savings for a comfortable living. But he works to raise funds for an orphanage in Uganda:

> On a visit to a charity in Kampala in 2002, I also visited an orphanage in a town called Mityana, 70 kilometers from the capital of Kampala. I was impressed with the director who, as I later found out, takes in orphans and vulnerable children and tries to feed them and give them basic education. He uses his $200 a month pension to pay for this. Realizing that the children were undernourished, the director tells me: "What can I do? This is all I can afford."[25]

Eutychios came to the United States from Crete as an orphan himself, and he sees the Ugandan orphanage as his way to give back what he received as a child. Since that visit to Africa he has been working and collecting money from friends, and he travels to Uganda every three to four months. With $500 per month he can buy beans, rice, flour, sugar, oil, soap, salt, and ground peanuts to enhance the meals of the children. He works hard now to pay for his trips to Uganda and for all the other needs the children have in the orphanage:

> The work I could not get before, I now do gladly driving for Uber. It offers the flexibility for me to travel for extended periods of time, and whenever I am in Boston I can work as hard as I want and earn as much as I need. What I do relaxes me much better because I have a reason to live. I get motivated to get up early in the morning every

day and go to work. I work ten hours a day and do not feel tired. I am excited to go to work having in mind the children I work for and seeing their smiling faces as I am driving around the city. I never get tired and am very happy in what I do. I meet very nice people, we have good conversations and my life gets fulfilled. I have 130 reasons to live for, that is how many children are at the orphanage.

Eutychios is a happy Uber driver. He does the work on a supplemental basis, benefits enormously from the flexible time, and can work as much or as little as he desires or needs. This type of zero-hours contract is close to perfect for him. For him, the zero-hours contract means a maximal-hours contract.

This is not true for some others: for example, the person who for one reason or another has chosen to make a career out of being an Uber driver. It is a full-time job, just like a taxi driver. After driving for some time the career driver now decides to lock in: they make an investment by buying a car and they need to drive to pay off the loan. This, by the way, is where the Uber subsidization model starts to pay off: Uber heavily subsidizes drivers to start driving in the hope of locking them in to staying with Uber. The reality is, however, that Uber sets wages as low as possible, and once the driver is locked in and needs to pay off the car and maintenance, not much is left of the apparent generous wage. Within the sector, Uber's wage policy is denominated as "minimum wage plus two": they pay two dollars above the minimum wage. That is approximately what they earn per hour, even though they are paid by the mile.

Large, dominant firms may of course do more harm than just paying the lowest market wage. As we have seen in chapter 4, when workers have few options for employment, a large company like Uber can use this monopsony power to pay lower wages. They can even use their dominance to blatantly exploit workers or deny them access to the usual rights and benefits that workers have. Everything should be done to stop that from happening. But it appears that the main reason for low wages in gig jobs is the same as low wages for low-skilled workers throughout the economy. Uber can pay "minimum wage plus two" because this is as much as what workers can get somewhere else.

This "minimum wage plus two" is very similar to what a New York City taxi driver who is employed by a medallion owner makes. In most cities the medallions are owned by companies, who then hire drivers for a fee who can keep the revenue and pay for gas. Of course, the medallion owner is a businessperson who pays just enough wages to get the driver to do the job. And if a driver wants to buy their own medallion, it will be close to what they earn after paying back the $1 million loan on the medallion. After paying back the loan, their take-home pay is likely to be close to the "minimum wage plus two." These are the brutal forces of a competitive labor market: low-skilled labor is compensated at low-skill wages. If demand for rideshare services goes up and competition is limited, then the driver still gets the same "minimum wage plus two," but the rideshare company makes profits. The opposite is true for medallion owners of traditional taxis who face competition from rideshare companies: they lose money. Medallions that were worth over $1 million in 2014 are trading at less than $140,000 now.[26]

Is Uber so much better for the customer? The rideshare technology does provide better coverage than traditional taxi services in less dense areas, such as suburbs.[27] And there are technological improvements that make the rideshare service superior: no exchange of cash money, GPS-oriented drivers that choose the optimal trajectory, safety for all because of registered owners and users, good incentives to provide excellent service with rating systems, and so on. But nothing is stopping traditional taxi services from adopting these new technological advances as well.

In part, Uber is successful mainly because the competition in many locations is so lousy, whether it is incumbents from private, unsubsidized taxis or public mass transportation. The medallion system generates huge barriers to entry and inefficiencies for credit-constrained drivers, ending up in a highly concentrated monopolistic market with a few companies owning the majority of the medallion fleet. Uber disrupts this noncompetitive economy in a substantive manner. But it seems a minor barrier for medallion-operated taxis to adopt those technological improvements themselves, and many of them do. The main contribution of ridesharing is probably the better service in less dense areas and the lower prices from competition that all lead to more users, and hence better-off customers.

Clearly, the business model of Uber is not just to offer more flexibility to drivers like Eutychios and riders like me; Uber is in business to make money. The danger is that in the wake of their disruptive technology they are building a big Buffettian moat around their castle. The network externalities that match up the drivers with the riders make this an industry where being large creates value, and you become large if you enter the market first and grow the fastest. Just like eBay in the online auction world or Amazon in online retail, the scale economies make space for only one or a few competitors.

With limited competition, those dominant firms pay "minimum wage plus two" to their workers and set prices to keep competitors out but otherwise make nice profits. For now, the rideshare companies are not making profits because they are still heavily subsidizing drivers in order to build the network, especially in China and India. But once they are declared winners, they will exert their market power and prices will slowly creep up. That is why investors are willing to pay huge amounts for stock in these companies. There may be none yet, but huge profits are expected.

As customers there is little that we can do. Some people propose to boycott the gig economy firms; this sends a signal to the company that it has to abide by ethical standards. Firms loathe the reputation cost these campaigns have, which have disciplined companies such as Nike to diligently supervise and select the companies they source from to avoid those companies that employ child labor. But from an economic viewpoint, activism, especially in the form of individually boycotting Uber or Deliveroo (an online food delivery company founded in the United Kingdom), can even hurt the worker. I learned this the hard way when I first traveled to India as a teenager. Walking out of the train station in Calcutta, I turned down a bicycle rickshaw driver and sought out a motor rickshaw instead. I found it unethical and inhumane that a poorly fed rider was sweating under the scorching sun, cycling me, a rich Westerner, to my destination. Through a shop owner who spoke some English, the rickshaw cyclists explained to me that if he didn't make enough rides he could not feed his young children. I ended up taking the bicycle rickshaw and left a generous tip, but there were some twenty other riders waiting in line.

A worker is driven to take on an Uber or Deliveroo job because that is the best option they have. The fact that the job is badly paid is not always exploitation; rather, it is a sign that there are no better alternatives. By personally boycotting those services we reduce the demand for their work, which eventually lowers their wages even more. And even if we wanted to boycott them, how can we avoid the fact that these services are in our supply chain? If the restaurant where I order fresh fish runs out of my favorite variety, it might have some additional fish delivered by an Uber or Deliveroo driver from a partner restaurant. I don't even *know* that I am using the gig economy.

In the current economy, the highly intertwined supply chain of goods and services, it is impossible to survive without accepting at least a small fraction of relatively low-wage labor. If we consider low-wage labor such as gig economy work unethical, everything we buy contains some unethical work done by someone. The point is that work in the gig economy is so badly paid because all other low-skilled jobs are badly paid. That is the profit paradox again: Erin's pay is similar to that of an Uber driver, and all wages are low because of the falling tide, driven by economy-wide market power.

Even if personal activism is not effective, it is not an excuse not to do anything about low wages in the gig economy. There is more hope for change in trying to stop Uber by lobbying local and national politicians or regulating the industry in exerting that market power. We will need to see whether the impact of riding services like Uber and driverless cars is beneficial or not. But in spite of the stagnating wages of low-skilled work, many workers seem to like the gig economy. Evidence on rideshare services shows that most drivers work fewer than ten hours per week, and only 19 percent work full-time.[28] Clearly, for most workers the added flexibility makes the gig job attractive: it allows them to supplement their earnings from another job, and they can work when and as much as they like. Within seconds of switching on the Uber app, a driver is active. If anything, many workers report to be willing to accept lower wages in exchange for the flexibility. Rather than a shift at Mc-Donald's, many prefer to drive when and how much they want to make, even if it pays slightly less.

The gig economy has many advantages and is not the culprit of low wages. It offers the opportunity for people who can't otherwise work to have a job, and wages are indeed low. In part, that is because the flexibility of the gig jobs is more attractive than many other low-paying jobs. But most importantly, gig jobs draw low pay because all low-skilled and routine work is paid badly. Market power by dominant firms all over the economy leads to a falling tide that lowers the demand for labor.

So if it is not the gig economy that threatens work, what does the future of work look like? That is the subject of the next chapter.

10

The Future of Work

AS AN AVID USER of Google Translate, I often look up individual words, but I also translate sentences or even entire pages of text. Even though researchers communicate exclusively in English, some grant agencies abroad require an application to be made in two languages, English and the language of the grant agency. Rather than have someone translate it for me or do it myself, I cut and paste the English text and pretty quickly get a translation, which most often I need in Spanish.

When I started using Google Translate fifteen years ago, I would get a text back that was a translation with many mistakes. In particular, it had a hard time picking the correct word if similar words had multiple usages, such as "minister" (priest in a religion or cabinet member of the government), and it would have strange sentence construction. But then, toward the end of 2016, I saw a sudden change in the quality of the translations. It was as if I was moving from a nineteenth-century streetcar to the Shinkansen, the Japanese bullet train. Everything was superior: speed, precision, comfort.

Initially, Google used statistical machine translation where there was a mapping of words or short phrases. Basically, every word in one language had its counterpart in the other language. Because the mapping between words is not unique (such as "minister"), Google used statistical models to decide on the translation. In order to decide which of the multiple translations was the best, they would use a large database of human translations. To make things more complex, Google would double translate between any non-English languages. For example, from

French to German, Google would translate French to English and English to German. Something to do to light up a boring rainy Sunday used to be to translate Google Translate (say, a phrase from English to Spanish and then back to English). It gave plenty of surprising answers.

But those Google Translate fails are harder to come by these days. In November 2016 Google switched to a neural machine translation system. This form of artificial intelligence (AI) uses examples of human translations to learn and improve the quality of the translation. It translates entire sentences rather than piece by piece, and key to the learning process is that it takes into account the context of the complete text. This avoids mistakenly translating "minister" as a priest when the text is talking about a cabinet member of the government. In addition, it uses commonality between different languages, which is consistent with the linguists' consensus view—following the linguist Noam Chomsky's early work—that language is modular in the brain. This manner of processing in different languages creates commonalities in the expressions that can be traced back to common origins.

AI is the next general-purpose technology, just like the steam engine, electricity, or computers were in past industrial revolutions. More specifically, most recent advances come from machine learning (ML). Rather than rule-based logic encoded in algorithms, in ML computers learn from sample data. There is still limited direct evidence of the economic impact of AI and ML translation services. However, one recent study shows that eBay's in-house machine translation system that is offered to buyers and sellers on the eBay platform has increased exports by 17.5 percent and that translation-related search costs have decreased substantially. It seems that now that container transportation has lowered the costs of trade, the dismantling of language barriers is leading to further integration between trading partners with different languages.[1]

While it is easy to make fun of algorithms and machines, it is amazing how well they perform and how much they improve the quality of decision making and, ultimately, of our lives. In the realm of work, algorithms are not only efficient—in some circumstances they may also correct biases inherent in human decision making.

A recent study at Columbia University of résumé selection for hiring computer programmers shows that algorithms do significantly better than humans.[2] The program parses résumés and converts them into measurable outcomes that can be compared and ranked. Using a database of past selection decisions, algorithms are trained to make a link between those quantified résumés and the outcomes—who makes it to an interview and who receives and accepts a job offer. During the selection process, humans base their decisions on limited information about the individual in order to make job offers to suitable candidates.

The study shows that candidates are significantly more likely to pass the interview, and they are substantially more likely to accept a job offer when it is extended. Moreover, there is no subgroup where humans outperform the algorithm. This works particularly well in an environment with limited information (a couple of pages of a résumé) and where decisions are typically not very accurate.

The algorithm outperforms humans in reducing the biases in the decision making. The algorithm tends to pick candidates that graduated from nonelite colleges who did not have connections, who have limited experience, and who have strong soft skills, such as empathy. Humans have those biases because they do not possess the full information that is in the database. They base their decisions on the limited number of cases they handled themselves, which is a lot smaller than the total number of past cases in the data set, and they use their own views to screen those candidates.

For example, even if on average programmers from MIT are better than those from the University of South Dakota, the top graduates from MIT would not apply for this job, whereas the best students from South Dakota would. The algorithm can pick up this selection because it has been trained on hundreds of thousands of applicants, whereas the human might never have seen a University of South Dakota or MIT applicant before.

AI and Firms

AI can improve efficiency, but it will also serve to build power in many spheres. Beyond the military power, there is no doubt that AI will be a tool to create, widen, and maintain the moat around new and existing business models to strengthen dominant firms. Now that I am talking about the future and playing Nostradamus to prophesize about what is to come, my approach is more to offer a personal opinion rather than reporting facts and existing research. After all, it is a challenge to find compelling evidence from the future.

The main question that is relevant for *The Profit Paradox* is how AI will affect and create market power. Like the earlier technological revolutions, such as steam and electricity, the technological change from AI is a force toward creating market power in each of three sources of market power that we discussed in chapter 2.

The first source consists of supply returns to scale that created the railway monopolies a century ago. Those are also at work here. New technologies using big data, AI, and ML have led to the success of apparently traditional retailers such as Walmart and the clothing company Zara. With the use of data-driven logistics, often to respond quickly to changes in consumer demand, Walmart can adjust the supply of energy bars and bottled water to its stores in an area where a hurricane is predicted to make landfall, when these areas are often determined at short notice. Zara also adjusts what is on offer in its stores depending on the demand, which affects design, production, and shipment decisions at very short notice. Through investment in physical logistics and data processing capacity, these firms can produce at a lower cost. At the same time, they use their advantage to build a moat. While their technological superiority brings lower prices, it also permits leaders to erect barriers.

The demand returns to scale, the second source of technology-induced market power, are those scale economies that derive from the thickness of the user base. If a lot of people use eBay or Tinder, then more people find it attractive to join. And while these platforms with technological scale economies have been around for a long time in traditional technologies—think newspapers, the stock market, and so on—there is no doubt that new technologies have taken this to a different level. The reason is simply the fact that it is much easier and cheaper to organize an online platform without the need for a physical marketplace. But at least as important is that the potential of ML algorithms to improve the match between daters, for example, is unlimited. This in turn increases the possibility to create market power. Larger pools increase the information, and hence the precision of match prediction. The larger the scale, the more potential for market power.

The third source of technologically generated market power is learning by doing. There are not necessarily any direct-scale effects from supply or demand, but the competitive advantage stems from being able to reduce unit costs when more data is available. The self-driving cars developed by Uber, Google Cars, and Toyota use ML algorithms that improve as more data from driving is available. The better the algorithm works, the cheaper the product. The main cost savings is the ability to dispose of the supervisor, who is there in case the car does not respond as expected. Those supervisors are necessary in the early stages, but when there have been enough autonomous driving hours and hence enough data, the cost of operating the car without the supervisor will be lot lower. That is the promise of self-driving cars. Still, even without a supervisor, performance continues to improve as more data is collected. Those who get in there first learn first, and they gain an edge on those who follow. This learning process therefore generates an advantage that is hard for competitors to overcome.

Rather than from scale economies in supply and demand or from learning, market power can also originate from strategic behavior, which is also influenced by technology—for example, by algorithmic collusion. It is illegal for firms to collude overtly and coordinate price setting. But under tacit collusion, where prices are set unilaterally without explicit agreement between the colluders, prices are kept high because firms can use intricate strategies to sustain implicit collusion. The most famous strategy is tit-for-tat: I set a high price until you undercut me, and then I respond likewise. This strategy can sustain collusion without any communication. The impact of algorithms and much faster trading is that it may be easier to sustain high prices from collusion. Such algorithmic collusion can, for example, ensure that undercutting a competitor is not beneficial because the competitor will respond immediately. As a result, there is no incentive to break the collusive outcome.[3]

A similar strategic approach using detailed data can be applied to price differentiation because it may become easier when more data is collected from the customer. The finer the detail of the data collected, the better the price can be adjusted to the customer. While in theory it is not clear whether more price discrimination is good or bad—for example, food prices for the poor come down when there is price discrimination[4]—it is clear that there are circumstances where firms extract a much higher surplus when they have data. Firms use cookies on browsers extensively in order to price differentiate. They even charge different prices whether the user connects from a Mac or a Windows machine. And airline ticket prices may change on a second visit to the website.

It is clear that new technologies provide tools to create a lopsided concentration of market power. What will the impact be on work? Let's take a look at what one of the most influential economists of the last century had to say about it.

Like Horses . . . Really?

When Wassily Leontief was giving his Nobel lecture in Stockholm in December 1973 on the input-output matrix—based on his 1941 analysis of the network connectivity of sectors in production—one of the physics laureates in the front row reputedly whispered to the other physics laureate: "I didn't know that you could get a Nobel Prize for inverting a matrix."

I have heard this story multiple times, but I have not been able to get a direct source confirming it. Despite the physicists' supposed disdain for his work, Leontief's idea has been enormously influential. Sergey Brin and Larry Page's PageRank algorithm to order web pages uses a similar iterative method to determine the relevance of a page (pun intended or not, Larry Page named PageRank after himself, not after web pages).[5] It does not merely matter how many link to your web page, but also how important those who link to you are. If a web page receives links from a thousand obscure web pages, it will be ranked as much less relevant than another page that is linked only a hundred times but whose links are the major news outlets, newspapers, and so on. It is not only a matter of how many friends you have, but how popular your friends are.

As Brin and Page found out, this is a powerful way to determine whether information is valuable. Of course, they went much further to create Google, but their method is built on Leontief's method, using matrix algebra to summarize the importance of connectivity of inputs and outputs.

Car producers sell not only to customers like you and me, but also to firms that use cars to deliver packages, to the police department, and so on. Some of the production is used as an input and some as a final output. And the car producer in turn requires its own inputs to build a car.

This creates a network of enormous complexity among firms around the globe who are both users of inputs and producers of output that is either used as a final good or as an input in production for another firm. With increasing specialization and division of labor, and with far-reaching connectedness from globalization, this network of input-output relations has become enormously detailed and complex. Leontief proposed a mathematical way to summarize that complexity. The eigenvalues and vectors—which require calculating the inverse of Leontief's input-output matrix—collapse this complex network into a simple ranking that takes into account the connections of your connections.

The insight of Leontief's method is that it allows us to evaluate the impact of any change on all inputs. For example, what is the effect of a shift in demand from combustion engines to electric engines on the demand for rubber boots used by oil drillers? It is important to study phenomena such as the evolution of specialization and the transmission of shocks in booms and recessions, and to evaluate policy interventions.

In the network of producing scientific knowledge with advisors and students, Leontief was a key player who was ranked at the top. Not only did he receive a Nobel Prize himself, he was also the doctoral advisor to four other recipients.[6]

As an early adopter of computers, by 1949 Leontief had already started applying his method to analyze the US economy. At that time computers were used predominantly to solve large systems of linear equations and thus inverting matrices. Doing this with pen and paper was a tedious task replete with errors. During the rest of his career he became a vocal proponent for economists to work with data and do quantitative analysis.

Leontief's embrace of new technologies also made him somewhat pessimistic. Toward the end of his life, at a symposium of the National Academy of Engineering, he made the following comparison: "The role of humans as the most important factor of production is bound to diminish in the same way that the role of horses in agricultural production was first diminished and then eliminated by the introduction of tractors."[7] The horse comparison has often been used as a dystopian prediction of what is to come for labor, especially in the popular press. Leontief's intellectual eminence has given this argument a lot of credibility but, like most current-day academic economists, I beg to disagree with this popular apocalyptic conclusion.

To start, there is no doubt in the facts about horses. In 1915 there were an estimated twenty horses per one hundred inhabitants in the United States. The horse population per capita reached a minimum of 0.78 per one hundred inhabitants in 1964 and has been increasing moderately again in recent years, remaining very low compared to a century ago. For the entire world we have data from 1961 only, when that number was 2.02, and it dropped to 0.76 in 2018.[8]

Humans are of course not horses. Humans can adapt and learn new tasks. If there is no work as a bank teller, there are jobs as a security guard or a retail manager. It may take time to retool, but it is possible. This substitutability creates a lot more opportunities. Moreover, humans are creative; they can invent new goods and services.

But what are the facts about humans? In the discussion of leisure in chapter 9, we have seen that we work fewer hours than in the past. This piece of evidence appears to support Leontief's argument. However, this requires some explanation. The fact that we work on average a lot less than we did in the past is a choice that gives us a better quality of life. Rather than spend Saturdays working as our ancestors did a hundred years ago, we prefer to watch a football game, have lunch at the beach, or play sports. Rather than an apocalyptic prediction, it shows that our quality of life has gone up tremendously. Instead of repetitively tightening screws on the assembly line, we now watch TV or go to the theatre. If people would work more hours our earnings would rise, but we already earn enough to live comfortably and prefer to have more leisure time rather than have the extra money and no time to spend it. I don't believe this is the interpretation Leontief had in mind.

Not only do humans work fewer hours, fewer of them actually work at all. I discussed earlier that labor force participation has decreased. Since the mid-1990s, fewer people of working age are working, both men and women. In spite of the enormous gains on the front of women going to work, for the past two decades the fraction of working-age people who have a job or are looking for one has declined.[9]

So that seems to go in favor of Leontief's argument, too. However, the decrease in the fraction of people working is driven by the decrease in wages, especially for those earning wages at or below the median. And I have argued that the rise in market power has a lot to do with this decline in the median wage. If markets were competitive and profits were zero, wages would be driven up again and low earners who now prefer to stay at home would not do so.

The key insight that takes the wind out of the sails of Leontief's horse parable is that in competitive markets the ownership of capital does not generate enormous profits. All the gains from innovation and techno-logical progress accrue to workers, after paying for the competitive price of capital investment. Technological progress raises output, and then in competitive markets this also raises wages. As a result, the worker ap-propriates all the gains from technological progress.

If in response to those higher earnings workers prefer to work fewer hours, they will definitely do so and go to the theatre on Saturdays. But technological progress does not make the humans disappear from the labor market as long as wages reflect productivity. The comparison of horses may hold with slavery, where the wage did not reflect the pro-ductivity of the worker. Instead, with paid labor and competition in the output market, workers extract all the surplus from technological pro-gress. In a competitive market, the worker is effectively the owner of the technology. All technological progress is embodied in labor. Even if on paper the firm holds the rights to capital and intellectual property, the owner of capital cannot make huge profits. Competition drives down output prices, and this in turn increases the real wage. Any technological advance therefore leads to an increase in wages.

Competition in the output markets and the resulting increase in wages ensures that workers stay active in the labor market as technology advances. The horse was paid only the same amount of oats. But there is one other caveat. What if there are two types of horses, say, draft horses that plow the field and racehorses that entertain people on Saturdays and feed the betting markets? Technological progress will give rise to more demand for racehorses and less for draft horses. In fact, the increase since the 1960s of the number of horses per capita is surely due more to the recreational use of horses than to their use in agriculture.

Likewise for humans. Technological change increases the productivity of high-skilled labor much more relative to that of low-skilled labor, and with it the dispersion of wages. If that gap keeps growing, an increasing number of low-skilled workers will drop out of the labor market. But without support from family or the government, people need work, so those most in need will continue to do so, albeit at wages that are enormously low compared to those in high-skill occupations. Those low earners will not enjoy more leisure time.

Technological Progress Favors the Skilled

The moral of Leontief's horse parable is that as long as markets are competitive, technological change is not so much a threat to jobs and work but to the wages of those who do low-skilled work. There will be plenty of work to do. Even if we think that all jobs are at risk from technological change and even ushers at a concert or health service workers will be substituted by robots, people will invent new activities and services that will require human labor.

I believe that people's fears of disappearing jobs are misguided. Part of this fear is rooted in our ignorance of what the future brings. Most of us now are doing jobs that didn't exist a century ago, and we have no way of knowing what jobs people will do a century from now. The past is testimony that we should not fear that there is a lump of labor. It has shown a constant creation of new jobs as technology progressed, and there is no reason to believe that today and the future are different. That said, we are completely agnostic about what those jobs will be. And even if there will be plenty of work to do, the biggest problem may be that many of those manual jobs will be very badly paid. Technological change that is biased against the low skilled and that disproportionately favors a few superstars will eventually have devastating outcomes. It is still not clear how great that biased technological change has been so far, and it is even more unclear what it will be in the future. But it is one of the more fundamental challenges that technological progress may pose to the economy in the future.

Imagine a world in which a few geniuses get better and better at their jobs and the rest of the workers are just pawns who execute menial, unrewarding tasks that are extremely badly paid. And with fewer and fewer superstars, there are not enough spouses to support stay-at-home husbands. That is potentially the biggest problem to address in the future.

In the meantime, though, things are certainly made worse when firms have market power. Not only does market power depress wages for all labor to the benefit of profits, but market power also increases the wage gap between the superstars and the rest, and between those with a college education and those without. If skill-biased technological change is an unstoppable chemical reaction that increases wage inequality, then market power is the catalyst that speeds up the process and exacerbates the differences between the haves and the have-nots.

Market power aggravates the impact of new technologies that already favor the superstars. In order to soften the impact of this lopsided dystopia, we need to tackle the root cause. Before we do so, we go on a quest for knowledge about work, or how we obtain the necessary data that allows us to formulate adequate policies.

11

The Quest for Facts

BEFORE WE CAN ADEQUATELY ADDRESS the impact of market power on work, we need to get the facts straight. To understand how labor markets work, to measure market power, and to evaluate how best to change undesirable outcomes, we need data in order to make informed decisions. Surprisingly, even in current times of data excess, researchers and policymakers are facing serious difficulties getting access to even the most crucial statistics. In this chapter it will become clear which aspects of the economy we cannot see immediately and how we can overcome those obstacles, as well as why we need the data to understand how the economy works and how those facts guide policy.

In the United States, for example, the all-important unemployment statistics that move stock markets every month and that determine whether a household is eligible for unemployment benefits are calculated after conducting a telephone survey of sixty thousand households around the country—a country with a total population of 330 million.

To ensure that the randomly selected sample is representative of minorities, geographical regions, and nonurban populations, intricate adjustments are made to balance the samples. It will come as no surprise that the numbers are not very precise and are revised substantially months or even years later.

Billions of dollars are spent differently depending on whether the unemployment rate comes out to be 5.9 percent or 6.1 percent. During recessions, an unemployment rate higher than 6 percent automatically triggers extensions of unemployment benefits from twenty-six to ninety-nine weeks. When months later those numbers are revised, millions of unemployed did not receive the benefits because the initial measure of unemployment was less than 6 percent, even though they were entitled because after the revision the unemployment rate was above 6 percent. Moreover, the numbers come out a month after the telephone survey has been conducted, so households who are eligible get those benefits with a delay.

The data collected by telephone has serious accuracy problems. We know that polls about the voting intentions of individuals have become less reliable in recent years, most notably during the last two US presidential elections. Those polls are typically based on a random sample of some one thousand telephone numbers. People wonder how a mere thousand people can inform us about the voting intentions of the 155 million Americans who are likely to vote. We know from basic statistics that a thousand random draws with few options—whether you are likely to vote and for whom out of two major candidates—generates a fairly precise prediction of the outcome, with a plus-or-minus three-percentage-point margin of error.

The problem with telephone polls is that the sampled pool of numbers has become less likely over time to be representative of the entire population. With more mobile phone users rather than users of landlines, it is harder to obtain a random sample of potential voters. In addition, the response rate has declined dramatically from 80 percent in the 1970s to 8 percent today.[1]

Aren't we all fed up with those marketeers calling us at the most inconvenient times of the day? Luckily we can block unwanted numbers or even go on registers that exclude us from being sampled. Those who do pick up and answer the telephone are increasingly unrepresentative of the entire population. These problems are even more pronounced for internet- rather than telephone-based polling.

In the current digital age, the data can be collected in a much more precise manner. Let every employer register their workers in an online portal. That would give us real-time data, not for a sample of sixty thousand individuals but for each of the 159 million working Americans, and no data revisions would be needed.

In times when Google Street View can generate the visual representation of any public place in the country in no time, when Walmart knows where billions of products are stored and in which of their stores there is demand, and Amazon knows what kind of cereal I prefer on Sundays, it seems that the government is using methods from the Stone Age to collect data about work. Work is the most important activity of most people, and it accounts for two-thirds of gross domestic product. Yet the way we collect information about work is comparable to using pigeons to communicate when we have wireless devices.

If a company like Google decided to tackle this problem, they would have a system operational in six months. It would cost them a few million dollars for the development—peanuts, knowing that one privately conducted monthly telephone survey of one thousand respondents costs around $1 million already—and the Internal Revenue Service (IRS), the US Census Bureau, and all researchers would have coded data on employment in real time.

To make things worse, most of that data is already collected electronically, often multiple times. Government agencies obtain administrative data for all kinds of reasons. As stipulated in the US Constitution, every ten years the Census Bureau collects demographic and economic data in order to allocate seats of the House of Representatives and to allocate federal funds to states, businesses, and cities for infrastructure, education, health, safety, and other services. The IRS and the Social Security Administration collect information on the annual income and taxes of citizens and companies and on their Social Security contributions.

Yet, US citizens, journalists, companies, and researchers do not have access to this information. This is not so everywhere around the globe. Enter Scandinavia.

Norway: Data Galore

A few decades after independence from Denmark in 1814, the Norwegian authorities started to produce a statistical account of the economic activity and population in the country. Those statistics were then published and made available in what is called *Statistisk sentralbyrå* (Statistics Norway).[2]

From the very beginning, those publications have been available for inspection by all citizens, which means that anyone can verify the total income of their neighbor. You cannot see the distinct sources, but you do know the total amount of income that is declared for tax purposes. Every year in October, media outlets rush to compile the list of the richest Norwegians as well as the incomes of politicians and public figures. Before the days of the internet you had to walk into the library or the local authority to obtain the data, but now it is available online. Because the increased accessibility online made abuse more prevalent, currently the person whose information you request is notified with the identity of the requestor, which has led to a substantial decrease in the number of searches.

Data transparency is common in the Scandinavian countries. We can speculate about whether this is the result of Protestant puritan ethics, humble lifestyles, or the norm not to show off wealth. But the main implication is that in present-day economic research, a lot of what we know about the work and the effectiveness of social policy is based on research using Scandinavian data. We have access to the information of all citizens on salary, bonus, hours worked, holidays, social security contributions, taxes, unemployment spells, and so on.

This allows researchers to calculate, for example, the wage inequality within firms, between firms, and the average duration of unemployment. Not surprisingly, we know a lot more about work and the impact of policies in Norway, a country with a population of 5.3 million, than we do about the United States, the most advanced economy, with a population of 330 million.

Privacy concerns are not to be taken lightly, and the right to privacy should not be overshadowed by the need for better data or even transparency. One of the main problems of market power is precisely that technology firms are collecting data on individuals in order to build and exploit that power. Privacy is a major concern for market power and hence antitrust. I will turn to this issue in chapter 12.

There is, however, a fundamental difference between a technology firm collecting detailed information on the comings and goings of an individual through Siri, in order to sell them breakfast cereal, and making data on people's incomes available. The income of an individual is an issue of government because of the tax liability, not because of an individual's private sphere. And here most advanced economies, and the United States in particular, maintain a schizophrenic position regarding the privacy of their citizens. While tech and communications firms are freely allowed to collect, use, and sell highly personal information, the government itself cannot use information on citizens' taxes, even if identities are anonymized.

Transparency of incomes is not totally unheard of in the United States. In Wisconsin income information is provided upon request, and as in Norway the authorities reveal the identity of the requester to those about whom information has been requested. When the US Congress levied the first taxes in 1861, the names and incomes of everyone were published. This transparency disappeared quickly until 1924, when the United States briefly made income information public again. This was met with massive resistance from the wealthy, precisely because with transparency they were forced to declare all of their high incomes.

Transparency in incomes has enormous benefits. First and foremost, it puts an additional control on fraud and tax evasion. Those with high incomes who avoid or evade taxes would rather not have more people wondering why. Transparency also improves efficiency because there is less dispersion in earnings due to opacity. People make better decisions about which jobs to accept and when to look for better jobs if they know what other people in similar positions make. The disclosure of pay data also closes pay gaps for different minorities such as gender, ethnicity, and age. It would lead to less discrimination and an easier implementation of fair pay.

"Secrecy is of the greatest aid to corruption" said Republican senator Robert Howell of Nebraska when the 1924 transparency law was introduced.[3] There is also evidence showing that transparency increases government tax revenue. Researchers have found that public disclosure leads to a 3 percent higher reported income.[4]

If the transparency of personal income increases efficiency and decreases inequality, the transparency of company accounts makes markets even more competitive. It is shocking that the accounts of nearly all US firms are not publicly available. This is of crucial importance for suppliers to vet their customers. When a firm ships a few million dollars' worth of goods with two-month terms of payment to a company across the country, it wants to know how solvent that customer is. Where better to look than the accounts of the firm? Yet, in the United States, only publicly traded firms—some five thousand firms out of a total of more than six million—mandatorily need to disclose their accounts. It is impossible to find the most basic information on privately held companies in the United States. So when shipping those goods across the country to a company you have never done business with before, you are often throwing a Hail Mary pass down the field.

We need to recalibrate the balance of where we promote privacy and transparency. We live in a time when a simple app on my smartphone collects, uses, and sells the most intimate information without my consent, from my live location to the personal hygiene products and medications I use. Yet, a small business cannot verify the financial health of a potential client. Without transparency, competition suffers. Moats are more effective when filled with muddy water.

Denmark: Data Is Not Enough

In the absence of transparency, only limited data is available and competition suffers. In addition, researchers analyzing market power and labor markets are driving with frosted windshields. High-quality data is a first requirement to draw precise conclusions, but it is not enough. There are many instances where even with perfect data we can reach erroneous conclusions. Consider the following example: people who use opioids tend to be from richer backgrounds, and those who use crack cocaine tend to be from poorer backgrounds. Therefore, in order to get rich, I should use opioids.

Wealth and opioid use are positively correlated, but this does not let us infer the cause. Most obviously, correlation does not tell us about the direction of the causality. Do opioids cause wealth, or does wealth cause opioids? More problematically, there may be no causation at all. For example, over a ten-year period, "US crude oil imports from Norway" and "drivers killed in collision with a railway train" are highly correlated (correlation coefficient 0.95).[5]

In this case we can be pretty sure that the correlation can be due to pure coincidence, and in other cases there may be a common cause: ice cream sales are correlated with swimming pool drownings. The fact that more people buy ice cream does not result in more drownings—it is simply that warm weather leads to both, with no relation between them.

The name of the game in economic research is to find settings where we can tease out what causes which outcomes. This is extremely important when we want to engage in policy. If we think opioid use causes wealth accumulation, then we should prescribe opioids to the poor. So let's do the science right before we activate the policy machinery. To get at the cause, scientists use different approaches; all of these methods require some form of indirect observation. It is a bit like shaving or putting on makeup in front of a steamy bathroom mirror: you go by what you know more than by what you see. You don't see exactly what you are looking for, but you infer it indirectly.

This is of course common to all scientific endeavors. For example, there is no way we can directly infer evidence that the universe is expanding, but we can measure the color spectrum of stars and we understand the Doppler effect. The color spectrum changes with the speed and distance at which a star moves. The inference needs precise measurement, but above all a hypothesis and therefore a theory of how the world works. Or in George Santayana's words, "Theory helps us to bear our ignorance of fact."[6] Research is constantly coming up with new theories and clever tricks to infer features that cannot be observed directly.

Any data that economists use therefore must have some combination of a theory and some form of an experiment. The experiment can be an explicit experiment, much like that of a biologist in a laboratory who changes a gene in one set of mice (the treatment group) and compares the outcomes relative to a set of mice that have had no genetic change (the control group). Economists design experiments where they can explicitly control the behavior of a population that is subject to a treatment and compare it to those who are not subject to the treatment. In light of the evidence, the scientific theory explains people's actions in response to the policy.

Experimental methods are more and more commonly used to tease out the causes of certain labor market phenomena. There is one salient aspect of experiments that is fairly unique to labor markets and economics in general, and that is less likely to be of importance in other sciences, which was evidenced in a large policy experiment in Denmark. In the early 1990s Denmark had a particularly harsh recession, with unemployment rates reaching 10 percent. Danish policymakers embarked on a profound overhaul of the Danish labor market. In a society with a marked work ethic, the relative absence of free riding and an institutionalized sense of compassion, it was deemed unacceptable that 10 percent of those who wanted to work could not find a job and were exposed to the economic insecurity and inequality inherent in job loss.

In 1994, Prime Minister Poul Nyrup Rasmussen introduced the idea of flexicurity, a contraction of the words "flexibility" and "security." Danish policymakers determined that the main culprit of high unemployment was the lack of flexibility in the labor market. Quite controversially, they considered that by introducing flexible labor contracting to induce job mobility, unemployment would drop.

Under flexicurity, firms are no longer bound by costly firing restrictions and they do not have to offer job contracts for life. The idea is that firms hire when they have a vacancy. If firms can easily let go of a worker who is underperforming, they will hire a new one. Therefore, firms do not have to think too much about long-term commitment when hiring because there is no cost to firing when economic times are bad.

In order to counter the negative effects of flexible labor markets (more job loss), flexicurity was accompanied by two measures that would guarantee security to the worker. The policy provides a modern social security system with adequate income support for those transitioning to other jobs—unemployment insurance benefits. In addition, government policies focus on active labor market policies, which provide active coaching and training for the unemployed in order to find a new job as well as lifelong education and skill upgrading.

The flexicurity policy was hailed as unprecedented success. The unemployment rate in Denmark is now among the lowest in the world, and most importantly, even in recessions, unemployment rate hikes are fairly muted and they come down relatively quickly. Even in the years following the Great Recession of 2008, the unemployment rate stayed below 8 percent (in Spain the unemployment rate exceeded 26 percent by the end of 2012).[7]

Part of the success is not merely the low unemployment rate but also the fact that unemployment duration has dropped significantly. As a result, workers are exposed to shorter periods of unemployment and hence face less income insecurity, which is covered by generous unemployment benefits. Especially young workers find a job quickly at the bottom of the job ladder, and older workers who fall off the top rungs of the ladder have plenty of job prospects, even close to retirement.

So the Scandinavian labor market policies are the darlings of researchers of labor markets and policymakers alike, but the Scandinavian policymakers are ready to admit that they do not own the truth—they are willing to experiment and find out which policies work best. One such experiment, also in Denmark, with an activation program to get the newly unemployed to work revealed quite a shocking insight.

Between November 2005 and February 2006, any newly unemployed worker in the southern counties of South Jutland (on the Atlantic coast) and Storstrøm (on the east coast, south of Copenhagen) entered in the experiment. Those born in the first half of the month (between the first and the fifteenth) were selected to participate in the mandatory activation program (the treatment group). Upon becoming unemployed, the selected workers participated in a course to guide them on how to focus their job search, and they met with a case worker on a weekly or biweekly basis. Throughout, the participant's activity was monitored.

Those born in the second half of the month (between the sixteenth and the last day) received the standard assistance: one meeting with a case worker every three months, followed by more intensive assistance after one year of unemployment. This is considered a legitimate experimental setting because birthdays are random and there is nothing that systematically differentiates those born in the first half of the month from those born in the second half. We can therefore be sure that this provides an adequate setting to test the policy impact.

When researchers analyzed the data from the experiment, they found that the impact of the activation program was large and positive: job searchers found work at a rate that was 30 percent faster. This implies that the average duration of unemployment was reduced by three weeks, from fourteen weeks to eleven.[8] Despite the cost of the program, the economic benefits were potentially huge. The worker earned an income for three additional weeks, and the government did not need to pay unemployment benefits. In Denmark, benefits are generous, at about 70 percent of the last wage. The total gain of wages earned and benefits foregone was therefore on the order of five weeks of wages (1.7 times 3 weeks), in addition to the nonmonetary satisfaction of the worker who had a job and reduced the time of unemployment. This is nothing short of an unequivocal policy victory.

Or is it? This success masks the fact that those workers born in the second half of the month and who do not receive the intensive guidance to find a job are competing with those who do. If firms create a fixed number of jobs (in this short period of time no jobs are displaced due to technological change; recall the discussion on the lump of labor), then each job that is taken up by one of those in the program cannot be taken up by someone who is not in the program. This is like a cycling race where half of the participants ride electric bikes and the others ride normal bikes. The electric bike racers are more likely to win, and as a result those on normal bikes are less likely to win. This is a zero-sum game.

The evidence on the Danish experiments confirms exactly that: those who did not receive the extra guidance found work at a lower rate. While there are some positive effects—firms tend to post more vacancies when the program is in place—the overall effect is neutral or even negative when taking into account the cost of the policy.[9] The Danish experience is not unique. In France, a similar experiment to help the long-term unemployed get jobs had similar effects.[10]

While these collateral effects are rarely present in laboratory experiments in the sciences, they are extremely common in economic experiments in the field. The keystone of all economic activity is equilibrium. If it rains, the demand for umbrellas at the subway exit sharply increases. Anyone selling them there can charge a higher price, especially to those who need to hurry to a job interview. The price ensures equilibrium of supply and demand.

When policymakers or researchers run experiments (for example, giving out umbrellas for free), they interfere with the behavior of some people, which in turn affects equilibrium: the price adjusts, how many are sold, and so on (in this case the researcher might also be harassed by the regular umbrella vendor, who sees prices and sales drop).

In the Danish experiment, the policy intervention changes the rate at which the unemployed find jobs because unemployment is an equilibrium outcome of the labor market. Equilibrium in markets is like communicating vessels, in this case one vessel with the unemployed who received the extra training and another vessel with the unemployed who didn't. The water marks in two vessels correspond to the speed at which you find a job. And those water marks are connected. If you apply pressure to decrease the mark in one vessel (offer training to one group of job seekers), it will increase the mark in the other vessel.

The Danish experience shows that data is not enough; you also need a scientific hypothesis. The theory makes explicit how workers respond to changes in the government program while recognizing that workers' behavior is also affected by changes in the behavior of all the others. These equilibrium effects can act through prices and wages as well as through the impact on other measures, such as the probability of finding a job.

Not All Data Is Created Equal

Often the data collected is less than ideal, in which case it is crucial to carefully interpret how data is collected and subsequently adjust for the biases in the collection process. To illustrate this, we take a look at a beautiful example described by Jordan Ellenberg in his book about mathematics, *How Not to Be Wrong*.[11] Abraham Wald was a Jewish mathematician who obtained his PhD in Austria under the supervision of Karl Menger, incidentally the son of the economist Carl Menger, founder of the Austrian school of economic thought and the intellectual father of Friedrich Hayek. After the Nazi invasion of Austria in 1938 Wald managed to escape to the United States where he started working at the Cowles Commission, then located at the University of Chicago. When World War II broke out, Wald applied his statistical knowledge to solve wartime problems. One of the challenges under investigation at the Center for Naval Analyses was to reduce the number of bombers that were shot down. To analyze the issue, engineers had collected data on the bullet holes in the airplanes that had returned from missions over enemy territory. They found particular concentrations of holes in the wings and tails of the airplanes, and they planned to use steel plates to reinforce those areas. Due to weight restrictions, only a limited amount of steel could be added. Protecting the areas most damaged, they argued, would lower the chances that the planes would be shot down.

To the surprise of the engineers, Wald instead recommended that steel plates were applied to the underbelly where there were hardly any bullet holes. The engineers protested and wondered out loud whether Wald wanted more pilots killed by enemy fire, not less. Then Wald made the case that changed the engineers' minds completely. He started out by asking them to think about the ideal evidence. He said the ideal evidence was somewhere at the bottom of the North Sea, between Dover and Calais. Inspection of the planes that were shot down would provide the perfect evidence where the bullets that brought down the plane had impacted.

He noted that instead, the only information they had was from bullet impact on planes that had survived their mission; they had no data for those bombers that had been shot down. He made them see that the data they had collected was highly selective. What that selective evidence showed is that damage to the wings and tail was not fatal and kept the bomber in the air long enough to return to the base. Instead, damage to the underbelly was fatal and led to the loss of the bomber.

Survival bias (also called selection bias) in the data collected is extremely common in economics. When Amazon or Walmart enters a market, some of the smaller mom-and-pop retail stores may go out of business. To analyze whether a firm has market power, we need not only know which firms are in the market but also those that are driven to bankruptcy and those that would have entered the market if Amazon was not there. The data rarely comes with information on firms that never enter a market to compete or on firms that left after bankruptcy. Therefore we need a hypothesis of which firms never entered the market in the first place, just like Wald's hypothesis of where the bullet holes were on the planes that didn't make it back.

Among other variables in the labor market, it is clear that executives have very different abilities and skills. Among the sample of executives, very few make it to CEO, and the characteristics of the survivors are therefore potentially very different from those who do not make it. Likewise, the characteristics of the CEO of a large firm are very different from those of the CEO of a small startup.

All this implies that there are certain biases in the data that we observe: competing firms have different characteristics than firms that decided not to enter the market or left because they went bankrupt. Recognizing the bias in the data and correcting for it is key to making correct policy prescriptions. When we only observe a selection of the data, theory helps us create what the missing data would have looked like. With a reasonable hypothesis of how and why the selection occurs, we can reconstruct the full data. That is exactly what Abraham Wald did. He had a theory of what had happened to the bombers that did not return from their missions. The theory was crucial for the recommended fix, and therefore to improve the pilots' chances of survival.

The Ship of Theseus

The story of Abraham Wald forces us to think carefully about how data is collected before blindly analyzing it. Another, though different, instance of data that does not reveal what is really underneath it is jobs data. Every month the US Department of Labor publishes the jobs report. Politicians are obsessed with creating jobs, but the reality is a lot more intricate. To get an idea, let's travel to mythical Greece and the ship of Theseus.

Theseus, a mythical king, sails his ship in a famous battle, and on his return from Crete to Athens the ship is kept for posterity in the Athens harbor. Over the years, as the wood deteriorates, ship carpenters apply new timber to repair the ship. Eventually they replace all of the planks and the ship is made entirely of new wood. Philosophers like Heraclitus and Plato ask whether the ship with new planks is still the ship of Theseus. Suppose we consider that the ship with the new planks is Theseus's, and suppose that all of the old planks are collected and treated against decay, and then a separate ship is built with the old, discarded planks. An equally intriguing philosophical question is whether this reconstructed ship is the ship of Theseus.

We are not preoccupied with the metaphysics of identity here, but there is a parallel in the job market. A firm is a ship and a plank is a worker. Workers in a form are continuously changing. Workers come and go, and before long everyone in the company is new. Yet the company remains the same. Today, Coca-Cola still sells the same old Coke (at least since 1929, when cocaine was finally eliminated from the drink). None of the workers from back then are left.

Something similar happens to the cells in our body. Cells have a limited life span and die, and new cells replace them. Skin cells last for two to three weeks, red blood cells last over a year, and some cells, such as neurons, are not replaced when they die. Eventually nearly all of the estimated 50 to 75 trillion cells in our body are replaced, multiple times, yet we tend to think that the person is still the same.

Workers move in and out of jobs all the time. They move from unemployment into a job, from one job to another, and from a job back into unemployment. One of the most salient facts about the labor market is the sheer amount of turnover. It is precisely this large amount of turnover that is often misunderstood and frequently ill-represented in the public debate.

When the jobs report of February 2020 stated that 273,000 new jobs were created, that meant that an estimated 4,611,000 people had lost their jobs and 4,884,000 had found new ones.[12] Those magnitudes in the job flows seem astronomical, but firms expand and contract all the time depending on how their business is doing. And workers switch jobs all the time as well because they move their families or because they find better opportunities.

Even if there are tumultuous currents of massive changes of jobs underneath, the surface level is still and unemployment moves relatively little. The job market therefore is more like a pressure cooker, where atoms bump into each other to form and destroy molecules. Even if you observe a stable temperature, the particles keep bumping.

The only exception, when the pressure cooker explodes, is during times of crisis. Then we tend to see only jobs destroyed and very few new ones formed. In the COVID-19 crisis, for example, in early May of 2020 over 14 percent of the population became unemployed and there were 38 million new jobless claims over a period of two months. The underlying currents come to the surface in those times of crisis. In normal times the water is flat, with equally strong undercurrents, but those undercurrents usually balance each other out. These crisis episodes illustrate the huge importance of those currents.

What's important is that jobs are created when firms become more productive and they are destroyed when firms face headwinds. And if workers leave for better opportunities, then a new replacement is needed: the firm is hiring. The more frequently workers move on to new jobs, the more the firms they are leaving will have vacancies.

This also indicates that many efforts to create jobs are a drop in a bucket. When a new job is created it is displacing another one, either because another job is destroyed or because no other new job is created. The obsession with creating jobs is like rain on an erupting volcano. From the Danish experiment helping the unemployed find jobs we have learned that there are indeed benefits to those receiving help, but this is to the detriment of the ones not receiving any help. Even if policy has an impact on who finds jobs, the bottom line is that little can be done about the total number of jobs, nor about the average rate at which people find or lose jobs.

Observe that the inability to create jobs does not contradict the lump of labor fallacy. When robots increase productivity with fewer workers, the displaced jobs disappear permanently. The affected workers eventually transition to other jobs, possibly switching occupations from assembling cars to health care services. Or when the supply of workers increases, as has been the case in the second half of the twentieth century when women massively joined the workforce, then those new workers' salaries will also generate new demand for other goods and hence jobs. When there is a change in technology (labor demand) or in the number of workers (labor supply), there is no lump of labor and new jobs are indeed created. Instead, under invariant conditions of labor supply and labor demand, the number of jobs do not change. In that case, creating jobs is a mirage.

In an ideal world we would like to have workers find jobs quickly and lose them slowly. That would mean that the unemployed workers have a lot of employment security because whenever they become unemployed, they find employment quickly. As a result, they face a short duration of unemployment. If workers lose their jobs at a slow rate, that means they also have a lot of job security. Once they have a job, that job is secure for a long time.

Wishing for both job security (long duration of jobs) and employment security (short duration of unemployment) is a noble aim, but it is like wishing that the laws of gravity did not apply. The job market is more like a children's carousel: if the rides are long, the waiting times are long, and if the rides are short, the waiting times are short. But with both short and long waiting times, the number of people lining up and the total time spent in the queue is always the same: frequent short waits versus infrequent long waits.

The same goes for unemployment. If job security is high and the duration of jobs is long, then employment security is low because it takes a long time to find a job. And vice versa, if job security is low, then employment security is high. All the while, the number of unemployed remains the same. This is a fundamental law in the economics of work: if there was both job security and employment security, the unemployment rate would necessarily have to tend to zero. The unemployment rate—the number of unemployed as a fraction of all those of working age and either working or looking for work—is remarkably stable over time and across regions and countries, except during recessions when it spikes, as we saw with the 38 million jobless claims in the United States due to the COVID-19 pandemic in the spring of 2020.

There are some notable exceptions, like Spain, with outlandish unemployment rates, and yes, unemployment is higher in recessions and lower in good times. Overall, though, there have been no major changes in the unemployment rate in recent decades; most economies have unemployment rates fluctuating between 5 and 10 percent. Yet, one of the most striking facts about work is that across countries there are enormous differences in job and employment security. The Anglo-Saxon countries (the United States, the United Kingdom, Canada, Australia, and New Zealand) and the Scandinavian countries tend to have the highest employment security (short unemployment duration) and the lowest job security (short job duration). The Mediterranean countries are at the other extreme (long job duration, long unemployment duration).

The United States is the absolute outlier at the top of those underwater currents, and Italy is at the bottom. And the differences are simply mind boggling. The United States has a median unemployment duration of about nine weeks (just over two months), whereas in Italy it is close to a year. And, of course, jobs in Italy on average last over twenty years, whereas in the United States they last about four years.[13]

Even at the surface (the unemployment rate), where these economies look similar, the undercurrents hide enormous differences. For example, youth unemployment in southern Europe is enormously high because it takes over a year on average to find any job and several years to find a first job fresh out of school. And older workers who are laid off past the age of fifty take a long time to enter a new job, and they are often forced into early retirement. The Mediterranean job security is nice work if you can get it, but it is a disaster for those who can't because it causes employment insecurity, which is especially calamitous for young and aging workers.

The bottom line is that in normal times without big structural changes in supply and demand, only as many new jobs are created as old jobs are destroyed. Legislation and policy can change the duration of jobs (for example, tilting the balance either toward job security at the detriment of employment security). But there is little policymakers can do to change unemployment, despite the constant political rhetoric about creating jobs. Jobs are more like taxi rides than owning a car. Politicians spend money giving citizens cars, but what people need are taxi rides, and that is what firms give us.

The job creator par excellence is business dynamism and innovation. Unfortunately, as we have discovered from the Gold Watch myth, market power is a drag on startups, innovation, and worker mobility. The game of musical chairs is increasingly played to the tune of slow crooners. Even the ultravibrant Anglo-Saxon and Scandinavian labor markets are atrophying under the greedy weight of dominant firms with moats. To improve employment outcomes, therefore, we need to tackle market power.

Now that we have the necessary facts on which to base policy, we turn in the next chapter to concrete proposals on how to rein in market power and how to drain the moats and fill them with rocks and sand.

12

Putting the Trust Back into Antitrust

MARKETS DO NOT WORK WELL in a vacuum: they do well when there is an institutional framework that supports the free exchange of goods without the danger of theft, expropriation, unbridled inflation, and political whims that create economic uncertainty. That is the major point made by Daron Acemoglu and James Robinson in their book *Why Nations Fail*.[1]

Well-functioning markets require a set of legal norms that ensure that property rights are respected and enforced in the case of violations. In the Bronze Age (3000 BC–1200 BC), free trade started to prosper in the Cyclades and Mesopotamia mainly due to the invention of bronze tools and weapons that made a military force possible and effective. This ensured that the exchange of goods with the resulting gains from trade was duly protected. For free markets to prosper, legal institutions are necessary—there is nothing free about markets in the first place. If markets were totally free, everything would be stolen.

Like in the Bronze Age, the markets in today's capitalist societies need a legal system that protects property rights and enforces the law. Because this is guaranteed in advanced economies—which is why those economies have managed to become advanced—free markets as we know them from textbooks work well. Adam Smith's "invisible hand" leads to prosperity. Individuals acting in their own self-interest is also in the interest of the greater public good. Free markets have given us wealth and brought billions out of poverty in less than a century.

But an institutional framework that guarantees law and order is not sufficient for all markets to work well. In too many markets, new technologies fundamentally transform how and what is produced, and this leads to failure of the invisible hand, just like in Chaplin's *Modern Times* a century ago. As we discussed earlier, network externalities, economies of scale, markets with free goods, and consumers with behavioral biases all lead to less-than-optimal outcomes and market failure. Often those are economic places with fierce competition *for* the market and virtually no competition *in* the market. The winner takes the entire market while being shielded by a massive moat from competitors.

Addressing these market failures requires institutions to protect not only property rights, like in the Bronze Age, but also the institutions that regulate the market. The idea that capitalism and free markets work without regulation is as big a misconception as the idea that free markets work without a legal framework and a police force to guarantee that property rights are respected.

The necessity of regulation is ubiquitous. In 2018 and 2019, within a six-month period, two Boeing 737 MAX planes crashed minutes after takeoff, killing everyone on board. In both cases the pilot lost control of the aircraft as it made sharp vertical movements. Later it became evident that this was due to the malfunctioning of the anti-stall software system that automatically lowers the nose without pilot action, especially at low speed. The 737 MAX was a new model aircraft and had been operational for just over a year before the first crash, of Lion Air Flight 610 in Indonesia, which killed 189 people. The day before a different pilot crew with one additional pilot experienced a similar loss of control on the same aircraft, but the third pilot diagnosed the problem and managed to disable the flight-control system. Following the second crash in Nairobi, Kenya, of Ethiopian Airlines Flight 302, killing 157 people, aviation authorities around the world grounded all 737 MAX aircraft.

From the investigation it has transpired that Boeing knew about the control issues even before the first aircraft rolled out. Under the existing design, there was only one probe taking measurements and no scope for correction in the case of erroneous readings. Boeing was downplaying these issues in communications with the regulator. It was in the interest of Boeing and its shareholders to convince the aviation authorities that the plane was safe. Adding a second probe and updating the software would be expensive and would delay the delivery of many of the planes. Even after the first plane went down, Boeing continued to argue that the crash was not due to the software or probe failure. To make things worse, pilots were not informed that the anti-stall software was installed until after the Lion Air crash. In a closed-door meeting after the crash, pilot representatives pushed Boeing for measures that would have likely led to an immediate grounding of the model. The Boeing executives resisted.

In this case, regulation ensures that private information hidden from the customer is evaluated by an independent party, the regulator. There is a fundamental tension between the economic interest of Boeing and the best interest of the customer. Admitting the problem early on meant delays in delivery and huge economic costs. Boeing was taking a gamble that the problem would be minor, and they lost. Still, even though Boeing's stock price suffered, especially after the second crash, with an 11 percent drop, the economic damage was remarkably small.

The free marketeer view on regulation argues that any market failure will be taken care of by the market. Rogue aircraft producers would have more crashes and would eventually go out of business. A firm's value depends on its reputation. But it is naive to think that customers will personally investigate the safety of a complex machine like an aircraft. Perhaps private safety agencies could sell safety reports, but they would have their own incentives to make money, as we saw with the financial rating agencies during the Great Recession.

That the airline industry (or any other industry, for that matter) will self-regulate is wishful thinking. The incentives to gamble are too high, the sophisticated machines are of unbounded complexity, and there is too much private information and scope for misrepresentation of the facts in the development process. Building unsafe aircraft has a huge return if no accident happens and Boeing makes a killing in the stock market. But if there is a genuine safety issue, even with low probability,

Boeing kills the families that fly with them. In the worst case Boeing goes bankrupt, but from a gambler's viewpoint the gains outweigh the losses. The result is unsafe air travel.

In any market that does not induce firms to make the decisions that ensure the level of safety that society demands, there is a need for regulation. If there was not a Food and Drug Administration, there would be plenty of deaths from people eating poisoned food and from patients using medication that has not been tested and shown to have the desired curative effects without undesired side effects.

The need for regulation in society has never been more acute than under the social distancing measures during the COVID-19 pandemic. Even if social distancing impeded trade and temporarily closed markets, it was necessary to minimize the lives lost and the long-term economic damage. Clearly, no market can properly price a spreading virus. After all, a restaurant owner does not take into account the economic cost they impose on all patrons who spread the virus and infect people who didn't have a meal there. A fast-spreading virus is the epitome of an externality, as economists call it, and these externalities can only be contained with some form of government intervention or regulation.

Regulation is needed not only to ensure health and safety, but also when firms create market power. In chapter 3 we discussed the circumstances in which platforms such as eBay's led to failure of the market to function in the best interests of all. To create pro-competitive regulation in circumstances where the free market fails to be competitive is the objective of antitrust institutions.

Monopoly in History

The word "monopoly" has its origin in the Ancient Greek word *monopōlion* (composed of *mónos* ["alone" or "single"] and *poleîn* ["to sell" or "seller"]). The word was adopted into Latin in the mid-sixteenth century and defined as "exclusive right of sale." A pure monopoly in the strict sense of the word probably does not exist, because for any good or service that is sold there is some better or worse substitute. Even

Comcast, the local US cable provider that had virtual monopoly power in many local markets in the 1990s, faced competition from satellite television.

Historically, regulation was implemented to *create* monopoly rather than to cure it. Most monopolies, in fact, were established by legal privilege, granting exclusive rights to sell goods or services, either as a gift to royal favorites or as compensation for some service a firm had rendered. Often the monopoly grantee had to agree on pricing and other restrictions, such as on alcohol and tobacco. The firm did not face competition, sold goods at high prices, and made profits. Some of those profits were shared with the monarch, either by providing the crown with the exclusive goods or by paying royalties. The firm and the crown were better off, but the customers and society were worse off. Customers paid higher prices and fewer customers purchased the goods, creating a loss to society.

The 1623 Statute of Monopolies in England was a first move toward a patent system, where monopoly rights were granted to reward innovation. The Dutch and British East India Companies, for example, were granted exclusive trading rights in goods from the colonies, such as the spice trade. Initially there surely were grounds for incentivizing ventures to discover unknown markets around the globe, but once markets were established, the East India Companies fully exerted their monopoly privilege and thwarted any competition. That led to protests and revolts.

One such revolt was the Boston Tea Party against Britain in December 1773, which was one of the causes of the American Revolutionary War. The main motivation behind the revolt was the Tea Act of 1773. The Tea Act relieved the British East India Company from taxes, effectively granting the company monopoly power to trade tea in the American colonies. Put simply, what led to the Revolutionary War started out as a revolt against the market power that the British East India Company exerted in America.

In these historical examples, monopoly and market power are the results of legal privilege where one sole company or group of companies has exclusive rights to selling in a market, which gives it complete control over that market. It is a form of what economists call "rent extraction" by a sovereign power because the monopoly rights were often granted in exchange for the payment of a fee. In such cases it is often a form of taxation whereby the customer pays a higher price than the cost of the good. The producer may or may not pocket some of the excess profits, depending on how much of them accrue to the Crown.

Like those examples, many present-day monopolies are similarly sanctioned by the authorities. Patents in particular are a legal means to temporarily grant monopoly power to the owners of newly invented products. For limited duration, typically fifteen years, the owner of a patent has exclusive rights to produce and sell goods and services that require the patented technology.

Patents are not new, of course; early mentions of patents date back to Ancient Greek times.[2] The objective of granting monopoly is much more noble than mere rent extraction or an inefficient way of taxation, as in the case of the East India Companies. The reason for granting temporary monopoly power through patents is to ensure that costly upfront investments are rewarded. After all, good ideas can easily be copied, and the copier can compete against the inventor without having laid out the upfront investment.

One of the few remaining bulwarks of monopoly explicitly granted by the government are patents. The reason is that the US Constitution was very weary of the British monopolistic institutions that were beneficial for London's royal coffers but were detrimental to the entrepreneurs and citizens in the American colonies. The Founding Fathers considered incorporating antimonopoly wording in the Constitution, and some lawyers consider the Equal Protection Clause in the Fourteenth Amendment as a stance against monopolies that get special protections under the law. One generous interpretation is that the independence of the United States as a nation is founded in the fight against government-sanctioned monopoly.

Despite the noble antimonopoly origins of the United States as a nation, the current patent system has gone haywire, so much so that some experts have called for the complete abolition of patents altogether.[3] One big problem is that it is a one-size-fits-all system. A fifteen-year monopoly is granted for the invention of a vaccine that cures malaria as well as for a piece of wireless technology in a smartphone. The use of smartphone technology is much shorter-lived and doesn't open up to competition until the technology is already outdated. Moreover, mobile devices are full of patent-protected technologies that require large companies with deep pockets, such as Apple and Samsung, to be able to buy the rights to produce devices with that patented technology.

The patent system is often gamed to make minor modifications to obtain extensions. There is mounting evidence that large firms create patent thickets around their intellectual property portfolios, exploiting patent legislation to build a moat.[4] Patents often have become a tool to build and maintain market power, especially in fast-moving, complex technologies such as communications. Rather than rewarding new ideas with a temporary monopoly, patents allow large communications device companies to build an intricate web of obstacles to competitors. While the idea of property rights protection in order to induce innovation is laudable, the patent system is not fine-tuned to modern-day innovation and often creates more distortions than it alleviates.

Corporate America, or at least part of it, has managed to turn the patent system, designed full of noble intentions to stimulate innovation, into excavators that dig moats. The evidence is mesmerizing. In 2018, 339,992 patents were issued in the United States, compared to 66,170 in 1980.[5] At face value the rise in patents may appear to be a wonderful development, as it is a sign of increased innovation and technological progress. But before we get the champagne out, let's take a look at the sobering reality. Out of the 4,700 patent lawsuits filed in the United States in 2012, 62 percent involved patent trolls, compared to 19 percent in 2006.[6] A patent troll is a firm whose exclusive raison d'être is to make money from obtaining patents and to find firms and citizens they can sue. In other words, patent trolls do not make any money from producing anything with the patents; they don't even invent the patent. They typically look for existing inventions that are already making money but for which no patent has been issued. The patent troll then makes those firms or individuals who invented the idea pay for the use of the patent.

Software patents in particular are the target of trolls because they can be defined broadly with a vague description. It often means that getting the patent today pays off in the future when new technologies are developed that fit the description of today's patent. Even though it is legal, the practice of looking for someone else's new technology and fitting it to vaguely defined past patents is totally contrary to the spirit and philosophy of patent legislation. This legalized intellectual property fraud works because patent litigation is expensive, and the trolls know that firms prefer to settle rather than delay further developments of their technologies. The trolls therefore find the maximum settlement amount firms are willing to pay to avoid continuing litigation. As a result, 90 percent of all patent lawsuits are settled.

To stimulate innovation when competitors can copy new technologies, society needs to reward those who make the investments. But is creating an artificial monopoly the best way to give such rewards? There are alternatives without the cost of monopoly, one of which is to incentivize innovation through prizes. Arguably one of the most pressing technological breakthroughs in history was incentivized with a cash prize in exchange for the freely available technology.

In 1707, four Royal Navy warships sank off the Isles of Scilly with the loss of between 1,400 and 2,000 lives; it is one of the worst maritime disasters in naval history. While pendulum clocks existed, they require stable positioning and are therefore of no use for timekeeping on ships, where accurate time is essential to determine longitude (the position of stars only allows you to deduce the exact longitudinal position if you also know the exact time). In an attempt to secure commercial and defense maritime traffic, in 1714 the British Parliament established the Longitude Prize, a £20,000 prize (worth nearly £3 million today[7]), as a reward for a practical method to determine longitude at sea. It took the carpenter John Harrison a lifetime to develop his H4 sea watch, and he didn't receive the full reward until 1773, when he was eighty years old. The main components of his invention are still used in mechanical watches today.

While prizes have their own issues—it is difficult to establish whether an invention truly satisfies the stated objectives, and whether the government can know how to set the prize to induce innovating firms to make the right investment—they have one huge advantage. Once invented, there is no patent that grants monopoly rights for exclusive production by the inventor, and the innovation can be used by competitors at no cost. The government finances the invention and then guarantees the full use of the invention by competing producers. Imagine if the World Health Organization or the US Food and Drug Administration had awarded a prize to the pharmaceutical company that first came up with the COVID-19 vaccine. We would have had dozens, if not hundreds, of producers simultaneously manufacturing vaccines in December 2020. There would be plenty of capacity of production, and the vaccine would be sold at competitive prices and delivered nearly instantaneously to the entire population. The world would have been vaccinated much faster. The economic and health cost of the monopoly power that derives from the patent system is outlandish.

But the patent system is the only system we currently have. While patents are meant to increase innovation, they can have the opposite effect. We can learn as much from a remarkable decision that Tesla, the maker of electric vehicles, made. In 2014 they decided to put all their information technology in the public domain and thus make their hardware and software open source. With access by other producers to the technology, one would expect a poorer performance by Tesla. Still, the effect on investment in the industry could go in both directions. The cost for competitors is lower, which might increase investment. Moreover, with lower barriers to enter the market, competition might further lower manufacturing costs. However, it may also lead to lower investment because competitors can freeride on Tesla's investment. Research shows that the overall effect was beneficial for both Tesla and the entire industry of electric vehicles.[8] Most surprising is that Tesla was made better off. The reason is that there are plenty of spillovers from innovation. And with short-lived innovations and quick improvements in software, for example, Tesla benefited from the innovations by others that were building on Tesla's early breakthroughs.

But patents are the last holdout of government-sanctioned monopoly. Present-day monopoly is protected by moats that are built by the monopolists themselves.

Antitrust: A Hard Problem

As a former antitrust official under President Franklin D. Roosevelt, Wendell Berge's view on monopoly shows how hard a problem antitrust can be: "The weapons of monopoly are as numerous as they are artful and varied. It is for this reason that monopoly conditions have often grown up almost unnoticed by the public until one day it is suddenly realized that an industry is no longer competitive but is governed by an economic oligarchy able to crush all competition."[9]

There is no panacea to resolving market power. There are no ready-made solutions, especially knowing that a large number of experts who think about antitrust for a living do not find easy solutions. Those experts include the employees, lawyers, and judges at the competition authorities; the experts working for the consulting firms that advise on mergers; and academic economists working on problems in antitrust and industrial organization. Many of those experts think hard about what can be done. An excellent review of the state of antitrust enforcement is the recent book by Jonathan Baker, *The Antitrust Paradigm*.[10] While you are not reading a book about antitrust, antitrust is at the root of resolving market power, which in turn is causing the major problems that work faces in modern times.

A simple, straightforward solution to market power that might come to mind is to tax a firm's profits. While this raises revenue that can be distributed to those who suffer from market power, it does not take away the source of the problem, that firms charge prices that are too high. If Apple makes $100 billion in profits by selling iPhones at $1,200 each, then even if the corporate tax rate goes from 10 percent to 80 percent, Apple will still sell the iPhone at $1,200—even with higher taxes it wants to set a price that generates the highest possible profits. When European authorities went after Apple's profits hidden in Ireland in 2014 there were major distributional implications, but it did not do anything to reduce the root cause of market power and high prices.

While taxing profits has some effect on investment and incentives for executives,[11] it has mainly distributional implications only. And contrary to what you often hear in the public opinion, maintaining high profits for firms is not an objective for society. Profits are there to reward investment, but excess profits will always be driven down to the bare minimum when the market is competitive. As Adam Smith eloquently advocated: "Consumption is the sole end and purpose of all production; and the interest of the producer ought to be attended to, only so far as it may be necessary for promoting that of the consumer."[12]

The reason, of course, is that consumers are best off under the lowest possible prices. Any profits the firm makes are transferred to the consumer when prices drop, so nothing is lost from lowering prices at the cost of lower profits. To the contrary, the added benefit of low prices is that more customers can afford to buy, which is the real gain of competition. The so-called consumer surplus is highest: prices are low and the number of buyers is maximal.

Moreover, when markets are competitive the corporate tax rate is irrelevant because there are barely any profits. Because corporate taxes can't attack the cause of market power, competition authorities have a complicated job. Regulation has to resort to more sophisticated measures that restore competition.

The most visible antitrust action often discussed in the media is merger review. When two firms merge, or one firm acquires another firm, the merging firms are reviewed under certain circumstances by the relevant government authority. In the United States that is typically the Federal Trade Commission (FTC) or the Department of Justice (DOJ).

Both authorities share the enforcement of civil antitrust laws, where the Antitrust Division of the DOJ can also enforce criminal matters. The FTC was set up by Woodrow Wilson in 1914 together with the Clayton Antitrust Act to rein in the powers of the trusts that were engaging in unfair competition. This legislation was building on earlier legislation, most notably the 1890 Sherman Antitrust Act, which is still the main legal basis of antitrust enforcement.

In the European Union (EU), each country has its own competition authority, but European competition law that promotes a competitive European single market is directed from the executive branch, the

European Commission. Procedures are different across continents, but the basic principles are common.

For example, in 2018 AT&T acquired the media company Time Warner. This deal had to be approved by the DOJ in the United States and by several antitrust authorities around the world where either of the companies is active. In such proceedings the justice ruling on the case hears arguments presented by the attorney general of the DOJ's Antitrust Division who argues the case for the US customers, while AT&T's lawyers argue the case for the company. The judge can rule to stop the acquisition, they can ask AT&T to divest (or sell off) some businesses that generate dominance in some markets—there was talk of divesting DirectTV or Turner Broadcasting, the owner of CNN—or they can approve the acquisition.

Key in these rulings and the antagonistic judicial system is of course the subjective views that each of the parties defends. Those views and facts differ, depending on the interests of each party arguing their case. In addition, there is also an active academic and policy debate, often linked to schools of thought. However . . .

There Are No Schools of Thought

There are only indvidual thinkers with an opinion and research to back up their claims. Still, in the quest for organizing ideas, the antitrust debate is often painted as a war between two ideological views, impersonated by two schools of thought, the Brandeisian school and the Chicago school. Moreover, these schools are often associated with simplistic political views of left and right. The reality is much more nuanced, not only because of the disagreement within each of these schools but also because many scholars and practitioners do not identify with either of them. At the risk of grossly oversimplifying, and with the irresponsibility of perpetuating this simplistic view, let me nonetheless reproduce how people often refer to these two broad schools of thought on antitrust.

The Brandeisian school of thought argues that monopoly and market power per se is bad. These views are based on ones initially formulated by Louis Brandeis.[13] Brandeis, who became a Supreme Court justice under President Woodrow Wilson, argued that monopolies and large firms were harming competitors, customers, and the firms' workers. He also pointed out that large monopolistic firms had a detrimental effect on innovation.

The Brandeisian view was formed at the beginning of the twentieth century—modern times—a time of high market power. The excess concentration of corporate wealth became so salient that it took President Theodore Roosevelt to break up those corporations and trusts that had cemented that market power. In his "Square Deal," Roosevelt advocated his three C's, for conservation, control of corporations, and consumer protection. He was in favor of trusts and organized labor but against the exploitation of market power by either. Roosevelt fought to regulate the fiefdom of the robber barons.

It was during the period of Roosevelt's presidency that Brandeis formed his opinion on antitrust. Large firms were considered harmful because they exerted market power, even if those firms were operating more efficiently. Most importantly, Brandeis argued that the concentration of market power and large firms was detrimental for innovation, stymied business dynamism, and hurt workers and suppliers. Brandeis labeled it "the Curse of Bigness." Moreover, large, profitable firms had enough cash to influence the political decisions in their favor, which led to even more consolidation and dominance.

Just after World War II, the Brandeisian view was prominently associated with Harvard, and therefore sometimes called the Harvard school. Up until the 1970s, Harvard and their structural approach dominated the era of activist antitrust enforcement, inspired by the works of Edward Chamberlain, Edward Mason, and Joe Bain, who argued that the simple fact of market concentration—that few firms hold the majority of the market share—leads to anticompetitive conduct.[14]

The half century following the Great Depression had been a period of low concentration and low market power. Still, the Brandeisian school would soon lose the fight for ideological dominance to the Chicago school in the early 1980s. In recent years, though, with mounting evidence of rising market power and concentration, the Brandeisian view has regained some of that lost luster, most notably with an article by legal scholar Lina Khan that has drawn attention to the broad impact of Amazon's monopoly power on suppliers, competitors, workers, and customers.[15]

One of the main criticisms of the Brandeisian school is that they advocate for competition per se and for keeping those inefficient producers artificially alive. Having competitors lowers prices only if those competitors are similarly productive. When some producers are much less productive than the leader—for example, Amazon in retail—it is as if those inefficient producers do not exist because they cannot really compete with the leader. That is both costly and ineffective.

By the late 1970s, the Chicago school started to gain prominence with a litigation approach that was built on empirical evidence. Lawyers such as Richard Posner and Robert Bork, and economists such as George Stigler, Arnold Harberger and Milton Friedman, all associated with the University of Chicago, believed that business should be let free. When a firm charges a price that is too high and generates abnormal profits, other firms will step in and compete to grab some of the profits. Usually, losses to consumers are very small—measured by the reputed Harberger's triangle of deadweight loss—and if there are any profits, this is merely an issue of redistribution, not of inefficiencies. If needed, profits can easily be taxed and redistributed.

But there are subtle differences even within the Chicago school. Milton Friedman, for example, wrote extensively on the role of the American Medical Association (AMA) in thwarting competition. Putting the main lobby of medical doctors in charge of regulating entry in the market for doctors leads to too little entry of new doctors, too little competition, and wages that are too high. In chapter 4, where we discussed the impact of licensing, we saw how too little entry affects health care.

The argument that the AMA puts forward is that only they can select the best doctors and that health care is too precious and has too much impact on people's lives to leave this unguarded by those in the know. This is a fine objective, but it does not rule out that those experts have enormous incentives to look after their own wallets. The result is AMA-sponsored regulation to create market power under the guise of efficiency. Friedman of the Chicago school argued fiercely against the AMA's self-regulation.[16]

The government has tried out the idea of letting industry regulate itself in other markets, too. In addition to the AMA, there are two other notable examples that Self-Regulatory Organizations (SROs) are detrimental to customers, if not to our health. The National Association of Realtors ensures that home buyers pay 6 percent agent fees, higher than in other countries; and the Financial Industry Regulatory Authority's oversight of brokerage firms and exchange markets leads to inefficiently high fees and lack of transparency.

If we extend the AMA's argument of SROs to other leaders and decision makers, such as the executives of, say, the tech firms, then we are supposed to believe that the CEOs of Google, Apple, and Facebook should regulate their industries in order to ensure a competitive outcome. It is no surprise that they will not do what is in society's best interest, knowing that their shareholders (often the executives themselves) reward them on making profits, and there is no better way to do that than by creating and maintaining market power.

The differences within the Chicago school became most notable during the debate over the breakup of the telecom giant AT&T, which began in 1974 and eventually led to the creation of the Baby Bells in 1984. Some Chicago economists had argued in favor of the breakup. Instead, the Chicago school's legal scholars made a case against it. They were relying on Harberger's work, which had provided a theoretical framework and evidence that the welfare loss of market power was small.[17] The period on which his evidence was based was one of high competitiveness and low market power and, most importantly, very few large, superstar firms. Those results do not necessarily hold up in the current economy.

The nonmonolithic nature of the Chicago school in the half century after World War II is made even more manifest by the fact that some prominent members changed their views over time. Initially, Milton Friedman and George Stigler were in favor of government intervention and strong antitrust enforcement in order to ensure more competition. They both moderated those views because they came to believe that the antitrust apparatus was hijacked by those who were benefiting from it. In the end, Friedman and Stigler saw antitrust regulation as more harmful to competition than no regulation at all.[18]

There is no better way to illustrate the internal division within the Chicago school than with the atmosphere that used to hang over the machine room where economic ideas and ideology are produced and taught. In the late 1980s, George Stigler and Lester Telser were coteaching PhD classes. Students called these classes "I hate government" and "I hate monopoly." Telser disagreed with almost everything Stigler thought about market power. According to Telser, large fixed costs in railroads, for example, imply that unregulated competition is ruinous. Stigler advocated against government intervention. Students asked Telser before the exam: "How should we answer questions on market power?" Telser responded: "Try to figure out who asked the question."[19]

Despite the divisions within the Chicago school and the eventual breakup of AT&T, the legal scholars obtained the upper hand. The most influential figure in policy circles was Robert Bork, who is best known for almost becoming a Supreme Court justice (he was nominated by Ronald Reagan but voted down by the Senate). He studied at the University of Chicago and was a professor at Yale Law School, where he was an advocate of originalism, the view that aligns with the Founding Fathers' "literal" understanding of the US Constitution.

Bork became the dominant antitrust scholar following the publication of his book *The Antitrust Paradox* in 1978, in which he argues that what matters for antitrust enforcement is not guaranteeing competition but rather consumer welfare.

The appeal of his argument is that if firms are large because they are efficient, then the regulator should not intervene in those markets and regulate those large firms. In fact, he argues that a firm is large *because* it is efficient. Regulation that breaks up the large firm into multiple small firms will lower efficiency and hence artificially raise prices. A paradox. This argument is particularly relevant today with the emergence of dominant firms such as Amazon. Amazon is so large because it is efficient.

While the main argument in Bork's book continues to have merit, especially when it comes to dealing with dominance due to technological superiority or network effects, Bork's view is too simplistic. If there are economies of scale, for example, firms still price their goods noncompetitively and exert market power. This requires regulatory intervention.

What is alarming is that since the 1980s, Bork's dogma has infiltrated antitrust enforcement across a large array of cases. First, large and efficient firms still exert market power, so regulation rather than splitting them up is typically required. Second, many firms are large not because of technological superiority but because of mergers and acquisitions (M&A). It is no technological advantage that thousands of beer brands are held by two companies, or that the Match Group, Inc. owns forty-five global dating companies (including Tinder, Match.com, and OkCupid), except that it allows these companies to set higher prices.

As a result of Bork's influence, merger guidelines were relaxed and the sole criterion for allowing mergers was consumer welfare, not the effect on suppliers or workers, for example. Interestingly enough, consumer welfare is not even mentioned in the legislation on which antitrust regulation is based, namely the Sherman Antitrust Act (1890) and the FTC and Clayton Acts (1914). Following Bork, attorneys general at the DOJ need to argue that merger activity leads to abuse of dominance and that it harms the customer.

Not only is this a tall order, it is hard to construct and calculate with sufficient certainty what the outcome will be of a merger that has not happened yet. Predicting the market environment in the hypothetical case of a merger requires a lot of assumptions with a wide range of potential outcomes that can all be very different. In this environment, the lawyers for merging firms argue that there are enormous cost reductions resulting from mergers, the so-called synergies. Those synergies, the lawyers of the merging firms argue, will be passed on to customers because firms will lower their prices when costs fall.

The reality of antitrust litigation is less idealistic. According to a study by Deloitte, the total economic value (synergies) claimed by merging firms is $1.6 to $1.9 trillion, the equivalent of Canada's gross domestic product (GDP).[20] However, there is ample evidence that market power has increased since 1980 and that markups rise in markets where mergers have taken place, without evidence of efficiency gains.[21] What is most damning of all is that merger review activity has dramatically declined. The number of cases brought against mergers went from an average of 15.7 cases per year during the period from 1970 to 1999 to 3 cases during the period from 2000 to 2014.[22] The Chicago school's insistence on using evidence in litigation had turned into a contest of convincing judges of soft projections rather than bringing on hard scientific facts.

The current antitrust system that is supposed to police competitive behavior is based on noncompetitive principles. Self-interested parties can argue their cases for what the benefits and losses are without a clear incentive structure to discipline those arguments. One of Friedrich Hayek's claims about the pitfalls of a planned economy is that prices are tremendously distorted. Self-interested actors in the economy will claim excessive valuations, something that does not occur in a competitive economy where competing suppliers undercut a firm's outlandish claims. It seems that the antitrust system looks more like a planned economy with apparatchiks in the merging firms whose claims are not disciplined by the market.

This system, devoid of competitive forces to value costs and benefits, is reminiscent of what happened to the selling off of broadband licenses for radio and mobile communication. Until the late 1990s, those licenses were assigned and priced in an arbitrary manner. Companies claimed that the values of the licenses were low. This changed drastically when the government started organizing the so-called spectrum auctions— selling off the broadband spectrum—where all providers bid competitively. Those auctions were huge successes not just for the government and its citizens, but also because they were a testament to the value of competition. Government officials immediately figured out that the supposedly low valuations they had been convinced of in earlier years disappeared into thin air when the providers could only operate a licensed mobile service if they bid the highest in a competitive auction. For a long time, economists have argued that competition enables a much more accurate valuation than simply letting self-interested parties argue their case.

While the juxtaposition of the Chicago and Brandeisian schools is still present in the debate, it is far too simplistic and outdated. Many practitioners and academics do not identify with either of the two. For example, there is an important constituency that critiques the Chicago views as wrong on the economics. These views attach fundamental importance in our understanding of market power to the game theory revolution in industrial organization where strategic interaction between competitors and customers is crucial in understanding the sources of market power. This in turn led to another Copernican revolution in modern empirical research, begun in the early 1990s, that identified market power founded in carefully specified market descriptions and the conduct of competitors.[23]

Yet, these critics of the Chicago view do not automatically subscribe to the Brandeisian view either. Quite to the contrary, they take a third view. A prominent example in this recent tradition is the Thurman Arnold Project at Yale. It is named for the assistant attorney general of the Franklin D. Roosevelt administration in the late 1930s and early 1940s, who launched a trust-busting campaign, to the dismay of President Roosevelt, who promoted him out of the DOJ's Antitrust Division into the US Court of Appeals.

To date, and despite the apparent differences between the Chicago school and the Brandeisian school, economists are in remarkable agreement about what constitutes monopoly, market power, and inefficiencies. Most economists see the virtues of market competition, yet they accept that regulation is necessary when the free market fails. The contention among economists is rather the question of how to best remedy those inefficiencies. A key concern in the debate is that even if regulation is needed, it has the potential to make things worse because it can create perverse incentives where firms exploit the regulation to build even more market power than without the regulation. To make things even worse, political influence leads to legislation that is in the interest of the regulated and is therefore counterproductive. This points to the inadequacy of the political system to implement effective regulation that restores competition.

The Vicious Circle of Market Power
and Political Influence

Even if there is agreement on the negative impact of market power, the opposing views on how to deal with regulation are made into a caricature by those with skin in the game. Among interest groups and lobbyists, the language is often misleading. Those against regulation tend to call themselves pro-business and argue that government interference is bad and anti-competitive. But when markets fail, the absence of regulation does exactly the opposite; it makes room for market power or anti-competitive behavior. Therefore, a so-called pro-business view of regulation leads to noncompetitive outcomes.

Instead, the pro-market view argues that whenever there is market failure, regulation is necessary to ensure that markets are competitive. The Chicago view in its purest form is pro-market, not pro-business. Still, the pro-business view hijacks the Chicago argument, in part by falsely claiming that markets are competitive and that no regulation is needed. Moreover, the central principle of the pro-business view is that what is good for business is good for the economy. Under this view, when firms make profits, those profits eventually lead to more jobs, not fewer, and to higher wages. We have shown that the opposite is true. That is precisely the profit paradox.

When the pro-business view does recognize that there is market power, it argues against intervention because regulation does more bad than good and distorts the market even further. In response, the pro-business view often offers regulation with an additional twist: self-regulation. The claim is that companies themselves can ensure pro-competitive behavior by self-imposed restrictions, but it stands squarely against the central tenet of Smith's invisible hand to ask firms not to act in their self-interest and maximize profits. Self-regulation requires firms to make lower profits and to take actions that are in the interest of competitors and stakeholders, such as customers and workers. Who believes that Google and Facebook will self-regulate the tech sector in order to attain pro-market prices and low profits? This is like asking the Koch family, who own most of the coal industry in North America, to reduce CO_2 emissions.

Currently, rather than self-regulate in order to reduce market power, the large corporations are doing exactly the opposite: they are exploiting the political system to help write regulation that increases rather than decreases their dominance. The influence of interested parties on legislation occurs in all spheres of society, but it is most acutely problematic when it comes to market power because it creates a vicious circle.

Political influence requires money, and money is precisely what dominant firms with market power have. So what do they use the money for? To lobby for legislation that consolidates and increases their market power, generating even higher profits for them. This is a vicious circle that gives firms with market power profits, and profits give them the money to influence politics, to buy even more market power. That in turn generates more profits.

It will come as no surprise that the big tech companies spend vast amounts of money on lobbying in order to influence legislation in their favor. No one is spending that money representing the duped customers or the workers whose wages stagnate due to rising market power.

Even if there was perfect agreement among specialists on how to implement regulation in order to reduce market power, the vicious circle of a few firms with market power buying even more market power would forcefully overturn those consensual recommendations that are in the interest of the entire economy.

Before I make concrete proposals for a solution to the broad problem of market power, I will zoom in on the solution to one particular problem for new technologies, data. In chapter 10 we saw that artificial intelligence (AI) and data hoarding are ideal sources to create market power. To that end, I argue the case for regulation that induces data sharing.

Data as a Public Good

The phenomenon of self-driving cars is an example where the initial data collection effort combined with the continuous learning process by itself is an extremely expensive operation. These algorithms only work if there are millions of observations, so it takes an enormous investment in time and resources to generate the data from which to learn. This creates a barrier to entry for competitors. Everyone in the industry agrees that having access to data, not the software, is the key to gaining a competitive advantage. When Google generously offered to make some of its AI code openly available, they were implicitly confirming that it is all about the data. You do not gain advantage over the competition with code: you gain advantage with data, lots of big data.

According to Hal Varian, the academic and chief economist of Google, data is like calories. "We used to be data poor, now the problem is data obesity."[24] The problem is not so much that there is too much data, but that it is distributed unequally. Some companies, like Google, have access to a glut of data while others are starving. Even the Big Five tech firms are complaining that their competitors are faster at hoarding all the data, and this creates a disadvantage for the one arriving second. This is a true winner-take-all market.

The tech firms are keen to get into cloud computing because it is another way to collect data. For whatever data projects you or your firm have, you need a data pipeline to channel the data. Instead of building your own data infrastructure and buying servers, you can rent space on cloud providers such as Amazon Web Services, Google Cloud Platform, or Microsoft Azure Cloud. Once your data is in the cloud, however, the landlord has access to your data. And since you are putting in a lot of effort to organize the data, they can even swallow the information without chewing.

Who owns data? If the data is mine as a user or contributor because I have clicked to identify a bridge in a photo, shouldn't I be the beneficiary of the value that the data generates? That is exactly what University of Chicago Law School professor Eric Posner and Microsoft economist Glen Weyl propose in their recent book *Radical Markets*, which offers a refreshing look on the role of markets.[25] The firms that benefit immensely should be held to reward the contributors of the data. They consider "Data as Labor" where you pay the data providers. The problem is that millions contribute, and however large the benefits to the tech firm that collects and exploits the data, once you divide them up by the sea of contributors, it comes down to small change. Estimates of value of data contributed by users is a few dollars per year, which makes it hard to administer.

An alternative way to induce the tech companies to compensate users for the value of their data is competition. More competition might lead social media platforms to offer rebates, or they might offer users more content. We love the services of Google and Facebook, but those companies love our data even more. Social networking sites are platforms that bring together advertisers and potential customers, just like newspapers and television channels. The platforms attract users by offering services and generate revenue by selling advertising to companies that want to draw users' attention. When a firm has monopoly power in any market, it charges more and gives less in return. In this case, platforms like Facebook and Google charge too much both to the companies running ads and to users, even if the price to users is zero.

In a competitive world, and to keep you from leaving their platform to the benefit of a competitor, tech firms will offer the user even more content—say, a Netflix or a Spotify subscription—that compensates you for the value of your data. Now, with the extra content on top of what they already offer, the zero price that you pay would be right. The reason why the current zero price plus all your data doesn't buy you all those services and content is because these companies do not face competition. Market power means that a firm offers too little in exchange for what you pay, whether that payment is in currency or in valuable data that you provide.

Note that when there is competition, this market with free apps needs no explicit intervention in order to determine that the price is right or that the package of services is adequate in exchange for your valuable data at zero price. Competitive pressure will ensure that the providers either give you financial rebates or enough services to keep you on their platform. The only intervention that is needed is for the regulator to ensure that there is enough competition between the platforms and on the platforms. That is of course easier said than done when there are huge economies of scale in these social networks. But some proven regulatory solutions exist that ensure competition without losing the benefits of scale of the network. One such solution is the concept of interoperability, to which I turn later in this chapter.

Not only is your data buying you too little in terms of services: the main problem is that those companies who have and hoard the data use the same data to create barriers for competitors to enter. Big data for use with AI and machine learning (ML) technologies is an ideal tool to build market power. And once the data moat is built, that market power is very hard to contest.

Where do we get the rocks and sand to fill in this moat? In economics lingo, data is nonrival. If one user consumes a rival good—say, food—no one else can consume it. But a nonrival good—whether it is an idea, data, or a walk in a noncongested park—does not preclude anyone else from consuming that same good; the cost to an additional user is zero. If you find out about Newton's law of universal gravitation, you know it and can explain it to someone else. If you are lucky you can sell it and make some money, but why would anyone pay for it if the laws are all over the internet and in books, and it can be spread by word of mouth at no cost?

In fact, data is not protected by copyright,[26] but owners can still keep the data private. That is where the value is. In order to encourage people to invest money in new ideas, most modern societies have a patent system, as we discussed earlier. It gives the creator temporary exclusivity rights and therefore market power. A pharmaceutical company is rewarded with a fifteen-year patent after it invents a new drug, which allows it to sell the drug at a much higher price because it has a monopoly. The profits from the monopoly are the carrot that pays for the huge upfront investment to develop the drug. This is inefficient once the drug is discovered, but it provides the necessary incentives in order to have the drug at all. And after the patent expires, competitors enter the market and drive down the price of the drug.

So if information is free and you cannot stop anyone from copying it, then what is the problem with big data for AI applications? The problem is that information is only free if someone makes it public. If Newton had hoarded the laws of gravitation we wouldn't have known about them then, and they would have had a different name as soon as someone else discovered them and made them public. The point is that despite that nonrival nature of data—that it can be consumed at no cost once it is made available—the owners of the data are hoarding it. They do everything they can to keep the data under cover—in part because it costs them a lot of money to collect it, but predominantly to avoid letting competitors use the data to train their algorithms to compete. When Google made public their algorithms, it was neither a mistake nor altruism. A truly generous act would have been to make their data available.

I therefore suggest a policy where those who collect our data to create market power are forced to make the anonymized data public. It is a sort of inverse data patent, similar to the traditional patent system as we know it now that was introduced in order to provide incentives to innovate. The point of a patent is to ensure competition after the patent expires and the idea has received a just reward for the upfront investment.

The inverse data patent creates a similar temporary reward. The difference is in what happens when the patent runs out. The traditional patent's knowledge has become freely available from the moment it was published or from the moment the first good was sold. That is why the law protects the inventor from competitors who can freely copy that knowledge. When the patent runs out, the patent holder loses that protection. Instead, the inverse data patent has information that no one can freely copy. When the inverse data patent runs out, the holder of the information must put the data in the public domain so that competitors can have free access to it. Versions of this exist in academic research. Authors of published papers must make their data and software available so that other researchers can replicate the results or use it to test new hypotheses.

Firms like Uber that collected data from their driverless cars in Tempe, Arizona, get exclusive access to it for some time, and then they need to make the data publicly available for use by competing driverless operators. Like a patent, the firm that collects the data temporarily gets the exclusive use of it. But it is the reverse of a patent because rather than granting exclusivity of an idea that can easily be copied, the inverse data patent takes away exclusivity of information that can easily be hidden.

The initial exclusivity ensures a temporary period of market power with higher prices and thus positive profits to pay for the initial costly investment. Afterward, however, because of the true nonrival nature of information, it would be available for free. And since we find strong evidence that the rise of market power extends across all industries and sectors, not just tech, those policies on data sharing may apply to other sectors where market power is driven by data.

As with the patent system, there will be plenty of distorted incentive effects, and possibly even more lawsuits. The greatest challenge will be to prevent firms from tampering with the data to make it useless or, worse, to lead the user to the wrong conclusions. Imagine that the data from driverless car accidents gives a 100 percent avoidance of an accident when swerving right, while only 50 percent when swerving left. Instead, if the data scientists tamper with the 273 cases on which this outcome is based such that it appears that veering off to the left causes no accidents while veering off to the right causes many accidents, then any company using that data will have disastrous accident numbers.

And even if there is no tampering with data, firms might gather and publish data that is of low value to competitors or that slows down their learning. Nonetheless, having access to more data in an environment where perverse incentives can be contained will be better than having access to no data at all. And as with patents, the temporary gains from monopoly power will make it worthwhile to give the incentives to collect and publish the sufficient quality data.

Like most new technological innovations throughout history, AI and ML are powerful improvements that will make life easier and will eventually save us from doing menial and boring tasks. But like many other technologies of the past, this new technology has a tendency to concentrate resources in the hands of a few. With AI and ML, that resource is the data. The problem is not that there is too much data or that we cannot process it; the problem is that a few have the data and others do not.

Unequal access to data creates huge scale advantages and, more importantly, it creates barriers to entry. As a result, the firms that own the data are able to sell their goods at prices well above cost, and there will be no competitors that can come even close to getting a foot in the door.

This concentration of productive resources in the hands of a very few is already well under way. The castles of the big tech giants are already largely protected by a data moat. And while the customer may not see the immediate link with higher prices, advertisers are paying higher prices for ads on Google, Facebook, and Instagram—and if advertisers are paying more to show you sneakers, you end up paying more to buy those sneakers.

Dealing with data in a clever manner may avoid the accumulation of market power, but this requires antitrust institutions that are effective.

Putting Back the Trust

Given the rise of market power that we have experienced in the past four decades, the existing institutions have not been able to stem the prevalence and growth of moats. There is plenty of work studying the history and workings of antitrust in detail and highlighting the difficulties and pitfalls of the current institutions. The bottom line is that the current focus on consumer welfare has not managed to rein in the rise of market power. Beginning in the 1980s, antitrust enforcement has weakened, allowing mergers to go through that shouldn't have. At the same time, in the wake of disruptive technological change, highly efficient superstar firms have emerged that exert excess market power.

That doesn't mean that what firms do now is illegal. They operate within the legal framework, which includes building moats and paying politicians to not pass legislation. As Arthur Daley, a character in the British crime drama *The Minder*, says: "Hitting little old ladies over the head and stealing their handbags is crime. Everything else is business."[27] It does indicate, however, that there is legislation and enforcement that can make the economy healthier.

Here, I propose concrete measures to reverse this ongoing trend. We can only be successful at reining in market power if we completely re-examine competition policy. The main objectives of my proposals are the following:

First, we need to go beyond the impact of market power on consumer welfare. The competition authority must also take into account the impact on all stakeholders—workers, suppliers, competitors—everyone with something to gain or lose.

Second, we need to incorporate the economy-wide implications of market power, not just the impact at the firm level. Even if Amazon is not lowering the wages of its own workers (i.e., it is not exerting monopsony power), the fact that there are hundreds of firms with market power lowers labor demand, which in turn affects the wage economywide—the falling tide. While putting workers on the boards of firms can reduce the impact of monopsony power, workers on boards cannot stop the impact of market power on economy-wide wages. That is also why social responsibility of firms will not resolve the problem. It can only be resolved by reining in market power directly—not just for one firm, but for all firms in the economy.

Third, we need to put a stop to M&A activities as we know them. Yes, there are cases where buying another firm has synergies, but in the majority of M&A cases, the main benefit is that it creates market power. Why on earth do we trick the customers into the illusion of choice of many brands—whether it is in beer, social media, or funerary services—when a handful of companies own nearly all of the brands?

Fourth, we need to embrace the impact of technological change on scale and large firms. Competition for competition's sake by artificially keeping alive inefficient firms, as those following Brandeis's ideas propose, is not helpful. Similarly, splitting up highly efficient companies is wasting all the potential of scale in order to tackle abuse of dominance. There are intermediate ways to ensure competition while keeping all the benefits of scale. One solution is the principle of interoperability, to which I will turn below. In short, interoperability exploits both the efficiencies of technology and scale while at the same time fostering competition on those efficient platforms.

In sum, I propose (1) to take into account all stakeholders; (2) to consider economy-wide implications of all firms, not just the direct effects of one firm; (3) to make M&A more difficult; and (4) to regulate large firms with scale economies without breaking them up.

More specifically, to achieve these four objectives I propose the following concrete measures. I start from the premise that government interventions that are pro-business are typically not pro-market or pro-competitive, and that the objective is to obtain pro-competitive outcomes. I will distinguish between policies that tackle market power as a result of mergers, such as the brewing giant AB InBev, and those that are the result of technological change, such as Amazon. The main difference between the two is that AB InBev has grown as a result of buying other companies, whereas Amazon (or Walmart, or Urban Outfitters) has become large because of organic growth, which is the simple process of breaking new ground and opening new operations or outlets in new locations. In the latter case, competition policy must ensure that all of the gains from scale and technological innovation are maintained while tackling the ability of firms to exploit the same innovations in order to exert market power.

Most experts agree that a lot of the antitrust regulation does not need new laws, even to address contemporaneous issues in advanced, technology-driven economies. The Sherman Antitrust Act and the FTC and Clayton Acts in the United States, and competition law in Europe, provide a perfectly suitable legal framework for the majority of antitrust issues. The rise of market power predominantly stems from the interpretation, enforcement, and implementation of the law rather than from pitfalls in the law itself.

Mergers and acquisitions lead to too much concentration, and there is little evidence that those mergers create synergies, decrease costs, and lower prices. To make M&A more difficult, we should invert the burden of proof: companies cannot merge unless they can provide evidence that the merger is beneficial. Currently firms propose to merge, and it is up to the competition authorities to find evidence that the merger is harmful. Instead, I propose that the burden of proof is on the merging parties to show that there are significant benefits.

This reversal of the burden of proof in itself might be only a minor change in the order of events, but it will make a huge difference if the implications of a merger are broadened beyond just affecting consumers and if the burden of proof is made much more stringent. If a firm wants to grow, then it is necessarily forced to do this through a competitive channel. It must first create a new operation elsewhere and compete with the existing incumbents in the output market. This is beneficial for the customer. With mergers instead, the only competitive force at work is to compete for ownership of competitors but not for customers. The customer sees no benefit of that competition for ownership. Even with mergers, firms compete *for* the market, not *in* the market.

By reversing the burden of proof and starting from the default where a merger is not allowed, mistakes will be made where a merger that does generate synergies and is beneficial to society is not allowed to proceed. Call this mistake a false negative. The issue is that currently there are way too many false positives, mergers that are allowed but should not have been. The evidence on the rise of market power is so overwhelming that the false positives are doing a lot of harm.

Particularly in a fast-changing world, mergers are a convenient vehicle for a firm to grow compared to starting new operations from scratch. But the rapid change also leads to rapid consolidation of market power. Merged firms make it hard to even imagine what competition could have been like had there been no merger.

Mark Zuckerberg notoriously argued that once WhatsApp, Instagram, and the original Facebook were all owned by Facebook, he would scramble the eggs so it would be impossible to undo the merger. The egg scrambling might involve some less-than-desirable changes. At some point there was talk that Facebook would combine Facebook Messenger, Instagram Direct Message (DM), and WhatsApp into one. It remains to be seen whether the ongoing US government lawsuit against Facebook will manage to recoup the eggs from the omelet.

First off, these different DM apps have their own value. As any teenager will tell you, there is so much information in the fact that a message is sent by WhatsApp or Instagram. You want to signal something, or you may want to insinuate things you know. Moreover, these different messaging apps have different features and privacy settings that render one app of better use when flirting than when asking for help with homework. My teenage daughters are horrified with the prospect of Instagram DM and WhatsApp merging (they do not care for Facebook Messenger, which in their eyes is for use by older generations only). Zuckerberg and his colleagues at Facebook of course understand the value of the different uses, but merging these messaging apps is too important strategically to ensure that the merger cannot be undone by antitrust. It is an effective strategy to scramble the eggs.

Reversing the burden of proof is also a way of putting more emphasis on preemptive regulation as opposed to enforcement or policing after the fact. With regulation there is less scope for egg scrambling, and possible mistakes are dealt with before the eggs are broken.

In addition to reversing the burden of proof, all mergers must be approved. Currently in the United States only mergers above $90 million need to be declared for merger review. Thomas Wollmann, a professor at the University of Chicago, calls this "stealth consolidation," the type of market power that stays under the radar. His research shows that merger activity increases sharply when there is reduced scrutiny.[28]

Mergers are, of course, not exclusively horizontal (between competitors), but also vertical (between firms at different levels of the value chain). As we saw in chapter 6, Amazon purchased the supplier of its Kiva robots because the robots had become so central in Amazon's logistics. This has had implications for innovation and competition of a successful technology. Since the takeover, Amazon decided to no longer sell the Kiva robots to competitors. The cases of vertical mergers are notoriously hard, but there is no doubt that in many situations they stifle competition and create market power. The complexity of vertical merger cases is all the more reason to build an antitrust authority with resources that can rely on specialists to analyze those mergers on a case-by-case basis.

Before I turn to the impact of technological change on market power, I have one important observation about tech firms. Even though tech firms have made enormous innovations to the benefit of the customer, they have also gained dominance from taking over competitors. The Facebook omelet is one example. Alphabet, the parent company of Google, is a superstar firm not only because of organic growth (it started with a novel technology and grew large even without taking over other firms); it also engages heavily in M&A activity to grow and create market power. Alphabet has bought one firm per month for the past eighteen years.[29]

Now, how do I propose to deal with market power that originates from technological change, where firms become large due to organic growth, like Amazon, instead of mergers? The market power of these superstar firms is a lot harder to regulate. Breaking up the firm is not the cookie-cutter solution. It may be in some isolated cases, but not in most.

A perfect example is the Microsoft antitrust case in 1999. Not only did the regulators enforce antitrust laws from 1890 and 1914 on the quintessential digital age company, the regulators used those laws to enforce antitrust action beyond the effect of prices. Robert Bork had argued that prices were the only relevant metric to measure the effect of market power. But in the Microsoft war over web browsers, the price for Explorer was zero. Explorer was bundled in the purchase of Windows, while the competing browser, Netscape, was excluded. The main point was that the regulator did not ask Microsoft and Explorer to break into two companies to ensure competition. Instead, it forced Microsoft to unbundle Explorer and give Netscape access to Microsoft's Windows operating system. Rather than breaking up companies with market power that have grown organically, the regulator fosters competition by forcing those companies to accept competitors on their platforms. This is an example of the notion of *interoperability* broadly defined; it is the best solution to deal with natural monopolies that obtain scale from technological origins.

Narrowly defined, interoperability refers to the ability of different systems to work interchangeably, and it typically refers to the realm of information technology. It can be the ability to store alphanumeric information in ASCII code, for example. Open standards and standardized protocols are all examples where different systems use the same file formats.

Firms use certain technological features to do exactly the opposite, to stymie interoperability, because it gives the firm market power. Apple, for example, has all the motivation to produce a charging adapter that can be used only on Apple products. This increases the demand for those chargers, for which they can set high prices. In order to avoid the costly waste of multiple chargers, regulators finally forced Apple to adopt a common standard to make adapters from other manufacturers work on Apple devices, despite heavy lobbying.

In its broadest definition, I use the term "interoperability" as a means to induce competition in the market rather than for the market. My monthly cell phone plan for standard service in the United States costs nearly double what it costs in Europe. This is not because the market in the United States is larger (contracts in any member state now cover the entirety of the EU) or that the service in the United States is better. For example, in the United States I cannot use my cell phone to connect my laptop via Bluetooth, unless I pay another $30 per month; in my European contract, "tethering" as such Bluetooth access is called, is included. The contract is more expensive because there is less competition in the United States.

Technology in the United States is not that different from technology in Europe, so what makes the European mobile phone market so much more competitive? It is regulation. In particular, it is what falls under this broad definition of interoperability. The source of market power in telecommunications is the highly expensive network of cell towers and infrastructure. A small competitor who wants to enter the US market needs to set up its own infrastructure of cell towers—a gargantuan investment. Moreover, when there is already a powerful incumbent who has a solid customer base, the competition for the market is already over.

What EU regulation does is stimulate competition in the market. Owners of cell towers and infrastructure are forced to allow other operators to use that technology, at a fee set by the regulator. The incumbent firm that does not want competition would set a prohibitively expensive user fee. Instead, with an appropriately set price that takes into account the true cost to the incumbent, the regulator can induce competition in the market. Like in telecom markets, similar regulation is at work in the United Kingdom for operating train services on the rail network owned by the public sector company Network Rail. Private train operators compete for lines, paying a fee to Network Rail.

The broadly defined concept of interoperability can also be applied to network platforms such as Amazon and eBay. This is of course not straightforward, and the shareholders of those companies will not accept competition on their platforms easily. Nor did Microsoft lightly accept the antitrust verdict in 1999 that prohibited them from bundling

Explorer and excluding Netscape. Even if Netscape is long gone, the customer benefit of the 1999 decision is that now you can install any internet browser on any machine, and there is stiff competition among browsers. The Microsoft case is a form of broadly defined interoperability that induces competition. Competition in these markets with network externalities can be achieved without breaking up these companies.

Breaking up companies may make sense in some cases, but when companies have scale for technological reasons, it is typically not a good idea. For some sectors, the opposite is true. For example, recent research shows that if Uber and Lyft were to join and operate on the same platform in New York City, customers would be better off.[30] This has to do with minimizing traffic congestion as much as exploiting the benefits of a large platform. Even if the joint platform is better for customers, the monopolist firm will fully exert market power and will extract rents from the customers. Therefore, the best solution is one joint platform with multiple providers competing on the same platform: interoperability. The unique platform ensures the right density of cars and network effects, and the competition on the platform ensures that prices are set competitively to the benefit of users.

Related to interoperability, but different, is the prohibition of exclusive dealing. One of the reasons why the beer market is so concentrated is that the distribution system is rigged against competition. Things vary in different countries, but in many markets bars, pubs, and restaurants are forced to sign exclusive contracts to serve beer brands from only one producer. In the United States, the three-tier system with producers, distributors, and retailers is even more restrictive: any beer brand in a local market can be sold by only one distributor. Many of those contracts are for eternity. These exclusive dealing arrangements effectively give local monopoly power.

Those local exclusive deals also help explain why large producers like AB InBev have managed to set up a globally dominant firm with monopoly power in many local markets. There is no real network aspect to beer distribution, but the exclusive deals generate network effects. An antitrust regulatory body that can undo exclusive dealing will surely lead to more competition in the beer market.

The greatest challenge for a reinvigorated competition authority is to deal with the impact of market power that reaches beyond the direct stakeholders in the firm, such as the customers and the employees, or even the suppliers. With an economy-wide rise in market power, a falling tide lowers all boats: wages fall for workers far beyond those who are employed in the firm. This equilibrium effect cannot be resolved at the firm level.

Nonetheless, more can be done to tackle market power economy wide. To that end, I propose a number of institutional changes that can achieve this. The first institutional measure gives a lot more power to a competition authority to implement mostly the same, existing legislation. More power means first the centralization of antitrust activities. To fight concentration, you need concentration of institutions that regulate antitrust.

Currently, one of the major weaknesses, most notably in the regulation of the financial sector, is the dispersion of agencies and authorities between the DOJ, the FTC, the FTC's Bureau of Consumer Protection, the Consumer Financial Protection Bureau, the Securities and Exchange Commission, and the Federal Reserve. Cash-rich corporations can always find a loophole at one of the authorities or pit them against each other. It may sound like an oxymoron, but in regulating to achieve pro-competitive behavior, having competing institutions makes regulation ineffective. To beat concentration we need a more concentrated authority.

I propose a competition authority that is modeled after the Federal Reserve System, which is designed to make the financial system work and, above all, to control inflation. The Federal Reserve is the poster child of successful economic policy around the world. Central banks in nearly all developed economies are independent of the political system, both the executive and the legislative branches. Independence is desirable because politicians are tempted to inflate the currency and look for a short-term gain (for example in the run-up to an election). This makes the politician look good in the short term, but it is costly for the economy in the long term.

Antitrust is even more subject to interference, from politicians and business leaders alike. In 2019, with the proposed merger of two industry giants, Siemens from Germany and Alstom from France, the political pressure on the European competition authorities was enormous. It took the gutsy Margreth Vestager, the Danish politician in charge of the EU competition authority at that time, to stand up and resist the political temptation.

In the United States, creating and maintaining market power is one of the main activities for lobbyists. The problem with the link between market power and campaign finance is that they reinforce each other. Firms that obtain market power generate profits and therefore the necessary cash to finance political activities to shield that market power. This leads to a vicious circle in which the more those firms can shield their market power, the more cash they have to continue financing politics. Sadly, Washington has become an ATM for large corporations with market power.

The link between market power and politics is where free markets pose a threat to democracy. The threat was there in the early 1900s with the political influence that J. P. Morgan wielded to expand his business empire. He influenced lawmakers to obtain favorable legislation that allowed him to build market power. That was, of course, until he came up against president Theodore Roosevelt. And political connections were the raison d'être of the British East India Company in the seventeenth century. The same threat to democracy is there now from the big corporations that lobby politicians on a wide range of issues, from data protection, to mergers, to rideshare regulation, which allows them to maintain and extend their position of dominance.

And it is not simply the link between politics and superstar firms— public opinion plays a key role. We are all users of Google, Facebook, and Apple products, and many of their services are offered for free. Those free services still hurt the customer because we pay with our data and our appeal to advertisers who pay for us. There is no widespread movement to rein in these practices, even if they hurt the customer. This lack of public awareness of harm was also evident in the 1999 Microsoft antitrust case. The vast majority of PC owners used Windows. Bill Gates was a business hero, the example of innovation and progress building a business empire out of his parents' garage. Led by the shining example of the American dream, Microsoft knew it had a lot of popular support during the antitrust case.

A powerful antitrust authority must be independent and shielded from political influence. Like the temptation for politicians to increase government spending and raise inflation before elections, politicians are tempted to accept vast sums of campaign money in exchange for antitrust leniency. The case for an independent central bank is beyond doubt.

There is an even stronger case for independence of the antitrust authority. Not only are the interests of firms with market power enormous, the cost to society is enormous, too. While the welfare cost of inflation has been estimated to hover around 1 percent of GDP,[31] the welfare cost of market power is estimated to be substantially higher, on the order of at least 7 percent of GDP.[32] The high welfare cost tells us how costly market power is for society. Indicative of the high welfare cost is of course the magnitude of profits. Profits as a share of value added in 2019 were 15 percent, whereas in the early 1980s they were 3 percent;[33] in a competitive economy they should be close to zero. The potential benefits to society of reining in market power are enormous.

In a sense, the FTC and the DOJ are independent institutions, just like the Federal Reserve. Still, the extent of interference of interested parties in antitrust appears greater than it is in monetary policy. This could be due to many causes, such as limited resources, the political influence in legislation, or the fact that the cases that are handled are extremely complex and technical. An independent, centralized competition authority is toothless if it doesn't have resources. Currently, between the FTC and the DOJ Antitrust Division there are fewer than two thousand employees who are responsible for competition policy, consumer protection, and expert knowledge.[34] Moreover, most judges ruling over the merger cases are not specialists.

In contrast, the Federal Reserve System, with its mission to control inflation, employs around twenty-three thousand employees, many of them specialists, bankers, and researchers.[35] Not only are the resources employed in antitrust low, since the 1970s they have not kept up with GDP growth. Even worse, in a time when antitrust is a growing concern, since 1990 the amount of resources spent on federal antitrust agencies has declined.[36] It is not surprising that the number of cases brought is declining and that the competition authorities face an uphill battle against the lawyers from cash-rich superstar firms.

There is a lot of unjustified antitrust bashing. Politicians and opinion makers often accuse the existing authorities of allowing market power to grow to the unprecedented levels we currently see. I would say the opposite: it is remarkable how much employees of competition authorities get done given the limited resources, the lack of institutional support, and the narrow legal mandate they have available.

There are success stories where the competition authorities have been able to force merging firms to divest certain goods that were creating market power. For example, AB InBev, in its merger with SABMiller, was forced to sell off Peroni, which had an effect on prices. That is of course a small drop in the huge bucket of the beer portfolio that AB InBev has managed to merge together.

It is a heroic achievement that the current system can wield any oversight at all. The problem is not the people working in antitrust; it is the system that is broken. So, what would regulation in an ideal antitrust world look like?

An Ideal World: The Federal Competition Authority

Imagine an independent, centralized authority of more than thirty thousand employees with a pro-market mandate to render the economy competitive. It would be an institution built on independent investigation conducted by specialists and backed up by researchers who are at the forefront of their fields. They would scrutinize markets even if there is no merger or case brought, with a presence in local economies around the country. Like the Federal Reserve System, the Federal Competition Authority would have offices around the country, close to local markets.

With mergers being the exception, the focus would be on regulation and prevention rather than on enforcement and merger review. Rather than sanctioning bad behavior, competition policy would move away from an adversarial system where large, cash-rich firms compete against understaffed competition authorities. For the big superstar companies that use new technology, much of the activity is the implementation of interoperability—how network effects can be mitigated by inducing competition in the market rather than for the market. Platform competition policy requires different points of attention, but it can be done under existing antitrust laws.[37]

In the exceptional case when there is a merger review, the competition authority would design market mechanisms to avoid completely unrealistic predictions of the benefits of a merger. The mechanism would induce the merging parties to commit to and reveal the value of the synergies the merger will generate and the lower prices they will charge in the future. Fines and rewards in function of future measurable outcomes would be put in place to provide the right incentives for merging firms to disclose the right expected synergies. If they did not deliver the synergies and the low prices, the merged corporation would pay for them.

The centralized authority would also oversee a number of other areas that are closely related to market power. Consumer protection is typically already under the umbrella of antitrust activity, but much more proactive regulation is needed to rein in firms that exploit consumers' behavioral biases. New technologies are much better suited to trick inattentive consumers, such as bait-and-switch tactics with low initial prices locking in at higher prices later or the illusion of zero cost for the use of apps where the users sell their data.

In the future, data and privacy issues will become an inherent piece of market power. The Bundeskartellamt (the German antitrust authority), for example, has argued that Facebook abuses its power by collecting data from third-party sites.[38] That data privacy is a competition policy issue became clear over a decade ago. To compete with MySpace, Facebook committed publicly to never using cookies and to put user privacy at the center of its mission. Once MySpace was gone and Facebook took over WhatsApp and Instagram, Facebook's commitment gradually eroded. Now Facebook records users' activities on third-party websites and collects data. The cost to the customer is the loss of privacy. Privacy would have been protected had MySpace or Instagram

continued to compete with Facebook.[39] The market power that originates from exclusive access to large data is likely to be one of the greatest
challenges for a well-functioning capitalist system.

Patent and intellectual property (IP) regulation as a government-
sanctioned monopoly should ideally be part of the new competition
authority. There are certainly good arguments in favor of this—not least
of which is fostering innovation—but the current system is too simplistic and creates as many problems as it solves, if not more. Patent regulation should be much more case based, depending on the sector and the
type of innovation. And where possible, the incentives to innovate
should be generated without having to grant a costly monopoly.

Finally, a lot of market power currently resides in financial markets
and banks. While there are many specific features to financial markets,
they should be regulated through the lens of competition. Financial
markets and the activities of banks also have economy-wide macro implications. The experience of dealing with systemic risk in financial markets can be helpful in nonfinancial markets where market power has
profound economy-wide implications on work. One insight that we do
learn from finance is that competition can solve "too-big-to-fail" issues
and systemic risk. If Facebook were to go bankrupt, dragging Instagram
and WhatsApp along with it, we would lose the majority of social networking platforms, which may pose a threat to communication and connectivity. It would have been less of a danger had they never merged in
the first place.

In addition to covering all these competencies, the authority should
make firm data available and easily accessible. Transparency facilitates
economic activity without barriers and is pro-competitive. Currently, if
I want to ship goods to a client with the expectation of payment two
months later, I need to evaluate the risk of nonpayment. To start, I
would get a quick idea of the client firm's financial health by inspecting
its balance sheet and income statement. Currently that information is
not available for firms that are not publicly traded in the United States.
At the same time, credit agencies and any firm that runs an app on my
phone has much more detailed private information. Privacy of individuals should be guarded, privacy of firms not so much.

Likewise, a competition authority should require market players to report real-time data as much as possible. There is already an airline pricing database. By making the data available, the regulator can favor competition. Similarly, in the finance industry, so-called over-the-counter transactions often are not recorded, leaving potential buyers and sellers in the dark about price determination. The large financial institutions use the lack of transparency to charge fees, to create a rationale for a market maker, and to extract rents. Transparency is the friend of competition. Opacity helps build market power.

This is of course all very idealistic and would require a lot of political will to implement. Even if the stars aligned politically, market power is now a global phenomenon, as much as climate change is, and needs international coordination. This requires even more political leadership and the willingness to engage in a project as big as putting a man on the moon or as urgent as the Manhattan Project.

Epilogue

THERE IS NO DOUBT THAT, on average, times are better than they have ever been. Technology has made life more pleasant, poverty has declined enormously, and health has improved massively. That was also the case in the beginning of the twentieth century when the second Industrial Revolution gave us electricity, telephone communication, and rail transport, all of which brought unprecedented progress and wealth. Because that well-being was the result of enormous economic integration with international trade and specialization, Norman Angell argued in his book *The Great Illusion* (1910) that it would be in nobody's interest to ever destroy such riches. It took only four years for the destruction to happen.

Like over a century ago, we're experiencing an epoch of similar progress, and, like then, the gains of that progress are unequally distributed. Since 1980, the few have amassed all the benefits of progress while most see no gains at all. There is a clear chain of events originating with dominant firms grabbing extreme market power. This has profound implications for work, the source of income for the majority of the people. Market power leads to wage stagnation and extreme wage inequality, and it stymies social mobility and economic dynamism. The deteriorating labor market in turn affects some people's health and overall well-being. But it is not only the workers who feel let down; the small and medium entrepreneurs are frustrated as well. They can barely keep their establishments afloat because market power is concentrated in a few dominant firms that squeeze their returns and shuts down their businesses.

Market forces—the lack of competition challenging big business— are not only failing the poor, they are also failing the middle class and small business owners. Big-business capitalism is failing the majority of the households, where most come out on the short end and do worse than their parents. Pro-market capitalism is losing out to pro-business.

The central thesis of *The Profit Paradox* is that technological innovation has a natural tendency toward accumulating wealth in few hands. New technologies favor the early adopter who can take the entire market while using the same technology to entrench power and limit competition in the market. Remember Orwell's words: "The trouble with competitions is that somebody wins them."

We therefore need strong institutions and independent regulation that guarantees and protects competition. One of the biggest misperceptions is that markets are free and that competition is a natural outcome. Most markets work perfectly fine, but in the advent of new technologies, market failure leads to dominance and the accumulation of wealth. Only pro-market capitalism can attain healthy competition, which is to the benefit of all stakeholders in society, including the customers and the workers. Only then can we guarantee that what is good for business is good for workers.

Often, stakeholder capitalism and corporate responsibility are hailed as the panacea. Unfortunately, they are no more than a drop in the ocean. Of course, it is beneficial if business owners care about their workers and make sure that they earn a good living. A large firm that exerts monopsony power can make life better for its captive workers. The German model of nonconflictual worker representation is an example of making work work.[1] Often, better treatment of workers raises productivity, which is in the interest of the shareholders, too.

Generally, though, corporate responsibility is high on good intentions but low on results; it simply doesn't work if we expect that the CEOs or the boards of companies take it upon themselves to reduce their market power, in the process lowering profits and increasing wages. That would lead to perverse economic decisions and inefficiency.

Moreover, the unilateral decision not to exert market power is to the benefit of the other competitors who do exert market power. Hence, only coordinated action, such as regulation, can resolve the negative effects of market power.

Most importantly, self-regulation does not work because the problem is economy-wide: it is like asking the major owners of fossil fuel–generating firms to self-regulate emissions and environmental standards. BP and Shell bombard us with advertising that praises how much they do for the environment, but they also keep selling oil that increases CO_2 emissions. What we need instead is policy that regulates the emissions, such as carbon taxes and cap and trade, for example. That regulation has to come from outside the industry. Once the regulation is in place, profit-maximizing firms will be as efficient as the market and the regulation demands to generate low emissions energy.

The same holds for the stakeholder capitalism that attempts to reduce the adverse effects of market power that operate economy wide. The social responsibility of the firm should be to maximize profits through innovation and the use of new technologies. However, we should not allow firms to make profits from using those technologies that build moats around their castles. Institutions should ensure that there is healthy competition. If a firm makes excess profits, regulation should facilitate entry of competitors, which leads to lower prices and lower profits in the long run. This brings innovation and growth, and it leads to more employment and higher wages.

Rather than stakeholder capitalism, I therefore advocate for stronger and independent institutions that attain the desired social goals. The mandate of a competition authority is to protect competition, not competitors or businesses. It should rein in market power and give power to the market. Most markets work well without much intervention or regulation, but when they don't, pro-competitive institutions that are independent of politics guarantee there is no market failure.

My proposal is therefore a separation of powers to achieve the social objectives: competition by firms *in* the market, and regulation *of* the market by the competition authority. On the level playing field of competition, firms should be allowed to make profits, as they should be prepared to go bankrupt without bailouts in bad times. The competition authority's visible hand will ensure that the market's "invisible hand," where firms seek their own gain, will unintendedly produce the greatest gain for all.

Unfortunately, in the absence of such institutions, the rise of market power has resulted in widespread discontent against the backdrop of enormous technological advances and economic progress. Some of this discontent is simply the wrong perception. Many forget that only over half a century ago people died of pneumonia, for example, or that poverty and standards of living were much worse than they are now. But only part of the discontent is misperception; a large part of it is real. And that is why opinions get extremely polarized, why the *gillets jaunes* (yellow vests) demonstrate in France, and why people lose faith in political and economic institutions.

And with the COVID-19 pandemic, society jumps out of the frying pan into the fire. Everything indicates that the fallout of the 2020 economic crisis is generating even more pronounced inequality. Those most negatively affected are the low skilled, the poor, minorities, the elderly, those in low-quality housing and in disadvantaged neighborhoods, the disabled, and the unhealthy. They are all more likely to lose their jobs, their incomes, and their lives.

Of course, not everything is the fault of market power, so let's not use the pandemic as an excuse to bash big business. But when, under the guise of a safety net for the unfortunate, a multitrillion-dollar rescue package disproportionately helps large companies, then the policy responses are making things worse in the long run. Eventually, workers have to pick up the tab in the form of taxes on labor (or high inflation).

The fact that in April 2020, in the middle of the crisis, US stocks had their best month since 1987 and that they reached new highs by the summer is bad news. Markets rally because of the multitrillion-dollar bailout with no strings attached and without a need to pay back the handouts, not because the economy is healthy. This bailout capitalism tilts the scales even more in favor of large companies with market power. In times of healthy capitalism, it is fine if an airline goes bust because it keeps investors in check to make the best decisions in the first place.

When an investor makes the right decisions and times are good, they make money. And if things go wrong, companies make losses or even go bankrupt, and the investor loses money. That is what investors in healthy capitalism sign up for.

The argument increasingly is that, like with banks, those mega-firms are too big to fail. In a massive downturn such as the COVID-19 recession, those large firms will drag with them hundreds of thousands of jobs if they go under. Moreover, the bankruptcy of one large firm will have a knock-on effect that leads to the contagion of bankruptcies among other, smaller firms. The contagion of a virus leads to the contagion of business failures. The problem with this argument is that those firms are too big because they have market power. Had there been more healthy competition with more firms in all markets, those firms would not have been too big to fail in the first place. In the theatre of a healthy competitive market, failing is part of the scenario. Now, only the small firms without market power fail.

This lopsided capitalism gets to the heart of the dominance of large corporations and the Profit Paradox. A number of large, thriving firms that make huge profits for prolonged periods of time is bad for the economy. We have to stop equating a rising stock market with a healthy economy. And if at the height of an economic recession, with small businesses closing and unemployment claims at record highs, those stock markets rally, then we know that market power is propping up some businesses at the expense of labor, today and in the future.

The greatest threat of market power is that its enormous concentration of wealth further entrenches that power. Market power generates huge profits that allow the few to buy political favors, which further cements that power. It is a vicious cycle that destroys democracy. In his grim description of exploitation in the Chicago meatpacking industry at the beginning of the twentieth century, Upton Sinclair writes in *The Jungle*: "[The businesses] own not merely the labor of society, they have bought the governments; and everywhere they use their raped and stolen power to intrench themselves in their privileges, to dig wider and deeper the channels through which the river of profits flows to them."[2]

This process of market power reinforces political power, and vice versa; wealth creating wealth is not sustainable in the long run. In Germany, the Weimar Republic had tight relations with big business, which led to a rise in industrial cartels. And only a few decades later the coal and steel conglomerates provided the defense apparatus for Nazi warmongering. The ensuing wars, the economic depression, and high inflation decimated small business and the middle class. After the war the alienated small merchants and entrepreneurs ensured that this vicious cycle between politics and big business was broken. The postwar economy was built around *Mittelstand* (small business), where procompetitive institutions made space for small and medium enterprises as the engine of growth for the recovering country.[3]

History has taught us that it is sufficient for a spark in one region to ignite the dynamite everywhere else. In 1914 the United States did not have the political problems that Germany had, and Teddy Roosevelt's trust busting was an attempt to restore the balance toward more equality. But it was not enough, and the globalized economy was brought down by World War I. Following the war, the United States had major discontent during the Great Depression, and in World War II the United States was dragged into the world conflict again.

In his recent book *The Great Leveler* (2017), Walter Scheidel argues that mass violence and catastrophes are the only forces that can reduce inequality.[4] He goes back to the Stone Age and carefully documents how only wars, revolutions, state collapse, and plagues have managed to restore more equal societies. The thesis is that inequality is so tenacious that only calamitous violence can dismantle it. Will it be any different now?

It appears that in our age of advanced medical technology and information, society has managed to avoid the COVID-19 virus becoming the next great leveler. Epidemiologists and scientists have educated us on how to use social distancing, face masks, and gloves to manage the spread of a disease that would in earlier times have been far more deadly. We may have managed to level the curve of contagion and death and avoided a needless social implosion. But COVID-19 has not leveled the inequality that has grown out of proportion in the past four decades— quite the contrary.

Inequality is as high as it was before World War I. Discontent is everywhere. Only very draconian measures will revert the course. It helps to look back: "Those who cannot remember the past are condemned to repeat it."[5] Incidentally, four Viennese intellectuals in exile, Friedrich von Hayek, Karl Popper, Joseph Schumpeter, and Stefan Zweig, set the tone for a postwar economic and social order with the objective of avoiding the concentration of power and totalitarianism. They all experienced the dire consequences of a collapsing order firsthand and dedicated the remainder of their lives to making sure no one else would experience the same ever again.

We cannot ignore how rapid technological progress and tightly interconnected global economies created enormous market power at the turn of the last century, in the last so-called modern times. The result was a Gilded Age—one where the majority of the workforce saw no gains. Today, in the current modern times, the economy is edging in the direction of a new Gilded Age. In the first half of the twentieth century we were able to stop the slow-drifting ship of inequality in the global economy, but it took two brutal wars and the Great Depression.

Today, the only way to avoid another calamity and restore the economic order is to bet on pro-market reforms that break the power of mega-firms. We need to put the trust back into antitrust, which requires the ambition of a moonshot and the resources of a Manhattan Project. And if that is not complicated enough, market power, like climate change, is a global problem that requires international coordination.

We also need to break the link between market power and political power, which are dangerously feeding off each other. We need to keep money out of politics and politics out of the economy. That means we need to minimize the role of lobbying. In the United States, campaign finance holds politicians hostage, who suffer acutely from Stockholm syndrome. Campaign finance has a role in many social problems, from mass shootings to the opioid crisis.

But the political influence of big business is also at the heart of the ailments of the economic system. Firms with market power have the resources to lobby politicians, and they use the lobbying to build larger uncontested empires, which in turn frees up more resources to lobby even further. In this vicious cycle, mega-firms kidnap politicians on issues ranging from data protection (the big tech firms) to the absence of environmental regulation (the Koch family), and most of all, on the power of those dominant firms to further extend their dominance. Lobbying is the main vehicle to create and perpetuate market power. It was like that for the East India Company, a master lobbyist, and it is nothing more than a legalized form of corruption.

Market power concentrates vast resources in the hands of a few, who use those resources and more to perpetuate market power. This poses a serious threat to democracy. To put it in the words that former US Supreme Court Justice Louis Brandeis reputedly has spoken, "Americans might have democracy . . . , or wealth concentrated in a few hands, but they could not have both."[6]

It is easy to blame the capitalist system. It is true that technology and markets inherently lead to concentration of wealth and inequality, but markets do not operate in a vacuum: even the most rogue form of capitalism needs institutions and regulation. It needs an army and a police force to guarantee that property rights are respected, and to foster trust between trading partners that encourages them to make long-term investment decisions. But from this rogue form of laissez-faire capitalism much more intervention and regulation is needed to ensure that capitalism is also competitive. The current institutions ensure that capitalism is pro-business. To safeguard democracy and a just division of what society produces, we need regulation and institutions that foster pro-competitive capitalism. We need that now, before it's too late!

ACKNOWLEDGMENTS

I HAVE HAD THE PRIVILEGE of benefiting from the help and support of many people as I wrote this book. Jay Mandel at WME skillfully navigated me through the writing process, and he has been instrumental in thinking about the audience. The entire team at Princeton University Press has been exceptionally supportive throughout the course of publishing the book. Joe Jackson, the editor, has been an ardent supporter of the project from the day we first met, around the time I started writing in the fall of 2017. He provided extremely valuable feedback on an earlier draft of the book, as well as an abundance of excellent ideas to incorporate. The advice on the writing at the early stages from Nic Albert, David Moldawer, and Erin Hobey has been invaluable. John Donohue of Westchester Publishing Services has been an exceptional copy editor.

I am indebted to my colleagues at UPF Barcelona and University College London for creating a productive atmosphere that is conducive to intellectual debate. I am grateful to the Department of Economics at Princeton for their hospitality during my sabbatical visit in 2017–2018. I also want to thank the support staff at UPF Barcelona. They take such good care that it makes our daily lives much easier. Because of them we can spend all our time on research and writing.

I want to thank all the academic researchers around the world on whose work this book is based. Research is a collaborative community endeavor, and I wouldn't know anything that I write about without the lifetime contributions of hundreds of the best researchers. As I stand on the shoulders of giants, I have a privileged view of all the latest developments in economics research. In addition to reading the work of hundreds of researchers, I have also had the benefit of discussions with Ufuk

Akcigit, Jose Azar, Jonathan Baker, Isaac Baley, Simcha Barkai, Tom Barkin, Susanto Basu, Richard Blundell, Markus Brunnermeier, James Bullard, Dean Corbae, Morris Davis, Ryan Decker, Maarten De Ridder, Matthias Doepke, David Dorn, Florian Ederer, Jordan Ellenberg, Emmanuel Farhi, John Fernald, Xavier Gabaix, Manuel García-Santana, Pinelopi Goldberg, Robert Hall, John Haltiwanger, Arshia Hashemi, Thomas Holmes, Henry Hyatt, Gregor Jarosch, Michael Kades, Greg Kaplan, Loukas Karabarbounis, Dmitry Kuvshinov, Jeremy Lise, Hanno Lustig, Alex Mas, Thierry Mayer, Branko Milanović, Thomas Philippon, Fabien Postel-Vinay, Jean-Marc Robin, Esteban Rossi-Hansberg, Pierre-Daniel Sarte, Edouard Schaal, Fiona Scott Morton, James Spletzer, Chad Syverson, Nicolas Trachter, James Traina, Tommaso Valletti, John Van Reenen, Gianluca Violante, Glen Weyl, Thomas Wollmann, and Arlene Wong. I also received detailed feedback on an earlier draft from Christian Gual and Ignasi Calvera.

I am eternally grateful to the coauthors with whom I have had the pleasure of working on related research papers over many years. They have sculpted the ideas in this book before I even started writing: Jan De Loecker, Hector Chade, Simon Mongey, Ilse Lindenlaub, Alireza Sepahsalari, Boyan Jovanovic, Philipp Kircher, Nezih Guner, Roberto Pinheiro, Kurt Schmidheiny, Christoph Hedtrich, Lawrence Warren, Xi Weng, Chunyang Fu, Wenjian Li, Gabriel Unger, and Lones Smith.

This book contains major contributions from all the collaborators of our research team at UPF Barcelona. They have engaged in countless discussions, they have helped with data analysis, and they have given detailed feedback on earlier drafts. I thank Korie Amberger, Renjie Bao, Elena Casanovas, Federica Daniele, Shubhdeep Deb, Patricia De Cea, Milena Djourelova, Julia Faltermeier, Ana Figueiredo, Ian Hsieh, Wei Hua, Akhil Lohia, Thomas Minten, Adria Morrón-Salmerón, Aseem Patel, Evangelia Spantidaki, Joanne Tan, and Inês Xavier.

One extremely rewarding discovery has been to meet the numerous people who kindly volunteered to be interviewed for the book. For most of them, their involvement was the result of a fortunate encounter. Yet, each of their stories helped me to think about the importance of market power in the daily lives of ordinary people. I thank them for their generosity. All first names are pseudonyms, except for Nancy and Eutychios. I donate part of the royalties from this book to Eutychios's orphanage in Uganda, http://www.ugandanorphans.org.

I could not have written the book without Elena, Emma, and Mireia. They engaged in endless discussions and gave me feedback on every little detail. Above all, their unconditional love and enthusiastic encouragement throughout has been the source of my inspiration. I dedicate this book to them.

NOTES

Chapter 1

1. See www.TheProfitParadox.com, figure I.

2. See www.TheProfitParadox.com, figure II.

3. Cortes, Jaimovich, Nekarda, & Siu (2020) found that in 2015, 31.2 percent of jobs involved routine activities.

4. See www.TheProfitParadox.com, figure I.

5. Figure 1 shows the evolution of average worker productivity of all workers in the economy, as well as the average wage of nonsupervisory production workers. If we include all nonsupervisory workers, not just production workers (see www.TheProfitParadox.com, figure III), the wage level is even lower. If we consider median wages (as opposed to average wages) and include all workers, including supervisors, we find the same pattern of stagnating (median) wages (see www.TheProfitParadox.com, figure IV).

6. See www.TheProfitParadox.com, figure V. See also Autor (2014).

7. See Rosen (1981).

8. See Bloom et al. (2019).

9. See Karabarbounis & Neiman (2014).

10. See www.TheProfitParadox.com, figure VI. See also Hyatt & Spletzer (2013).

11. See www.TheProfitParadox.com, figure VII for the decline in the job switching probability. We calculate the average job switching probability as the inverse of the job duration in months. See also Moscarini & Thomsson (2007) for 1994–2006 data and Bosler & Petrosky-Nadeau (2016) for 1997–2013 data. See www.TheProfitParadox.com, figure VIII for the decline in business dynamism. See also Davis & Haltiwanger (2014); Decker et al. (2014, 2020).

12. See Kaplan & Schulhofer-Wohl (2017).

13. The average annual rate of net employment growth rate from small firms with one to four employees is about 15.2 percent higher than that for large firms with 500 or more employees. See Haltiwanger, Jarmin, & Miranda (2014).

14. See www.TheProfitParadox.com, figure IX. See also Karahan, Pugsley, & Şahin (2019); Pugsley & Şahin (2019).

15. The startup rate has declined from 60 percent in 1980 to 38 percent by 2011 in high-tech sectors. See Haltiwanger, Hathaway, & Miranda (2014).

16. The unemployment rate in the United States is estimated to have been over 20 percent of the labor force. See Coen (1973). The numbers were similar in the United Kingdom, most of Europe, and, for that matter, around the world.

17. Measured as total trade (imports plus exports as a share of GDP). See Klasing & Milionis (2014).

18. Cornelius Vanderbilt built the first Grand Central Terminal in 1871; Edward Durell Stone & Associates with Emery Roth & Sons built the General Motors Building in 1968.

19. See Zweig (1943).

20. See Angell (1910).

21. It issued bonds and shares to finance its rapid expansion, and it was the precursor to the modern multinational corporation.

22. See Zweig (2015 [1941]).

Chapter 2

1. See Buffett (2007), start minute 2:31.

2. The rate of return that compensates the investment, appropriately taking into account the risk-free market return on capital, inflation, depreciation, and a premium for the risk born.

3. See Schumpeter (1942).

4. See Pilon (2015).

5. See Orwell (1944).

6. See Orwell (1944).

7. See Open Markets Institute (2019). For pacemakers, see https://concentrationcrisis.openmarketsinstitute.org/industry/pacemaker-manufacturing/. For baby formula, see https://concentrationcrisis.openmarketsinstitute.org/industry/baby-formula/. For dry cat food, see https://concentrationcrisis.openmarketsinstitute.org/industry/dry-cat-food/. For mayonnaise, see https://concentrationcrisis.openmarketsinstitute.org/industry/mayonnaise/. For social networking sites, see https://concentrationcrisis.openmarketsinstitute.org/industry/social-networking-sites/. For domestic airlines, see https://concentrationcrisis.openmarketsinstitute.org/industry/domestic-airlines/. For home improvement stores, see https://concentrationcrisis.openmarketsinstitute.org/industry/hardware-and-home-stores/. For coffin and casket manufacturers, see https://concentrationcrisis.openmarketsinstitute.org/industry/coffin-casket-manufacturing/ (all accessed November 11, 2020).

8. See Hall (1988).

9. See De Loecker & Eeckhout (2018).

10. Personal conversation at ECB Forum on Central Banking, Sintra, Portugal, June 18–20, 2018.

11. In addition, measures of concentration show an increase over the past four decades. See Council of Economic Advisors (2016); Grullon, Larkin, & Michaely (2019); Gutierrez & Philippon (2017).

12. The profit rate in figure 5 is for the publicly traded firms, based on De Loecker, Eeckhout, & Unger (2020). A similar pattern of increasing profit rates is observed in the national accounts, for all firms and starting in the late 1920s. See www.TheProfitParadox.com, figure X.

13. Based on the calculations underlying figure 6.

14. See "AB InBev," Wikipedia, accessed November 11, 2020, https://en.wikipedia.org/wiki/AB_InBev; and "Anheuser-Busch InBev's (AB InBev) Beer Market Share Worldwide in 2015, by Country," Statista, accessed November 11, 2020, https://www.statista.com/statistics/199024/ab-inbev-beer-market-share-by-country/.

15. See Alviarez, Head, & Mayer (2020).

16. See Lafontaine & Morton (2010).

17. See Cunningham, Ederer, & Ma (2021).

18. See Bogle (2018).

19. See Azar, Schmalz, & Tecu (2018).

20. See Anton et al. (2020) on how owners incentivize their managers when there is common ownership.

21. From American Airlines, TWA, America West, US Airways, Delta, Northwest, United, Continental, Southwest, and AirTran to American Airlines, Delta, United, and Southwest.

22. See Noack (2017).

Chapter 3

1. See "Sears," Wikipedia, accessed November 11, 2020, https://en.wikipedia.org/wiki/Sears.

2. See Holmes (2011); Houde, Newberry, & Seim (2017).

3. In 2019, total US retail sales were $5.45 trillion; see U.S. Census (2020). For Walmart, total 2019 sales were $524 billion; see "Walmart," accessed November 11, 2020, https://s2.q4cdn.com /056532643/files/doc_financials/2020/q4/Earnings-Release-1.31.2020-Final.pdf. For Amazon, total 2019 sales were $280 billion; see "Amazon (company)," Wikipedia, accessed November 11, 2020, https://en.wikipedia.org/wiki/Amazon_(company). In 2019, total sales for Walmart and Amazon were $804 billion, or 14.8 percent of total US retail sales. In 1930, total US retail sales were $53 billion; see U.S. Census Bureau (1930), 14. For A&P, total 1930 sales were $2.9 billion, or 5.4 percent of total US retail sales, which was twice as large as Sears, the second largest retailer; hence the total share of A&P and Sears was 8.1 percent. See Levinson (2011); "Red Circle & Gold Leaf," *Time*, November 13, 1950, http://content.time.com/time/subscriber/article/0,33009,821397,00.html; "The Great Atlantic & Pacific Tea Company," Wikipedia, accessed November 11, 2020, https://en.wikipedia.org/wiki /The_Great_Atlantic_%26_Pacific_Tea_Company.

4. See Ambridge (2015).

5. See Wilson (2012); see also Tong (2017).

6. See De Loecker & Warzynski (2012).

7. See Dasgupta & Stiglitz (1980); Sutton (1991, 1998).

8. See De Loecker, Eeckhout, & Unger (2020).

9. See Haskel & Westlake (2017).

10. See Coyle (2014).

11. See Schumpeter (1942).

12. See Schmitz (2020).

13. See Carpenter (2014).

Chapter 4

1. For the original paper documenting the facts, see Kaldor (1957). Kaldor (1961, 178) first used the term "stylized fact."

2. See Coyle (2014).

3. See www.TheProfitParadox.com, figure XI. See also Barkai (2020); De Loecker, Eeckhout, & Unger (2020); Karabarbounis & Neiman (2014). For the Penn World Tables, see Feenstra, Inklaar, & Timmer (2015).

4. See Barkai (2019); De Loecker & Eeckhout (2017); De Loecker, Eeckhout, & Unger (2020); Gutierrez & Philippon (2017); Hartman-Glaser, Lustig, & Xialong (2019); Philippon (2019).

5. See www.TheProfitParadox.com, figures X and XI.

6. See www.TheProfitParadox.com, figure XI. See also Autor, Dorn, Katz, Patterson, & Van Reenen (2020); De Loecker, Eeckhout, & Unger (2020); Karabarbounis & Neiman (2014).

7. See De Loecker, Eeckhout, & Unger (2020), table V.

8. It could of course also be because one goes down a lot (say, the number of workers) and the other rises modestly (say, wages). The net effect then is still a decline in the expenditure on labor. And then there is of course the issue of hours worked. The labor share could decline because the same people are at work, but they work fewer hours due to more leisure time or the rise in temporary employment.

9. See www.TheProfitParadox.com, figure XII.

10. See www.TheProfitParadox.com, figure XIII.

11. See www.TheProfitParadox.com, figure XIV.

12. See www.TheProfitParadox.com, figure XV. Figure XV shows the wages of the bottom twenty-fifth percentile of the wage distribution. In nominal terms, wages have increased, but in real terms (adjusted for inflation), wages are flat.

13. See www.TheProfitParadox.com, figure II.

14. See De Loecker, Eeckhout, & Unger (2020), figure X(B).

15. See Maynard (2012).

16. "The World's Billionaires," Wikipedia, accessed November 11, 2020, https://en.wikipedia .org/wiki/The_World's_Billionaires.

17. Since Wick sold the White Dog Café in 2009, the new owner has done exactly that: they opened two more White Dog Cafés.

18. See Eeckhout (2020); Rossi-Hansberg, Sarte, & Trachter (2020).

19. See Azar, Berry, & Marinescu (2019); Azar, Marinescu, Steinbaum, & Taska (2019); Berger, Herkenhoff, & Mongey (2019); Deb, Eeckhout, & Warren (2021); Goolsbee & Syverson (2020).

20. See Deb, Eeckhout, Patel, & Warren (2021); Goolsbee & Syverson (2020).

21. See Naidu, Nyarko, & Wang (2016).

22. See Marx & Nunn (2018).

23. See World Bank Group (2020a).

24. See Friedman & Friedman (1980), 231.

25. See Kleiner (2006).

26. See Ogilvie (2004).

27. "It is to prevent this reduction of price, and consequently of wages and profit, by restraining that free competition which would most certainly occasion it, that all corporations, and the greater part of corporation laws, have been established. . . . And when any particular class of

artificers or traders thought proper to act as a corporation without a charter, such adulterine guilds, as they were called, were not always disfranchised upon that account, but obliged to fine annually to the king for permission to exercise their usurped privileges." See Smith (1776), Book 1, chapter 10, part 2.

28. See "Le Chapelier Law 1791," Wikipedia, accessed November 11, 2020, https://en.wikipedia.org/wiki/Le_Chapelier_Law_1791.

29. See Kleiner (2015), 1.

30. See Kleiner and Kruger (2013), S176–S177.

31. See Kleiner and Kruger (2013), S175.

32. See Johnson & Kleiner (2020), 370.

Chapter 5

1. See Harris (1995).

2. See "The Meaning and Origin of the Expression: Oversexed, Overpaid and Over Here," Phrase Finder, accessed November 5, 2020, https://www.phrases.org.uk/meanings/oversexed-overpaid-and-over-here.html. Later the GIs responded with "undersexed, underpaid, and under Eisenhower."

3. As Steven Pinker describes in his work on evolutionary psychology, the notion of romantic love has an evolutionary origin. Emotions are adaptive strategies that are useful for reproduction and survival among humans. See Pinker (1997), "Fools for Love," 417, and "Men and Women," 460.

4. Quoted in Mukherjee (2011 [2010]), 139. See also Patlak (2001).

5. See Bertrand & Mullainathan (2001).

6. See Akerlof (1981), 37; emphasis added.

7. See "Nadeshot," Wikipedia, accessed November 11, 2020, https://en.wikipedia.org/wiki/Nadeshot; Dougherty (2014).

8. See Rosen (1981).

9. See Metz (2017).

10. See Nomad Health (2019); Smith (2012).

11. See Kaplan & Rauh (2013).

12. See Guvenen & Kaplan (2017).

13. See Dubrow & Adamas (2012).

14. See Du, Huasheng, & Maurice (2012). The probability reported is 0.29 = 4.91/16.91, from table 1 in the paper. The role of luck is the main thesis of several books: Robert Frank's *Success and Luck: Good Fortune and the Myth of Meritocracy* (2016); Malcom Gladwell's *Outliers: The Story of True Success* (2008); and Nassim Taleb's *Fooled by Randomness: The Hidden Role of Chance in Life and in the Markets* (2008).

15. See Streufert & Streufert (1969). See also Stephan, Bernstein, Stephan, & Davis (1979).

16. See De Botton (2004).

17. See Kindermann & Krueger (2021).

18. See Kleven, Landais, & Saez (2013).

19. See Henry (2013).

20. See Mishel (2014).

21. See Bertrand & Mullainathan (2001).

22. See Chade & Eeckhout (2017).

23. See Bhasin (2013).

24. Lowe (1997), 101, quoted in Davis (2008), 83.

25. See Surowiecki (2004).

26. See www.TheProfitParadox.com, figure XVI. See also Bloom, Guvenen, Price, Song, & Watcher (2019); Mishel (2014); Sommeiller & Price (2018).

27. See Chandler (1977).

28. This income effectively taxed at a lower rate is called pass-through business income, not to be confused with the pass-through of costs to prices of firms with market power.

29. See Smith, Yagan, Zidar, & Zwick (2019), 1677.

Chapter 6

1. Remarks made during the presentation of the Inaugural Lecture of the academic year of the Department of Economics at UPF Barcelona in October 1997.

2. See Levingston, Lorin, & McDonald (2018).

3. See National Institute on Drug Abuse (n.d.).

4. See Keefe (2017).

5. See Reich (2020), 4.

6. See Luce (2018).

7. Two recent books question the effectiveness and even the good intentions of charitable giving: see Giridharadas (2018) and Reich (2018).

8. See www.TheProfitParadox.com, figure XVI.

9. See www.TheProfitParadox.com, figure V.

10. See www.TheProfitParadox.com, figure I.

11. See Katz & Murphy (1992).

12. See Krusell, Ohanian, Ríos-Rull, & Violante (2000).

13. See Altonji & Pierret (2001).

14. See Goldschmidt & Schmieder (2017).

15. For the United States, see Barth, Bryson, Davis, & Freeman (2016); Bloom, Guvenen, Price, Song, & Watcher (2019). For Germany, see Card, Heining, & Kline (2013). For Sweden, see Håkanson, Lindqvist, & Vlachos (2020).

16. Barth, Bryson, Davis, & Freeman (2016) and Bloom, Guvenen, Price, Song, & Watcher (2019) find that two-thirds of the rise in wage inequality is accounted for by the change during the past four decades.

17. See Cavalli-Sforza (1997); Cavalli-Sforza & Feldman (1981).

18. See Baziki, Ginja, & Milicevic (2016).

19. See Traiberman (2019). For the median worker, a 1 percent decrease in wages increases the occupation switching probability by 3 percent. This also affects wages. Import competition declines lifetime earnings by up to 0.5 percent and increases the variance substantially.

20. See Simpson (1951).

21. See www.TheProfitParadox.com, figure XVII. See also Bourguignon & Morrisson (2002); Lakner & Milanovic (2013); Milanovic (2016); Ravallion (2018); Roser (2013).

22. See Eeckhout & Jovanovic (2010).

23. The wage data for the two cities is from the U.S. Bureau of Labor Statistics (2019a, 2019b); the population data is from the U.S. Census Bureau (2019a, 2019b).

24. See Eeckhout, Pinheiro, & Schmidheiny (2014).

25. See Davis & Ortalo-Magné (2011).

26. Observe that since households on average spend one-quarter of their after-tax income on housing, to have a proportionate increase in the spending on housing, house price differences between Janesville and New York are much larger than income differences. Housing prices per square meter in New York are over 160 percent higher. That is why New Yorkers who spend a quarter of their income on housing need to live in small spaces.

27. See Eeckhout, Pinheiro, & Schmidheiny (2014).

28. See Eeckhout, Pinheiro, & Schmidheiny (2014).

29. See De la Roca & Puga (2017).

30. See Eeckhout, Hedtrich, & Pinheiro (2021).

31. See www.TheProfitParadox.com, figure XVIII. Using the markup estimates of De Loecker, Eeckhout, & Unger (2020), we find that markups are higher for firms located in big cities than those in small cities. See also Anderson, Rebelo, & Wong (2020), who find a positive relation between local income and local markups.

32. See Jaimovich, Rebelo, & Wong (2019).

33. See Autor & Dorn (2013); Goos & Manning (2007); Goos, Manning, & Salomons (2009, 2014).

34. See Autor, Levy, & Murane (2003).

35. See Michaels, Natraj, & Reenen (2014).

36. See Autor, Levy, & Murane (2003), according to whom routinization contributes 60 percent to the college premium.

Chapter 7

1. See www.TheProfitParadox.com, figure VI.

2. See www.TheProfitParadox.com, figure VII.

3. See www.TheProfitParadox.com, figure VIII.

4. See Hyatt & Spletzer (2013). From yet another viewpoint, Cowen (2017) recounts the same facts of declining dynamism and attributes the decline in the thirst to innovate to a change in the norms due to the comfortable life that technology offers. However, this is a thesis that is hard to corroborate quantitatively.

5. See Campa & Goldberg (2005).

6. "H&R Block," Wikipedia, accessed November 11, 2020, https://en.wikipedia.org/wiki/H%26R_Block.

7. See www.TheProfitParadox.com, figure VII.

8. See Hyatt, McEntarfer, Ueda, & Zhang (2018); Kaplan & Schulhofer-Wohl (2017).

9. The three brothers traveled from Bambrugge to Ellis Island. In March 1914 Alfons Ottoy traveled on the SS *Vaderland*. After arriving at Ellis Island he later moved to Montana, where he married Irma Van Hemelrijck. They had three children, Susanne, Rene, and Betty. On April 18, 1914, Leopold Ottoy traveled on the SS *Vaderland*. After arriving at Ellis Island he later moved to Detroit. Rene Ottoy traveled on the SS *Rotterdam*, and after arriving at Ellis Island on May 28, 1915, he also moved to Detroit. The information about landing immigrants can be searched on the Statue of Liberty–Ellis Island Foundation website, accessed November 11, 2020, https://heritage.statueofliberty.org/passenger-result.

10. See World Tourism Organization (2018).

Chapter 8

1. See Fogli & Guerrieri (2018).

2. See Hobijn, Schoellman, & Vindas (2017) for an analysis of structural transformation and technological change that differs by cohort.

3. See www.TheProfitParadox.com, figure XIX. See also Mitchell (2007).

4. A bus has fifty seats. During rush hour all seats are taken; outside rush hour five seats are taken. Rush and peak hour each occur half the time. When we sample two buses and ask each passenger on the bus how many people they have seen, fifty people on the rush hour bus report having seen fifty passengers (including themselves) and five people on the off-peak bus report having seen five passengers. Hence, the average number of reported passengers is $50 \times 50 + 5 \times 5/55$, or 45.9. The average number of passengers on each bus is 27.5. There is no puzzle or surprise here; this example simply reflects the fact that many more people (fifty of them) experience a congested bus and only five people experience a lightly occupied bus.

5. See Case & Deaton (2015, 2020).

6. See Chetty et al. (2016). In the United States, life expectancy for men is eighty-seven years for the top 1 percent of household income versus seventy-two years for the ninety-ninth percentile. For women, life expectancy is eighty-nine years for the top 1 percent of household income versus seventy-nine years for the ninety-ninth percentile.

7. Also in Chetty et al. (2016).

8. See www.TheProfitParadox.com, figure XX. See also Kuvshinov & Zimmermann (2020), who show there is zero capital gains before 1980 and a sharp increase to 4 percent from 1980 onward. Meanwhile, the dividend yield hardly changes, with a slight drop from 1980 on.

9. See De Loecker, Eeckhout, & Unger (2020).

10. See www.TheProfitParadox.com, figure IX.

11. See Ritter (2020), 3, table 1.

12. See Levack, Muir, & Veldman (2011).

13. See www.TheProfitParadox.com, figure XXI. For other measures of the risk-free rate that show a similar decline, see Del Negro, Giannone, Giannoni, & Tambalott (2019); Eggertsson, Robbins, & Wold (2018).

14. See chapter 2, figure 3.

15. See Barkai (2020); De Loecker, Eeckhout, & Unger (2020).

16. See www.TheProfitParadox.com, figure XXII. See also Ordonez & Piguillem (2020).

17. See www.TheProfitParadox.com, figure X.

18. See chapter 2, figure 5 for the profit rate as a share of sales going from 1–2 percent in the early 1980s to 7–8 percent in 2016; sales (comparable to gross output in the aggregate economy) are roughly twice the value added (comparable to GDP in the aggregate economy), so the profit rate as a share of value added is roughly twice the profit rate as a share of sales, from 3 percent in the early 1980s to 15 percent in 2016.

19. See www.TheProfitParadox.com, figure XXI.

Chapter 9

1. See Bastian (2006).

2. See Eurostat (2019) and www.TheProfitParadox.com, figure XXIV.

3. See World Bank Group (2020b). The World Bank defines the poverty rate as the poverty headcount ratio at $3.20 a day (2011 PPP) as a percent of the population.

4. See Bourguignon & Morrisson (2002).

5. See www.TheProfitParadox.com, figure XXIII.

6. See Forbes (2020); Mohamud (2019).

7. See Rosling, Rönnlund, & Rosling (2018); Rosling & Rosling (2014).

8. Johnston & Williamson (2020).

9. See www.TheProfitParadox.com, figure XXIV.

10. Norwegian had 29.3 million passengers and 5,796 employees in 2016; Scandinavian Airlines had 29.4 million passengers and 10,710 employees in 2016. See "Norwegian Air Shuttle," Wikipedia, accessed November 11, 2020, https://en.wikipedia.org/wiki/Norwegian_Air _Shuttle; "Scandinavian Airlines," Wikipedia, accessed November 11, 2020, https://en.wikipedia .org/wiki/Scandinavian_Airlines.

11. See U.S. Bureau of Labor Statistics (2006).

12. See Orwell (1944).

13. See Goodman (2017): "Boliden has expanded annual production to close to 600,000 tons from about 350,000 tons three decades ago—while the work force has remained about 200."

14. See George (1879), 43. Malthusianism is an economic theory proposed by the Reverend Thomas Malthus (as laid out in his 1798 work *An Essay on the Principle of Population*). He argues that population tends to increase at a faster rate than food and natural resources, and that unless it is checked by moral restraint or disaster, such as disease, famine, or war, widespread poverty and degradation inevitably result. Incidentally, Malthus's theory has been very influential in biology, as it shaped Charles Darwin's views on natural selection and the role of overpopulation and competition between members of the same species.

15. See www.TheProfitParadox.com, figure XIV. Notice that the labor force participation rate is 1 minus the inactivity rate, as measured in figure XIV.

16. See Noack (2017).

17. Kambourov & Manovskii (2009) find that the wage drop after displacement is three times larger when the worker switches occupations, compared to a worker who stays in the same occupation.

18. See Jarosch (2015).

19. Smith (1776), Book 1, chapter 3.

20. Smith (1776), Book 1, chapter 5.

21. See Boppart & Krusell (2020). This is for postindustrial times. Some evidence suggests that in the prehistoric hunter-gatherer societies, hours of work were less than today, on average 4.86 hours per day. See "Average Working Hours (Statistical Data 2020)," Clockify, accessed November 11, 2020, https://clockify.me/working-hours.

22. See Keynes (1963), 371: "Three-hour shifts or a fifteen-hour week may put off the problem for a great while. For three hours a day is quite enough to satisfy the old Adam in most of us!"

23. If today we work thirty-four hours per week, and hours decline at 0.4 percent per year, we will reach fifteen hours 204 years later.

24. Aristotle (1925), Book X, 7.

25. Based on telephone conversation on September 29, 2016.

26. "Taxi Medallion," Wikipedia, accessed November 11, 2020, https://en.wikipedia.org /wiki/Taxi_medallion : "On July 11, 2019, sixteen medallions were offered at auction. Three sold for $137,000, $136,000 and $138,000. The other thirteen had no bidders."

27. See Fréchette, Lizzeri, & Salz (2019).

28. See Hall & Krueger (2015).

Chapter 10

1. See Brynjolfsson, Hui, & Liu (2019).

2. See Cowgill (2020).

3. See Borenstein, Bushnell, & Stoft (1997); Varian (2000).

4. See DellaVigna & Gentzkow (2019).

5. See https://web.archive.org/web/20010715123343/https://www.google.com/press /funfacts.html, accessed November 11, 2020.

6. They were Paul Samuelson, Robert Solow, Vernon Smith, and Thomas Schelling. This feat of being an advisor to so many Nobel Prize recipients in economics has probably been equaled only by Kenneth Arrow.

7. See Leontief (1983), 3: "Computers and robots replace humans in the exercise of mental functions in the same way as mechanical power replaced them in the performance of physical tasks. As time goes on, more and more complex mental functions will be performed by machines. Any worker who now performs his task by following specific instructions can, in principle, be replaced by a machine. That means that the role of humans as the most important factor of production is bound to diminish—in the same way that the role of horses in agricultural production was first diminished and then eliminated by the introduction of tractors."

8. The US horse population is from "Horses in the United States," Wikipedia, accessed November 11, 2020, https://en.wikipedia.org/wiki/Horses_in_the_United_States; the world horse population is from Food and Agriculture Organization of the United Nations, "Live Animals," accessed November 11, 2020, http://www.fao.org/faostat/en/#data/QA. The US population is from Federal Reserve Bank of St. Louis, "National Population," accessed November 11, 2020, https://fred.stlouisfed.org/series/POPH; the world population is from United Nations, "World Population Prospects 2019," accessed November 11, 2020, https://population.un.org /wpp/DataQuery/.

9. See www.TheProfitParadox.com, figure XXV.

Chapter 11

1. Zukin 2015.

2. See Bore (n.d.); Collinson (2016).

3. See Lenter, Slemrod, & Shackelford (2003).

4. See Bø, Slemrod, & Thoresen (2015).

5. See "Spurious Correlations," Tylervigen, accessed November 10, 2020, http://tylervigen .com/page?page=1.

6. Santayana 1941 [1896], part III, 125.

7. See OECD (2020).

8. See Graversen & Van Ours (2008); Rosholm (2008).

9. See Gautier, Muller, van der Klaauw, Rosholm, & Svarer (2018).

10. See Crépon, Duflo, Gurgand, Rathelot, & Zamora (2013). The displacement effect of active labor market policies has been observed in the literature at least since the 1970s; see Johnson (1979).

11. Ellenberg 2014.

12. See U.S. Bureau of Labor Statistics (2020). To calculate the total number of jobs lost we multiply the total active population (159 million) by the average job separation rate (2.9 percent, from www.TheProfitParadox.com, figure VII), which indicates that 4,611,000 jobs were lost. Since the net job creation reported by the U.S. Bureau of Labor Statistics is 273,000, the estimated number of jobs created was 4,884,000.

13. For the US job finding rate, see Federal Reserve Bank of St. Louis, table A-12, "Unemployed Persons by Duration of Unemployment," accessed November 10, 2020, https://fred .stlouisfed.org/release/tables?rid=50&eid=3142&od=2020-01-01#. For the US job separation rate, see www.TheProfitParadox.com, figure VII. For the job finding and job separation rate in Italy, see Elsby, Hobijn, & Sahin (2013).

Chapter 12

1. See Acemoglu & Robinson (2012).

2. "History of Patent Law," Wikipedia, accessed November 11, 2020, https://en.wikipedia .org/wiki/History_of_patent_law.

3. See Boldrin & Levine (2008).

4. See Abrams, Akcigit, & Grennan (2018).

5. See U.S. Patent and Trademark Office (2020).

6. See Chien (2013). See also Abrams, Akcigit, Oz, & Pearce (2019).

7. See "Longitude Rewards," Wikipedia, accessed November 11, 2020, https://en.wikipedia .org/wiki/Longitude_rewards.

8. See Yihan (2020).

9. See Berge (1947), 362–363; also quoted in Schmitz (2020).

10. See Baker (2019); see also Wu (2018).

11. See Eeckhout, Fu, Li, & Weng (2021).

12. See Smith (1776), Book 4, chapter 8.

13. See Brandeis (2009).

14. See Piraino (2007).

15. See Khan (2017).

16. See Friedman & Friedman (1980); Friedman & Kuznets (1945).

17. See Harberger (1954).

18. See Friedman (1999); Stigler (1952).

19. I am grateful to Lones Smith, who at the time was a PhD candidate in economics at the University of Chicago and is now a professor of economics at the University of Wisconsin, for providing me with this anecdote.

20. See Gordon (2015).

21. See Alviarez, Head, & Mayer (2020); Ashenfelter, Hosken, & Weinberg (2014); Blonigen & Pierce (2016); Kwoka, Greenfield, & Gu (2014); Peltzman (2014). David (2021) does find evidence of the benefit of mergers, though even there, there are too many mergers and the regulator should levy a tax on mergers.

22. See Grullon, Larkin, & Michaely (2019); Tepper (2019).

23. See Berry, Levinsohn, & Pakes (1995); Bresnahan (1989). These approaches go far beyond the mere measurement of market power by means of concentration indexes, such as the Herfindahl–Hirschman Index, that have proven to be problematic measures of market power (see, for example, Eeckhout 2020). Still, the use of HHI continues to be very widespread in litigation.

24. See Finn (2011).

25. See Posner & Weyl (2018).

26. "Feist Publications, Inc., v. Rural Telephone Service Co.," Wikipedia, accessed November 11, 2020, https://en.wikipedia.org/wiki/Feist_Publications,_Inc.,_v._Rural_Telephone _Service_Co.

27. "*Minder* (TV Series)," Wikipedia, accessed November 11, 2020, https://en.wikipedia.org /wiki/Minder_(TV_series). I am grateful to Jeff Borland for this quote.

28. See Wollmann (2019).

29. "List of Mergers and Acquisitions by Alphabet," Wikpedia, https://en.wikipedia.org /wiki/List_of_mergers_and_acquisitions_by_Alphabet.

30. See Rosaia (2020).

31. See Lucas (2000); "Welfare Cost of Inflation," Wikipedia, accessed November 11, 2020, https://en.wikipedia.org/wiki/Welfare_cost_of_inflation.

32. See De Loecker, Eeckhout, & Mongey (2021).

33. See De Loecker, Eeckhout, & Unger (2020), and chapter 8, note 18.

34. As of December 2011 the FTC had 1,131 employees; as of 2018 the DOJ Antitrust Division (ATR) had 695 employees. See "Federal Trade Commission," Wikipedia, accessed November 11, 2020, https://en.wikipedia.org/wiki/Federal_Trade_Commission; Department of Justice, "Antitrust Division (ATR), FY 2018 Budget Request at a Glance," accessed November 11, 2020, https://www.justice.gov/jmd/page/file/968396/download.

35. For 2017: Federal Reserve, "System Budgets Overview," last updated July 19, 2018, https:// www.federalreserve.gov/publications/2017-ar-federal-system-budgets.htm#xsystem budgetsoverview-690774ba.

36. See Kades (2019).

37. See Hovenkamp (2018).

38. See https://www.bundeskartellamt.de/SharedDocs/Entscheidung/EN/Entscheidungen /Missbrauchsaufsicht/2019/B6-22-16.pdf?__blob=publicationFile&v=5, accessed November 11, 2020.

39. See Srinivasan (2019).

Epilogue

1. See Jäger, Schoefer, & Heining (2021).

2. See Sinclair (2001 [1906]), 256.

3. See Munchau (2018).

4. See Scheidel (2017).

5. See Santayana (2001 [1905]), 284.

6. See Campbell (2013), 255.

BIBLIOGRAPHY

Abrams, D. S., Akcigit, U., & Grennan, J. 2018. Patent Value and Citations: Creative Destruction or Strategic Disruption? NBER Working Paper no. 19647. http://www.nber.org/papers/w19647.

Abrams, D. S., Akcigit, U., Oz, G., & Pearce, J. G. 2019. The Patent Troll: Benign Middleman or Stick-Up Artist? NBER Working Paper no. 25713. http://www.nber.org/papers/w25713.

Acemoglu, D., & Robinson, J. A. 2012. *Why Nations Fail.* New York: Crown.

Akerlof, G. A. 1981. Jobs as Dam Sites. *Review of Economic Studies, 48*(1), 37–49.

Altonji, J. G., & Pierret, C. R. 2001. Employer Learning and Statistical Discrimination. *Quarterly Journal of Economics, 116*(1), 313–350.

Alviarez, V., Head, K., & Mayer, T. 2020. Global Giants and Local Stars: How Changes in Brand Ownership Affect Competition. CEPR Discussion Paper no. DP14628. https://ssrn.com/abstract=3594259.

Ambridge, B. 2015. The Coca-Cola Wars: Can Anybody Really Tell the Difference? *JSTOR Daily,* April 9. https://daily.jstor.org/the-coca-cola-wars-can-anybody-really-tell-the-difference/.

Andersen, E., Rebelo, S., & Wong, A. 2020. Markups across Space and Time. NBER Working Paper no. 24434. https://www.nber.org/papers/w24434.

Angell, N. 1910. *The Great Illusion.* New York: G. P. Putnam's Sons.

Anton, M., Ederer, F., Giné, M., & Schmalz, M. C. 2020. Common Ownership, Competition, and Top Management Incentives. CESifo Working Paper No. 6178. https://ssrn.com/abstract=2885826.

Aristotle. 1925 [350 BCE]. *Nicomachean Ethics.* Book X. Translated by W. D. Ross. http://classics.mit.edu/Aristotle/nicomachaen.10.x.html.

Ashenfelter, O., Hosken, D., & Weinberg, M. 2014. Did Robert Bork Understate the Competitive Impact of Mergers? Evidence from Consummated Mergers. *Journal of Law and Economics, 57*(S3), S67–S100.

Autor, D. 2014. Skills, Education, and the Rise of Earnings Inequality among the "Other 99 Percent." *Science, 344*(6186), 843–851.

Autor, D., Dorn, D., Katz, L., Patterson, C., & Van Reenen, J. 2020. The Fall of the Labor Share and the Rise of Superstar Firms. *Quarterly Journal of Economics, 135*(2), 645–709.

Autor, D. H., & Dorn, D. 2013. The Growth of Low-Skill Service Jobs and the Polarization of the US Labor Market. *American Economic Review, 103*(5), 1553–1597.

Autor, D. H., Levy, F., & Murane, R. J. 2003. The Skill Content of Recent Technological Change: An Empirical Exploration. *Quarterly Journal of Economics, 118*(4), 1279–1333.

Azar, J., Berry, S., & Marinescu, I. E. 2019. Estimating Labor Market Power. Yale University, mimeo. https://dx.doi.org/10.2139/ssrn.3456277.

Azar, J., Marinescu, I., Steinbaum, M., & Taska, B. 2020. Concentration in US Labor Markets: Evidence from Online Vacancy Data. *Labour Economics, 66.* https://doi.org/10.1016/j.labeco.2020.101886.

Azar, J., Schmalz, M., & Tecu, I. 2018. Anti-Competitive Effects of Common Ownership. *Journal of Finance,* May 25. https://doi.org/10.1111/jofi.12698.

Baker, J. B. 2019. *The Antitrust Paradigm: Restoring a Competitive Economy.* Cambridge, MA: Harvard University Press.

Barkai, S. 2019. The Anticompetitive Effects of Low Interest Rates. *ProMarket,* February 21. https://promarket.org/2019/02/21/anticompetitive-effects-low-interest-rates/#:~:text=At%20low%20interest%20rates%2C%20dominant,much%20longer%20periods%20of%20time.

Barkai, S. 2020. Declining Labor and Capital Shares. *Journal of Finance,* April 26. https://doi.org/10.1111/jofi.12909.

Barth, E., Bryson, A., Davis, J. C., & Freeman, R. 2016. It's Where You Work: Increases in the Dispersion of Earnings across Establishments and Individuals in the United States. *Journal of Labor Economics, 34*(S2), 67–97.

Bastian, H. 2006. Down and Almost Out in Scotland: George Orwell, Tuberculosis and Getting Streptomycin in 1948. *Journal of the Royal Society of Medicine, 99*(2), 95–98.

Baziki, S. B., Ginja, R., & Milicevic, T. B. 2016. *Trade Competition, Technology and Labour Reallocation.* Institute of Labor Economics (IZA) Discussion Papers no. 10034. https://www.iza.org/publications/dp/10034/trade-competition-technology-and-labour-reallocation.

Berge, W. 1947. Monopoly and the South. *Southern Economic Journal, 13*(4), 360–369. https://doi.org/10.2307/1052300.

Berger, D., Herkenhoff, K., & Mongey, S. 2019. Labor Market Power. NBER Working Paper no. 25719. https://www.nber.org/papers/w25719.

Berry, S., Levinsohn, J., & Pakes, A. 1995. Automobile Prices in Market Equilibrium. *Econometrica, 64*(4), 841–890.

Bertrand, M., & Mullainathan, S. 2001. Are CEOs Rewarded for Luck? The Ones without Principals Are. *Quarterly Journal of Economics, 116*(3), 901–932.

Bhasin, K. 2013. JC Penney CEO Ron Johnson's Pay Package Plummeted 97%. *Business Insider,* April 3. https://www.businessinsider.in/JCPenney-CEO-Ron-Johnsons-Pay-Package-Plummeted-97/articleshow/21205670.cms.

Blonigen, B. A., & Pierce, J. R. 2016. Evidence for the Effects of Mergers on Market Power and Efficiency. NBER Working Paper no. 22750. https://www.nber.org/papers/w22750.

Bloom, N., Guvenen, F., Price, D., Song, J., & Watcher, T. v. 2019. Firming Up Inequality. *Quarterly Journal of Economics, 134*(1), 1–50.

Bø, E. E., Slemrod, J., & Thoresen, T. O. 2015. Taxes on the Internet: Deterrence Effects of Public Disclosure. *American Economic Journal: Economic Policy, 7*(1), 36–62.

Bogle, J. C. 2018. Bogle Sounds a Warning on Index Funds. *Wall Street Journal,* November 29. https://www.wsj.com/articles/bogle-sounds-a-warning-on-index-funds-1543504551.

Boldrin, M., & Levine, D. K. 2008. *Against Intellectual Monopoly.* Cambridge: Cambridge University Press.

Boppart, T., & Krusell, P. 2020. Labor Supply in the Past, Present, and Future: A Balanced-Growth Perspective. *Journal of Political Economy, 128*(1), 118–157.

Bore, R. R. n.d. Some Remarks on the History of Official Statistics. Statistics Norway, accessed November 8, 2020. https://www.ssb.no/en/omssb/om-oss/historie.

Borenstein, S., Bushnell, J., & Stoft, S. 1997. The Competitive Effects of Transmission Capacity in a Deregulated Electricity Industry. NBER Working Paper no. 6293. https://www.nber.org/papers/w6293.

Bosler, C., & Petrosky-Nadeau, N. 2016. Job-to-Job Transitions in an Evolving Labor Market. FRBSF Economic Letter, Federal Reserve Bank of San Francisco, November 14.

Bourguignon, F., & Morrisson, C. 2002. Inequality among World Citizens: 1820–1992. *American Economic Review, 92*(4), 727–744.

Bowley, S. 1937. *Wages and Income in the United Kingdom since 1860.* Cambridge: Cambridge University Press.

Brandeis, L. 2009. *Other People's Money and How the Bankers Use It.* New York: Cosimo.

Bresnahan, T. 1989. Empirical Studies of Industries with Market Power. In *Handbook of Industrial Organization,* vol. 2, edited by R. Schmalensee & R. D. Willig, 1011–1057. Amsterdam: North-Holland.

Brynjolfsson, E., Hui, X., & Liu, M. 2019. Does Machine Translation Affect International Trade? Evidence from a Large Digital Platform. *Management Science, 65*(12). https://doi.org/10.1287/mnsc.2019.3388.

Buffett, W. 2007. Warren Buffett MBA Talk—Part 3. May 23. YouTube video, 9:07. https://www.youtube.com/watch?v=r7m7ifUz7ro.

Campa, J. M., & Goldberg, L. S. 2005. Exchange Rate Pass-Through into Import Prices. *Review of Economics and Statistics, 87*(4), 679–690.

Campbell, P. S. 2013. Democracy v. Concentrated Wealth: In Search of a Louis D. Brandeis Quote. 16 Green Bag 2D 251, University of Louisville School of Law Legal Studies Research Paper Series no. 2014-11. http://greenbag.org/v16n3/v16n3_articles_campbell.pdf.

Card, D., Heining, J., & Kline, P. 2013. Workplace Heterogeneity and the Rise of West German Wage Inequality. *Quarterly Journal of Economics, 128*(3), 967–1015.

Carpenter, M. 2014. *Caffeinated: How Our Daily Habit Helps, Hurts, and Hooks Us.* New York: Hudson Street Press.

Case, A., & Deaton, A. 2015. Rising Morbidity and Mortality in Midlife among White Non-Hispanic Americans in the 21st Century. *Proceedings of the National Academy of Sciences of the United States of America, 112*(49), 15078–15083.

Case, A., & Deaton, A. 2020. *Deaths of Despair and the Future of Capitalism.* Princeton, NJ: Princeton University Press.

Cavalli-Sforza, L. L. 1997. Genes, Peoples, and Languages. *Proceedings of the National Academy of Sciences of the United States of America, 94*(15), 7719–7724.

Cavalli-Sforza, L. L., & Feldman, W. M. 1981. *Cultural Transmission and Evolution: A Quantitative Approach.* Princeton, NJ: Princeton University Press.

Chade, H., & Eeckhout, J. 2017. Stochastic Sorting. UPF, mimeo. https://www.janeeckhout.com/wp-content/uploads/SS.pdf.

Chandler, A. D., Jr. 1977. *The Visible Hand: The Managerial Revolution in American Business.* Cambridge, MA: Belknap Press.

Chetty, R., Stepner, M., Abraham, S., Lin, S., Scuderi, B., Turner, N., Bergeron, A., and Cutler, D. 2016. The Association between Income and Life Expectancy in the United States, 2001–2014. *Journal of the American Medical Association, 315*(16), 1750–1766.

Chien, C. V. 2013. Patent Trolls by the Numbers. Santa Clara University Legal Studies Research Paper no. 08-13. http://dx.doi.org/10.2139/ssrn.2233041.

Coen, R. M. 1973. Labor Force and Unemployment in the 1920's and 1930's: A Re-Examination Based on Postwar Experience. *Review of Economics and Statistics, 55*(1), 46–55.

Collinson, P. 2016. Norway, the Country Where You Can See Everyone's Tax Returns. *Guardian*, April 11. https://www.theguardian.com/money/blog/2016/apr/11/when-it-comes-to-tax-transparency-norway-leads-the-field.

Cortes, G. M., Jaimovich, N., Nekarda, C. J., & Siu, H. E. 2020. The Dynamics of Disappearing Routine Jobs: A Flows Approach. *Labour Economics, 65*. https://doi.org/10.1016/j.labeco.2020.101823.

Council of Economic Advisors. 2016. Benefits of Competition and Indicators of Market-Power. Issue Brief, May. https://obamawhitehouse.archives.gov/sites/default/files/page/files/20160414_cea_competition_issue_brief.pdf.

Cowen, T. 2017. *The Complacent Class: The Self-Defeating Quest for the American Dream.* New York: St. Martin's Press.

Cowgill, B. 2020. Bias and Productivity in Humans and Algorithms: Theory and Evidence from Résumé Screening. Columbia University, mimeo. http://conference.iza.org/conference_files/MacroEcon_2017/cowgill_b8981.pdf.

Coyle, D. 2014. *GDP: A Brief But Affectionate History.* Princeton, NJ: Princeton University Press.

Crépon, B., Duflo, E., Gurgand, M., Rathelot, R., & Zamora, P. 2013. Do Labor Market Policies Have Displacement Effects? Evidence from a Clustered Randomized Experiment. *Quarterly Journal of Economics, 128*(2), 531–580.

Cunningham, C., Ederer, F., & Ma, S. 2021. Killer Acquisitions. *Journal of Political Economy,* forthcoming. https://doi.org/10.1086/712506.

Dasgupta, P., & Stiglitz, J. 1980. Industrial Structure and the Nature of Innovative Activity. *Economic Journal, 90*(358), 266–293.

David, J. M. 2021. The Aggregate Implications of Mergers and Acquisitions. *Review of Economic Studies,* forthcoming. https://doi.org/10.1093/restud/rdaa077.

Davis, D. 2008. *The Dick Davis Dividend: Straight Talk on Making Money from 40 Years on Wall Street.* Hoboken, NJ: Wiley.

Davis, M. A., & Ortalo-Magné, F. 2011. Household Expenditures, Wages, Rents. *Review of Economic Dynamics, 14*(2), 248–261.

Davis, S. J., & Haltiwanger, J. 2014. Labor Market Fluidity and Economic Performance. NBER Working Paper no. 20479. https://www.nber.org/papers/w20479.

Deb, S., Eeckhout, J., Patel, A., & Warren, L. 2021. Market Power and Wage Inequality. UPF Barcelona, mimeo. https://www.janeeckhout.com/wp-content/uploads/Wage_Inequality.pdf.

Deb, S., Eeckhout, J., & Warren, L. 2021. The Macroeconomics of Market Power and Monopsony. UPF Barcelona, mimeo. https://www.janeeckhout.com/wp-content/uploads/Monopsony.pdf.

De Botton, A. 2004. *Status Anxiety.* London: Hamish Hamilton.

Decker, R., Haltiwanger, J., Jarmin, R., & Miranda, J. 2014. The Role of Entrepreneurship in US Job Creation and Economic Dynamism. *Journal of Economic Perspectives, 28*(3), 3–24.

Decker, R. A., Haltiwanger, J., Jarmin, R. S., & Miranda, J. 2020. Changing Business Dynamism and Productivity: Shocks versus Responsiveness. *American Economic Review, 110*(12), 3952–3990.

De la Roca, J., & Puga, D. 2017. Learning by Working in Big Cities. *Review of Economic Studies, 84*(1), 106–142.

DellaVigna, S., & Gentzkow, M. 2019. Uniform Pricing in U.S. Retail Chains. *Quarterly Journal of Economics, 134*(4), 2011–2084.

Del Negro, M., Giannone, D., Giannoni, M. P., & Tambalotti, A. 2019. Global Trends in Interest Rates. *Journal of International Economics, 118*, 248–262.

De Loecker, J., & Eeckhout, J. 2017. The Rise of Market Power and the Macroeconomic Implications. NBER Working Paper no. 23687. https://www.nber.org/papers/w23687.

De Loecker, J., & Eeckhout, J. 2018. Global Market Power. NBER Working Paper no. 24768. https://www.nber.org/papers/w24768.

De Loecker, J., Eeckhout, J., & Mongey, S. 2021. Quantifying Market Power. https://www.janeeckhout.com/wp-content/uploads/QMP.pdf.

De Loecker, J., Eeckhout, J., & Unger, G. 2020. The Rise of Market Power and the Macroeconomic Implications. *Quarterly Journal of Economics, 135*(2), 561–644.

De Loecker, J., & Warzynski, F. 2012. Markups and Firm-Level Export Status. *American Economic Review, 102*(6), 2437–2471.

Dougherty, C. 2014. No. 1 With a Bullet: "Nadeshot" Becomes a Call of Duty Star. *New York Times,* November 15. https://www.nytimes.com/2014/11/16/technology/esports-call-of-duty-nadeshot-celebrity-success.html.

Du, Q., Huasheng, G., & Maurice, L. D. 2012. The Relative-Age Effect and Career Success: Evidence from Corporate CEOs. *Economics Letters, 117*(3), 660–662.

Dubrow, J. K., & Adamas, J. 2012. Hoop Inequalities: Race, Class and Family Structure Background and the Odds of Playing in the National Basketball Association. *International Review for the Sociology of Sport, 47*(1), 43–59.

Eeckhout, J. 2020. Comment on "Diverging Trends in National and Local Concentration." In *NBER Macroeconomics Annual, 35.* https://www.nber.org/books-and-chapters/nber-macroeconomics-annual-2020-volume-35/comment-diverging-trends-national-and-local-concentration-hall.

Eeckhout, J., Fu, C., Li, W., & Weng, X. 2021. Optimal Taxation and Market Power. UPF Barcelona, mimeo. https://www.janeeckhout.com/wp-content/uploads/Optimal_Taxation.pdf.

Eeckhout, J., Hedtrich, C., & Pinheiro, R. 2021. Urban Job Polarization. UPF Barcelona, mimeo. https://www.janeeckhout.com/wp-content/uploads/Urban.pdf.

Eeckhout, J., & Jovanovic, B. 2010. Occupational Choice and Development. *Journal of Economic Theory, 147*, 657–683.

Eeckhout, J., Pinheiro, R., & Schmidheiny, K. 2014. Spatial Sorting. *Journal of Political Economy, 122*(3), 554–620.

Eggertsson, G. B., Robbins, J. A., & Wold, E. G. 2018. Kaldor and Piketty's Facts: The Rise of Monopoly Power in the United States. NBER Working Paper no. 24287. https://www.nber.org/papers/w24287.

Ellenberg, J. 2014. *How Not to Be Wrong: The Power of Mathematical Thinking*. New York: Penguin.

Elsby, M. W., Hobijn, B., & Sahin, A. 2013. Unemployment Dynamics in the OECD. *Review of Economics and Statistics*, 95(2), 530–548.

Eurostat. 2019. How Much Are Households Spending on Food? December 9. https://ec.europa.eu/eurostat/web/products-eurostat-news/-/DDN-20191209-1.

Feenstra, R. C., Inklaar R., & Timmer M. P. 2015. The Next Generation of the Penn World Table. *American Economic Review*, 105(10), 3150–3182.

Finn, H. 2011. Lunch with Hal. *Think Quarterly—01 Data*, March 19, 30–33. https://issuu.com/thinkquarterly/docs/01-data.

Fogli, A., & Guerrieri, V. 2018. The End of the American Dream? Inequality and Segregation in US Cities. NBER Working Paper no. 26143. https://www.nber.org/papers/w26143.

Forbes. 2020. Jeff Bezos Profile. www.forbes.com/profile/jeff-bezos/.

Frank, R. 2016. *Success and Luck: Good Fortune and the Myth of Meritocracy*. Princeton, NJ: Princeton University Press.

Fréchette, G. R., Lizzeri, A., & Salz, T. 2019. Frictions in a Competitive, Regulated Market: Evidence From Taxis. *American Economic Review*, 109(8), 2954–2992.

Friedman, M. 1999. Policy Forum: "Milton Friedman on Business Suicide." *CATO Policy Report*, March/April. https://www.cato.org/policy-report/marchapril-1999/policy-forum-milton-friedman-business-suicide.

Friedman, M., & Friedman, R. 1980. *Free to Choose: A Personal Statement*. New York: Harcourt Brace Jovanovich.

Friedman, M., & Kuznets, S. 1945. *Income from Independent Professional Practice*. New York: National Bureau of Economic Research.

Gautier, P., Muller, P., van der Klaauw, B., Rosholm, M., & Svarer, M. 2018. Estimating Equilibrium Effects of Job Search Assistance. *Estimating Equilibrium Effects of Job Search Assistance*, 36(4), 1073–1125.

George, H. 1879. *Progress and Poverty*. N.p.: Dodo Press.

Giridharadas, A. 2018. *Winners Take All: The Elite Charade of Changing the World*. New York: Alfred A. Knopf.

Gladwell, M. 2008. *Outliers: The Story of True Success*. New York: Little, Brown and Company.

Goldschmidt, D., & Schmieder, J. F. 2017. The Rise of Domestic Outsourcing and the Evolution of the German Wage Structure. *Quarterly Journal of Economics*, 132(3), 1165–1217.

Goodman, P. S. 2017. The Robots Are Coming, and Sweden Is Fine. *New York Times*, December 27. https://www.nytimes.com/2017/12/27/business/the-robots-are-coming-and-sweden-is-fine.html.

Goolsbee, A., & Syverson, C. 2020. Monopsony Power in Higher Education: A Tale of Two Tracks. NBER Working Paper no. 26070. https://www.nber.org/papers/w26070.

Goos, M., & Manning, A. 2007. Lousy and Lovely Jobs: The Rising Polarization of Work in Britain. *Review of Economics and Statistics*, 89(1), 118–133.

Goos, M., Manning, A., & Salomons, A. 2009. Job Polarization in Europe. *American Economic Review*, 99(2), 58–63.

Goos, M., Manning, A., & Salomons, A. 2014. Explaining Job Polarization: Routine-Biased Technological Change and Offshoring. *American Economic Review, 104*(8), 2509–2526.

Gordon, S. 2015. Record Year for M&A with Big Deals and Big Promises. *Financial Times*, December 16. https://www.ft.com/content/0fd15156-9e5b-11e5-b45d-4812f209f861.

Graversen, B. K., & Van Ours, J. C. 2008. How to Help Unemployed Find Jobs Quickly: Experimental Evidence from a Mandatory Activation Program. *Journal of Public Economics, 92*(10–11), 2020–2035.

Grullon, G., Larkin, Y., & Michaely, R. 2019. Are U.S. Industries Becoming More Concentrated? *Review of Finance, 23*(4), 697–743.

Gutierrez, G., & Philippon, T. 2017. Declining Competition and Investment in the U.S. NBER Working Paper no. 23583. https://www.nber.org/papers/w23583.

Guvenen, F., & Kaplan, G. 2017. Top Income Inequality in the 21st Century: Some Cautionary Notes. NBER Working Paper no. 23321. https://www.nber.org/papers/w23321.

Håkanson, C., Lindqvist, E., & Vlachos, J. 2020. Firms and Skills: The Evolution of Worker Sorting. *Journal of Human Resources*, September 21. http://jhr.uwpress.org/content/early/2020/09/16/jhr.56.2.0517-8801R2.full.pdf+html.

Hall, J., & Krueger, A. 2015. An Analysis of the Labor Market for Uber's Driver-Partners in the United States. *ILR Review, 71*(3), 705–732.

Hall, R. E. 1988. The Relation between Price and Marginal Cost in U.S. Industry. *Journal of Political Economy, 96*(5), 921–947.

Haltiwanger, J., Hathaway, I., & Miranda, J. 2014. *Declining Business Dynamism in the U.S. High-Technology Sector*. Kansas City, MO: Ewing Marion Kauffman Foundation.

Haltiwanger, J., Jarmin, R. S., & Miranda, J. 2013. Who Creates Jobs? Small versus Large versus Young. *Review of Economics and Statistics, 95*(2), 347–361.

Harberger, A. C. 1954. Monopoly and Resource Allocation. *American Economic Review, 44*(2), 77–87.

Harris, K. 1995. Oversexed, Overfed, Over Here. *New York Times*, February 15. https://www.nytimes.com/1995/02/12/books/oversexed-overfed-over-here.html.

Hartman-Glaser, B., Lustig, H., & Xiaolang, M. Z. 2019. Capital Share Dynamics When Firms Insure Workers. *Journal of Finance, 74*, 1707–1751.

Haskel, J., & Westlake, S. 2017. *Capitalism without Capital: The Rise of the Intangible Economy*. Princeton, NJ: Princeton University Press.

Henry, B. 2013. TO BE CLEAR: JC Penney May Have Just Had The Worst Quarter In Retail History. *Business Insider*, February 28. https://www.businessinsider.com/jc-penney-worst-quarter-in-retail-history-2013-2.

Hobijn, B., Schoellman, T., & Vindas Q., A. 2017. Structural Transformation by Cohort. 2017 Meeting Papers 1417, Society for Economic Dynamics. https://ideas.repec.org/p/red/sed017/1417.html.

Holmes, T. J. 2011. The Diffusion of Wal-Mart and Economies of Density. *Econometrica, 79*(1), 253–302.

Houde, J.-F., Newberry, P., & Seim, K. 2017. Economies of Density in E-Commerce: A Study of Amazon's Fulfillment Center Network. NBER Working Paper no. 23361. https://www.nber.org/papers/w23361.

Hovenkamp, E. 2018. Platform Antitrust. *Journal of Corporation Law, 44,* 713.

Hyatt, H., McEntarfer, E., Ueda, K., & Zhang, A. 2018. Interstate Migration and Employer-to-Employer Transitions in the U.S.: New Evidence from Administrative Records Data. *Demography, 55*(6), 2161–2180.

Hyatt, H. R., & Spletzer, J. R. 2013. The Recent Decline in Employment Dynamics. *IZA Journal of Labor Economics, 2,* article no. 5. https://doi.org/10.1186/2193-8997-2-5.

Jäger, S., Schoefer, B., & Heining, J. 2021. Labor in the Boardroom. *Quarterly Journal of Economics,* forthcoming.

Jaimovich, N., Rebelo, S., & Wong, A. 2019. Trading Down and the Business Cycle. *Journal of Monetary Economics, 102,* 96–121.

Jarosch, G. 2015. Searching for Job Security and the Consequences of Job Loss. Princeton University, mimeo. https://drive.google.com/open?id=1YVZz8ow8h3nlSxLUdDIWe3APovPAGNUx.

Johnson, G. E. 1979. The Labor Market Displacement Effect in the Analysis of the Net Impact of Manpower Training Programs. In *Evaluating Manpower Training Programs,* edited by F. E. Bloch, 227–254. Greenwich, CT: JAI Press.

Johnson, J. E., & Kleiner, M. M. 2020. Is Occupational Licensing a Barrier to Interstate Migration? *American Economic Journal: Economic Policy 12*(3), 347–373.

Johnston, L., & Williamson, S. H. 2020. What Was the U.S. GDP Then? Measuring Worth. http://www.measuringworth.org/usgdp/.

Kades, M. 2019. *The State of U.S. Federal Antitrust Enforcement.* Washington, DC: Washington Center for Equitable Growth.

Kaldor, N. 1957. A Model of Economic Growth. *Economic Journal, 67*(268), 591–624.

Kaldor, N. 1961. Capital Accumulation and Economic Growth. In *The Theory of Capital: Proceedings of a Conference Held by the International Economic Association,* edited by Friedrich A. Lutz & D. C. Hague, 177–222. London: Macmillan.

Kambourov, G., & Manovskii, I. 2009. Occupational Specificity of Human Capital. *International Economic Review, 50*(1), 63–115.

Kaplan, G., & Schulhofer-Wohl, S. 2017. Understanding the Long-Run Decline in Interstate Migration. *International Economic Review,* February 3, 57–94.

Kaplan, S. N., & Rauh, J. 2013. It's the Market: The Broad-Based Rise in the Return to Top Talent. *Journal of Economic Perspectives, 27*(3), 35–56.

Karabarbounis, L., & Neiman, B. 2014. The Global Decline of the Labor Share. *Quarterly Journal of Economics, 129*(1), 61–103.

Karahan, F., Pugsley, B., & Şahin, A. 2019. Demographic Origins of the Startup Deficit. NBER Working Paper no. 25874. https://www.nber.org/papers/w25874.

Katz, L. F., & Murphy, K. M. 1992. Changes in Relative Wages, 1963–1987: Supply and Demand Factors. *Quarterly Journal of Economics, 107*(1), 35–78.

Keefe, P. R. 2017. The Family That Built an Empire of Pain. *New Yorker,* October 23. https://www.newyorker.com/magazine/2017/10/30/the-family-that-built-an-empire-of-pain.

Keynes, J. M. 1963. *Essays in Persuasion.* New York: W. W. Norton & Co.

Khan, L. 2017. Amazon's Antitrust Paradox. *Yale Law Journal, 126*(3), 564–907.

Kindermann, F., & Krueger, D. 2021. High Marginal Tax Rates on the Top 1%? Lessons from a Life Cycle Model with Idiosyncratic Income Risk. *American Economic Journal: Macroeconomics,* forthcoming.

Klasing, J. M., & Milionis, P. 2014. Quantifying the Evolution of World Trade, 1870–1949. *Journal of International Economics*, 92(1), 185–197.

Kleiner, M. M. 2006. *Licensing Occupations: Ensuring Quality or Restricting Competition?* Kalamazoo, MI: W. E. Upjohn Institute for Employment Research.

Kleiner, M. M. 2015. *Guild-Ridden Labor Markets: The Curious Case of Occupational Licensing.* Kalamazoo, MI: W. E. Upjohn Institute for Employment Research.

Kleiner, M., & Krueger, A. 2013. Analyzing the Extent and Influence of Occupational Licensing on the Labor Market. *Journal of Labor Economics*, 31(2), S173–S202.

Kleven, H. J., Landais, C., & Saez, E. 2013. Taxation and International Migration of Superstars: Evidence from the European Football Market. *American Economic Review*, 103(5), 1892–1924.

Krusell, P., Ohanian, L. E., Ríos-Rull, J.-V., & Violante, G. L. 2000. Capital-Skill Complementarity and Inequality: A Macroeconomic Analysis. *Econometrica*, 65(5), 1029–1053.

Kuvshinov, D., & Zimmermann, K. 2020. The Big Bang: Stock Market Capitalization in the Long Run. CEPR Discussion Paper no. 14468. https://cepr.org/active/publications/discussion_papers/dp.php?dpno=14468.

Kwoka, J. E., Greenfield, D., & Gu, C. 2014. *Mergers, Merger Control, and Remedies: A Retrospective Analysis of U.S. Policy.* Cambridge, MA: MIT Press.

Lafontaine, F., & Morton, F. S. 2010. State Franchise Laws, Dealer Terminations, and the Auto Crisis. *Journal of Economic Perspectives*, 24(3), 233–250.

Lakner, C., & Milanovic, B. 2013. *Global Income Distribution: From the Fall of the Berlin Wall to the Great Recession.* Washington, DC: World Bank.

Lenter, D., Slemrod, J., & Shackelford, D. 2003. Public Disclosure of Corporate Tax Return Information: Accounting, Economics, and Legal Perspectives. *National Tax Journal*, 56(4), 803–830.

Leontief, W. 1983. *National Perspective: The Definition of Problems and Opportunities.* Washington, DC: National Academy Press.

Levack, B. P., Muir, E., & Veldman, M. 2011. *The West: Encounters & Transformations.* 3rd ed. Upper Saddle River, NJ: Longman/Pearson.

Levingston, I., Lorin, J., & McDonald, M. 2018. Harvard Billionaires Bail Out Alma Mater from Poor Fund Returns. *Bloomberg Businessweek*, June 26. https://www.bloomberg.com/news/articles/2018-06-26/harvard-billionaires-bail-out-alma-mater-from-poor-fund-returns.

Levinson, M. 2011. *The Great A&P and the Struggle for Small Business in America.* New York: Hill and Wang.

Lowe, J. 1997. *Warren Buffett Speaks: Wit and Wisdom from the World's Greatest Investor.* Hoboken, NJ: Wiley.

Lucas, R. E., Jr. 2000. Inflation and Welfare. *Econometrica*, 68(2), 247–274.

Luce, E. 2018. Is Wealthy Philanthropy Doing More Harm than Good? *Financial Times*, December 21. https://www.ft.com/content/64d70736-0212-11e9-9d01-cd4d49afbbe3.

Marx, M., & Nunn, R. 2018. The Chilling Effect of Non-Compete Agreements. EconoFact, May 20. https://econofact.org/the-chilling-effect-of-non-compete-agreements.

Maynard, M. 2012. BALLE Founder Judy Wicks on the Origins of Urban Outfitters, the Birth of the Localist Movement, and the Necessity of Local Ownership. MarkMaynard, June 23. http://markmaynard.com/2012/06/balle-founder-judy-wicks-on-the-origins-of-urban-outfitters-the-birth-of-the-localist-movement-and-the-necessity-of-local-ownership/.

Metz, C. 2017. Tech Giants Are Paying Huge Salaries for Scarce A.I. Talent. *New York Times*, October 22. https://www.nytimes.com/2017/10/22/technology/artificial-intelligence -experts-salaries.html.

Michaels, G., Natraj, A., & Reenen, J. V. 2014. Has ICT Polarized Skill Demand? Evidence from Eleven Countries over Twenty-Five Years. *Review of Economics and Statistics, 96*(1), 60–77.

Milanovic, B. 2016. *Global Inequality: A New Approach for the Age of Globalization.* Cambridge, MA: Harvard University Press.

Mishel, L. 2014. *Wages for the Top One Percent Have Grown Far Faster than Those of Other High Wage Earners.* Economic Policy Institute, May 29. https://www.epi.org/publication/wages -for-top-1-percent-grow-faster/.

Mitchell, B. 2007. *International Historical Statistics: The Americas 1750–1988.* 6th ed. Houndmills, UK: Palgrave Macmillan.

Mohamud, N. 2019. Is Mansa Musa the Richest Man Who Ever Lived? BBC, March 10. https:// www.bbc.com/news/world-africa-47379458.

Moscarini, G., & Thomsson, K. 2007. Occupational and Job Mobility in the US. *Scandinavian Journal of Economics, 109*(4), 807–836.

Mukherjee, S. 2011 [2010]. *The Emperor of All Maladies: A Biography of Cancer.* London: Fourth Estate.

Munchau, W. 2018. The Crisis of Modern Liberalism Is Down to Market Forces. *Financial Times*, December 23. https://www.ft.com/content/9dfea428-0538-11e9-9d01-cd4d49afbbe3.

Naidu, S., Nyarko, Y., & Wang, S.-Y. 2016. Monopsony Power in Migrant Labor Markets: Evidence from the United Arab Emirates. *Journal of Political Economy, 124*(6), 1735–1792.

National Institute on Drug Abuse. n.d. Overdose Death Rates. National Institutes of Health, accessed November 6, 2020. https://www.drugabuse.gov/drug-topics/trends-statistics /overdose-death-rates.

Noack, R. 2017. Why Are Flights So Much Cheaper in Europe than in the U.S.? *Washington Post*, October 12. https://www.washingtonpost.com/news/worldviews/wp/2017/10/12/why-are -flights-so-much-cheaper-in-europe-than-in-the-u-s/.

Nomad Health. 2019. Complete List of Average Doctor Salaries by Specialty. May 13. https://blog .nomadhealth.com/complete-list-of-average-doctor-salaries-by-specialty-locum-tenens/.

OECD. 2020. Unemployment rate (indicator). Accessed December 11, 2020. https://data.oecd .org/unemp/unemployment-rate.htm.

Ogilvie, S. 2004. Guilds, Efficiency, and Social Capital: Evidence from German Proto-Industry. *Economic History Review, 57*(2), 286–333.

Open Markets Institute. 2019. *America's Concentration Crisis.* https://concentrationcrisis .openmarketsinstitute.org/.

Ordonez, G., & Piguillem, F. 2020. Savings Rates: Up or Down? NBER Working Paper no. w27179. https://www.nber.org/papers/w27179.

Orwell, G. 1944. Grounds for Dismay. Review of *The Road to Serfdom* by F. A. Hayek and *The Mirror of the Past* by K. Zilliacus. *Observer*, April 9.

Patlak, M. 2001. *Targeting Leukemia: From Bench to Bedside.* Bethesda, MD: Federation of American Societies for Experimental Biology. https://www.faseb.org/portals/2/pdfs/opa/leukemia.pdf.

Peltzman, S. 2014. Industrial Concentration under the Rule of Reason. *Journal of Law & Economics, 57*(S3), S101–S120.

Philippon, T. 2019. *The Great Reversal. How America Gave Up on Free Markets.* Cambridge, MA: Harvard University Press.

Pilon, M. 2015. *The Monopolists: Obsession, Fury, and the Scandal behind the World's Favorite Board Game.* New York: Bloomsbury.

Pinker, S. 1997. *How the Mind Works.* New York: W. W. Norton.

Piraino, T. A., Jr. 2007. Reconciling the Harvard and Chicago Schools: A New Antitrust Approach for the 21st Century. *Indiana Law Journal, 82*(2), 345.

Posner, E., & Weyl, G. 2018. *Radical Markets: Uprooting Capitalism and Democracy for a Just Society.* Princeton, NJ: Princeton University Press.

Pugsley, B., & Şahin, A. 2019. Grown-Up Business Cycles. *Review of Financial Studies, 32*(3), 1102–1147.

Ravallion, M. 2018. Inequality and Globalization: A Review Essay. *Journal of Economic Literature, 56*(2), 620–642.

Reich, D. 2018. *Who We Are and How We Got Here.* Oxford: Oxford University Press.

Reich, R. 2020. *Just Giving: Why Philanthropy Is Failing Democracy and How It Can Do Better.* Princeton, NJ: Princeton University Press.

Ritter, J. R. 2020. *Initial Public Offerings: Updated Statistics.* https://site.warrington.ufl.edu/ritter/files/IPOs2019Statistics.pdf.

Robinson, Joan. 1933. *The Economics of Imperfect Competition.* London: Macmillan and Co.

Rosaia, N. 2020. Competing Platforms and Transport Equilibrium: Evidence from New York City. Harvard University, mimeo. https://scholar.harvard.edu/files/rosaia/files/draft.pdf.

Rosen, S. 1981. The Economics of Superstars. *American Economic Review, 71*(5), 845–858.

Roser, M. 2013. Global Economic Inequality. Our World in Data. https://ourworldindata.org/global-economic-inequality.

Rosholm, M. 2008. Experimental Evidence on the Nature of the Danish Employment Miracle. IZA Working Paper no. 3620. http://ftp.iza.org/dp3620.pdf.

Rosling, H., Rönnlund, A. R., & Rosling, O. 2018. *Factfulness: Ten Reasons We're Wrong about the World—and Why Things Are Better than You Think.* New York: Flatiron Books.

Rosling, H., & Rosling, O. 2014. *How Not to Be Ignorant about the World.* TED video, 18:51. June. https://www.ted.com/talks/hans_and_ola_rosling_how_not_to_be_ignorant_about_the_world#t-2304.

Rossi-Hansberg, E., Sarte, P.-D., & Trachter, N. 2020. Diverging Trends in National and Local Concentration. In *NBER Macroeconomics Annual, 35.* https://www.nber.org/books-and-chapters/nber-macroeconomics-annual-2020-volume-35/diverging-trends-national-and-local-concentration.

Samuelson, P. 1964. *Economics: An Introductory Analysis.* 6th ed. New York: McGraw-Hill.

Santayana, G. 1941 [1896]. *The Sense of Beauty.* Mineola, NY: Dover.

Santayana, G. 2001 [1905]. *The Life of Reason: Reason in Common Sense.* New York: Scribner.

Scheidel, W. 2017. *The Great Leveler: Violence and the History of Inequality from the Stone Age to the Twenty-First Century.* Princeton, NJ: Princeton University Press.

Schmitz, J. A., Jr. 2020. *Monopolies Inflict Great Harm on Low- and Middle-Income Americans.* Federal Reserve Bank of Minneapolis Research Department Staff Report, May. https://doi.org/10.21034/sr.601.

Schumpeter, J. A. 1994 [1942]. *Capitalism, Socialism and Democracy*. London: Routledge.

Simpson, E. H. 1951. The Interpretation of Interaction in Contingency Tables. *Journal of the Royal Statistical Society, 13*(2), 238–241.

Sinclair, U. 2001 [1906]. *The Jungle*. Mineola, NY: Dover.

Smith, A. 1776. *The Wealth of Nations*. New York: Bantam.

Smith, M., Yagan, D., Zidar, O., & Zwick, E. 2019. Capitalists in the Twenty-First Century. *Quarterly Journal of Economics, 134*(4), 1675–1745.

Sommeiller, E., & Price, M. 2018. The New Gilded Age: Income Inequality in the U.S. by State, Metropolitan Area, and County. Economic Policy Institute, July 19. https://www.epi.org /publication/the-new-gilded-age-income-inequality-in-the-u-s-by-state-metropolitan-area -and-county/.

Srinivasan, D. 2019. Why Privacy Is an Antitrust Issue. *New York Times*, May 28. https://www .nytimes.com/2019/05/28/opinion/privacy-antitrust-facebook.html.

Stephan, W. G., Bernstein, W. M., Stephan, C., & Davis, M. H. 1979. Attributions for Achievement: Egotism vs. Expectancy Confirmation. *Social Psychology Quarterly, 42*(1), 5–17.

Stigler, G. J. 1952. The Case against Big Business. *Fortune, 145* (May), 123.

Streufert, S., & Streufert, S. C. 1969. Effects of Conceptual Structure, Failure, and Success on Attribution of Causality and Interpersonal Attitudes. *Journal of Personality and Social Psychology*, 138–147. https://www.semanticscholar.org/paper/THE-EFFECT-OF-CONCEPTUAL -STRUCTURE%2C-FAILURE%2C-AND-ON-Streufert-Streufert/afb53f6973194f88850b 8adbaa59d8bcbe46a219.

Surowiecki, J. 2004. *The Wisdom of Crowds: Why the Many Are Smarter than the Few and How Collective Wisdom Shapes Business, Economies, Societies, and Nations*. New York: Doubleday.

Sutton, J. 1991. *Sunk Costs and Market Structure*. Cambridge, MA: MIT Press.

Sutton, J. 1998. *Technology and Market Structure*. Cambridge, MA: MIT Press.

Taleb, N. N. 2008. *Fooled by Randomness: The Hidden Role of Chance in Life and in the Markets*. New York: Random House.

Tepper, J. 2019. Why Regulators Went Soft on Monopolies. *American Conservative*, January 9. https://www.theamericanconservative.com/articles/why-the-regulators-went-soft-on -monopolies/.

Tong, S. 2017. When It Comes to NAFTA and Autos, the Parts Are Well Traveled. *Marketplace*, March 24. https://www.marketplace.org/2017/03/24/world/when-it-cones-nafta-and -autos-parts-are-well-traveled/.

Traiberman, S. 2019. Occupations and Import Competition: Evidence from Denmark. *American Economic Review, 109*(12), 4260–4301.

U.S. Bureau of Labor Statistics. 2006. *100 Years of U.S. Consumer Spending: Data for the Nation, New York City, and Boston*. Washington, DC: US Department of Labor, US Bureau of Labor Statistics.

U.S. Bureau of Labor Statistics. 2019a. May 2019 Metropolitan and Nonmetropolitan Area Occupational Employment and Wage Estimates: Janesville-Beloit, WI. Department of Labor, last modified March 31, 2020. https://www.bls.gov/oes/current/oes_27500.htm.

U.S. Bureau of Labor Statistics. 2019b. May 2019 Metropolitan and Nonmetropolitan Area Occupational Employment and Wage Estimates: New York–Newark–Jersey City, NY-NJ-PA.U.S.

Department of Labor, last modified March 31, 2020. https://www.bls.gov/oes/current/oes
_35620.htm.

U.S. Bureau of Labor Statistics. 2020. The Employment Situation—February 2020. March 6.
https://www.bls.gov/news.release/archives/empsit_03062020.pdf.

U.S. Census Bureau. 1930. Retail Distribution: 1929. https://www2.census.gov/library
/publications/decennial/1930/distribution-volume-1/00269599v1p1ch01.pdf.

U.S. Census Bureau. 2019a. Janesville-Beloit, WI Metro Area. Census Reporter, accessed November 8, 2020. https://censusreporter.org/profiles/31000US27500-janesville-beloit-wi
-metro-area/.

U.S. Census Bureau. 2019b. New York–Newark–Jersey City, NY-NJ-PA Metro Area. Census
Reporter, accessed November 8, 2020. https://censusreporter.org/profiles/31000US35620
-new-york-newark-jersey-city-ny-nj-pa-metro-area/.

U.S. Census Bureau. 2020. Table 2a. Revised (Not Adjusted) Estimates of Monthly Sales for
Manufacturers, Retailers, and Merchant Wholesalers: January 1992 through September 2020. https://www.census.gov/mtis/www/data/text/timeseries2.xlsx.

U.S. Patent and Trademark Office. 2020. U.S. Patent Statistics Chart, Calendar Years 1963–2019.
U.S. Patent and Trademark Office, last updated November 11, 2020. https://www.uspto.gov
/web/offices/ac/ido/oeip/taf/us_stat.htm.

Varian, H. 2000. Managing Online Security Risks. *New York Times*, June 1. https://archive
.nytimes.com/www.nytimes.com/library/financial/columns/060100econ-scene.html
?printpage=yes.

Wilson, C. 2012. U.S. Competitiveness: The Mexican Connection. *Issues in Science and Technology, 28*(4), 27–30.

Wollmann, T. G. 2019. Stealth Consolidation: Evidence from an Amendment to the Hart-Scott-
Rodino Act. *American Economic Review: Insights, 1*(1), 77–94.

World Bank Group. 2020a. World Development Indicators: Physicians (Per 1,000 People).
World Bank, accessed November 5, 2020. https://data.worldbank.org/indicator/sh.med
.phys.zs?end=2016&start=2016&view=bar.

World Bank Group. 2020b. World Development Indicators: Poverty Headcount Ratio at $3.20.
World Bank, accessed November 8, 2020. https://databank.worldbank.org/reports.aspx
?source=2&Topic=11.

World Tourism Organization. 2018. UNWTO Tourism Highlights, 2018 edition, September 13.
https://www.e-unwto.org/doi/pdf/10.18111/9789284419876.

Wu, T. 2018. *The Curse of Bigness: Antitrust in the New Gilded Age.* New York: Columbia Global
Reports.

Yihan, Y. 2020. Does Open Source Pay off in the Plug-in Hybrid and Electric Vehicle Industry?
A Study of Tesla's Open-Source Initiative. CRC TR 224 Discussion Paper Series, no. 218,
University of Mannheim, Germany. https://www.crctr224.de/en/research-output
/discussion-papers/archive/2020/DP218.

Zukin, C. 2015. What's the Matter with Polling? *New York Times*, June 20. https://www.nytimes
.com/2015/06/21/opinion/sunday/whats-the-matter-with-polling.html.

Zweig, S. 1943. *The World of Yesterday.* New York: Viking Press.

Zweig, S. 2015 [1941]. *Montaigne.* London: Pushkin Press.

INDEX

Note: Page numbers in *italics* indicate figures and tables.